FOR THOSE WHO DOUBT:

Is It Because of Jesus?

Conversations for Those Deconstructing Their Faith

By Pedro R. García

D6 FAMILY MINISTRY
114 BUSH RD · NASHVILLE, TN 37217 · 800.877.7030 · D6FAMILY.COM

Published by D6 Family Ministry

D6 Family Ministry
114 Bush Road
Nashville, TN 37217
d6family.com

ISBN: 9781614842057

Printed in the United States of America

To my wife, **Rebecca**: the messenger,

my children, **Alice** & **Peter**: the gifts,

my father **Pedro José**: the unconditional,

my mother **María**: the silent wisdom,

everyone who helped me become who I am today,

and to **Jesus**: the **One** who was, is, and will always be.

Foreword

By Justin Brierley

Conversations matter. That's a phrase I've often invoked across the course of my working life hosting debates and dialogues between Christians and non-believers on podcast and radio.

Sadly, we live in a digital age where good conversations are increasingly rare. The algorithms of our social-media-fueled timelines mean that we only hear from sources we already agree with, and tend to demonize those we disagree with. Our polarized online echo chambers have led to the breakdown of civil conversation or mutual understanding.

Part of the problem is that our conversations are increasingly mediated by the screens in our palms and pockets. When we only interact with others through online avatars on social media it's easy to forget that the person we are addressing is another human being, made in the image of God.

However, something very different happens when we sit down together face-to-face. We see a real person in front of us. So much more than mere words is conveyed by our tone and our posture when we talk to each other in the way we were meant to.

First Peter 3:15—"Always be ready to give an answer to anyone who asks you about the reason for the hope that you have" is a verse often appealed to in the world of *apologetics* (the intellectual defense of Christian faith). But the final words of the verse are just as important—"but do this with gentleness and respect."

If our world adopted this maxim it would transform so many aspects of our toxic culture wars and polarized politics. Sadly, in the anonymized world of keyboard warriors, any hint of "gentleness and respect" is quickly thrown out the window! That's why good conversations matter so much.

You are holding in your hands a book that is full of conversations. Yes, the characters and conversations are fictional, but the substance of what is being said is very real.

Perhaps the reason they resonate so much is because their author, Pedro Garcia, has himself pursued such conversations with seekers and skeptics through the "Ask And Wonder" event series he hosted for years. As a former atheist whose own journey to faith has been full of questions and objections (and continues to be), Pedro is wonderfully suited to writing this imagined dialogue.

For over seventeen years I presented a radio show and podcast *Unbelievable?* that aimed to do the same. I was privileged to chair hundreds of conversations between Christians, atheists, agnostics, and those of other worldviews. Yet even the hour or so of conversation I hosted each week was limited in its scope. The setting of a recording studio, with microphones and video cameras can make conversations more about "winning an argument" than "understanding." A podcast studio doesn't truly replicate the place where most conversations happen in reality—face to face between people who are friends.

Often the most natural conversation between my guests would happen after the recording was over, and the microphones were switched off. Relieved of the pressure of "performing," they would often share things that were much more personal and meaningful.

Even better was when there was a chance to go eat afterwards to talk and chat. You could really get to know someone over a meal.

If our conversations remain at the level of winning arguments they can certainly be entertaining to watch. However, that kind of interaction is often more like pushing playing pieces around a chessboard to win a game—it won't result in real change.

Real conversations happen between real people in real relationships. They are rarely completed in a single sitting. They rarely come to definitive conclusions. There are plenty of loose ends and unsettled questions. They can make us feel vulnerable and uncertain because they leave room for doubt. But these conversations also humanize the person in front of us. They enable us to understand the other person, not only intellectually, but emotionally and spiritually. They are often the gateway to real transformation.

I believe we need to get comfortable with open-ended conversations that don't always reach a definitive conclusion.

Jesus had lots of them Himself. Conversations that leave you wondering what happened next…

A conversation in the dead of night with a leading member of the Sanhedrin about spiritual rebirth. We don't know how Nicodemus responded. A conversation that challenged a rich young man give away all his belongings to the poor, and follow him. The man went away troubled. An imagined conversation between a father and his older son, imploring him to join a celebration feast… we don't know if the son accepted.

Likewise, *For Those Who Doubt: Is It Because of Jesus* is a book that doesn't try to give you neat and tidy "evangelistic" conversations.

No one gets led in the sinner's prayer at the end of it. It's much more realistic than that. But in the process, Pedro models what healthy, gracious, and Christ-like dialogue might look like in the lives of the varied characters that walk into The Shire coffee shop.

In our polarized culture we need this kind of example. Better conversations can transform individual lives and the world at large.

Whether you are a seeker or skeptic, a convinced Christian or a deconstructing doubter, this book offers a beautiful way of modeling how to engage in better conversations that will lead, in the end, to truth.

—Justin Brierley, author of *The Surprising Rebirth of Belief In God* and *Why I'm Still a Christian*, and host of the video podcast *Uncommon Ground*.

Why This Book Matters

I've never read a book like this. It's an unusual story, unusually written and unusually engaging. Pedro Garcia has spent decades engaging skeptics of Christianity. Now he lets us eavesdrop, as it were, on life-and-death dialogue. If you have doubts in your mind or doubters among your friends, you'll find yourself at home in these compelling pages!

—Robert J. Morgan, author, podcaster, and associate pastor at World Outreach Church

In a world where questions about faith often feel unsafe to ask, Pedro Garcia offers a courageous and imaginative story that creates room for honest wrestling. Through compelling characters and authentic dialogue, *For Those Who Doubt: Is It Because of Jesus?* demonstrates that the core of our doubts is rarely Jesus Himself; in fact, it's in Him that we find the clarity and hope we're searching for! This book is both a mirror for those in the midst of deconstruction and a gentle guide back to the person of Christ. A timely, thought-provoking read that invites doubters and believers alike to lean in closer to Jesus.

—Tommy Swindol, lead pastor, The Donelson Fellowship

Have you ever wrestled with the deepest questions of life? Have you ever experienced doubts about faith or God? Do you have any students who have begun to deconstruct their faith? This book is a great resource for exactly that. *For Those Who Doubt: Is It Because of Jesus?* tells the story of two friends walking through heavy difficulties, trying to make sense of all of it. But the heart of the story is actually the conversation itself. *For Those Who Doubt: Is It Because of Jesus?* reminds us of how important it is to keep talking to one another, to cultivate the conversation, and to not be afraid to spar over ideas with good dialogue and care. This book will be an excellent resource for anyone who is considering walking away from the church, or for those who have loved ones that already have. Keep the conversation going; always point to Jesus!

—Aaron Pontious, husband, father, pastor, M.A. in Christian Apologetics – Biola University

Some books are more than projects—and *For Those Who Doubt: Is It Because of Jesus?* is one of them. Pedro Garcia's journey from unbelief to faith has been marked by hard questions, careful thought, and honest conversations. At its heart, his story is all about Jesus. Readers will benefit not only from his study and experience, but from the way he brings it all down to earth in an engaging, personal way. The relatable characters, great conversations, and intelligently presented truths in this book will be a lifeline for those wrestling with doubt or deconstructing their faith, and a valuable resource for anyone walking alongside them.

—Mark McPeak, senior vice president of market research at 5by5 Agency

Table of Contents

Prologue.......13

Chapter 1: **Doubts Are Creeping**.......17

Chapter 2: **Nothing Is Forever**.......41

Chapter 3: **Unexpected Turns**.......65

Chapter 4: **Truth Is a Journey**.......95

Chapter 5: **For the Bible Tells Me So**.......129

Chapter 6: **Justice for All**.......175

Chapter 7: **Proud of My Weaknesses**.......223

Chapter 8: **Soul's Carving Party**.......255

Chapter 9: **A Prison of My Own**.......287

Chapter 10: **Nothing**.......309

Chapter 11: **No More**.......347

Chapter 12: **Peace in Uncertainty**.......357

Chapter 13: **THE Conversation**.......377

Chapter 14: **The Day Before**.......397

Chapter 15: **Thank You**.......409

Prologue

Doubting, deconstructing (the process of critically and systematically re-examining, questioning, and often dismantling—and hopefully rebuilding or reforming—the beliefs, doctrines, and practices that one has inherited or previously held, willingly or unwillingly, consciously aware or unaware) or feeling as though you are losing your Christian faith is a deeply complex experience. It often isolates us, making us feel alone, even when we are not. You might be surrounded by a loving church family or supportive relatives at home, yet the loneliness lingers.

Your Christian faith isn't just a belief system; it's an ideal that shapes your identity—your worldview, how you see others, and how you understand yourself. It is how you process and filter reality. This is what makes the process of doubt so daunting. As you doubt or deconstruct your faith, you are also (intentionally or unintentionally) challenging the person you thought you were. It's no wonder it can feel overwhelming, even frightening at times. "Who am I?" or "Who can I be after this?"

You might hesitate to share your questions with Christian friends, fearing you'll make them uncomfortable—or worse, that you might sow doubt in them. But trust me, shutting yourself off is the first real step toward isolation and resentment, which can wound you for years to come. Many who start down this path eventually feel that it was *faith* that abandoned *them*, rather than the other way around. Years later, some may even convince themselves it was all a mere intellectual journey and nothing more. However, deep down, their hearts may say otherwise.

Perhaps you've tried to be honest about your struggles, only to be met with simplistic or passive answers (a lack of faith, not enough time in prayer or Scripture, etc.). And while those offering advice genuinely care, they often don't know how to help. Maybe you confided in someone you trusted, only to feel dismissed or judged instead of heard.

If that's the case, I understand why you would pull away. However, I encourage you not to give up. There are countless churches and people who would walk with you through your questions, emotional struggles, and doubts. You might be surprised to find that many Christians—historical and modern—have faced the same challenges. Did you know that all the great figures in Scripture experienced doubt at some point? Oftentimes, when an individual battles his doubt with sincerity and honesty, it ends up becoming a necessary step toward the realization that God is calling him to be the kind of Christian he hopes to see in others.

If you are unsure where to turn or who to talk to, know that *you* are the reason I wrote this book. I don't want you to feel alone. I wish I could sit with you at a quiet coffee shop, listen to your story, and be your friend. Since I can't do that in person, I've chosen the most meaningful way to do it instead: through storytelling.

You will immediately notice the unique format in which this story is written. It will feel quite unconventional, but that is intentional. I want this to read more like a drama script than a novel. Why? Because at the heart of this book is a conversation and a central character in this story. The story is intended to feel like a living and breathing conversation between two friends, happening right in front of you. My reason? Too many people—Christian and non-Christian—shy away from open conversations about faith. It is a topic that simply is not discussed, and therefore, does not have space within relationships to grow and develop through a healthy and honest dialogue. I want to remove the stigma of having honest and caring conversations about the most important questions in life. This book is designed to make you feel like you are part of a discussion, sitting with the characters, engaging in their back-and-forth as they explore faith, questions, doubts, truth, and everything in between.

The story you are about to read, the characters you'll meet, and the situations you'll experience are a collection of moments from my own journey—from atheism to Jesus over the past 13 years. While the characters are not real, this story is inspired by my life. My hope is that you experience an array of emotions as you read: comfort and discomfort; reflection and introspection; frustration and satisfaction; despair and hope.

In my experience, it is rare that intellectual arguments are the root of the deconstruction. Deep inside, we all have an inner child yearning to belong, to feel fully known, to find answers about why the world isn't as it should be. Intellectual arguments can engage your mind, but they don't reach the parts of you that ache when no one is watching. Sometimes what we genuinely need can't be found in books but in a simple, sincere embrace. So, as you wrestle with your doubts, approach them with your heart *and* mind—not one or the other.

I wish I could hear your story. If I could, I'd ask you the one question that inspired me to write this book. When you finish reading, you'll find that question waiting for you. When you do, pause, look around, breathe deeply, and answer honestly. But no more spoilers for now.

Go ahead, my friend.

Thursday, September 14

Thomas: *(phone ringing . . .)*

Peter: *(answers the call)* Are you alright, mate? I cannot believe you are calling me, Thomas. This better be good enough to have made you overcome your "aversion" to phone calls, haha.

Thomas: *(smiles)* Hey man, *(his voice sounds down and somber)* I was wondering if you had time to grab coffee with me today . . .

(Thomas takes an uncomfortable pause before he speaks again.)

Thomas: There is something I need to tell you.

After hearing Thomas' voice, Peter's tone changes to a concerned one.

Peter: Of course, Thomas. You don't sound good at all. Are you alright?

Thomas: Well . . . I'm not doing well and don't know what to do about it. You are the only person I trust with what I am going through.

Peter: You don't sound quite good, mate. Let me make a few phone calls to cancel a meeting I have in a few minutes so we can spend time together.

Thomas: Dude . . . you don't have to do that. I can wait.

Peter: Rubbish, Thomas. Work and meetings can wait. You cannot.

Thomas: Thank you, Peter. Man . . . are you sure?

Peter: You know what I would say, wouldn't you?

Thomas: Yes . . . I know . . . "If I say it, then I mean it."

Peter: That's right. Let me call you back in a few minutes.

Thomas: OK.

A few minutes later.

Peter: *(phone ringing)*

Thomas: Yes?

Peter: Thomas, fancy a cup of coffee at *The Shire* in 20 minutes?

Thomas: That works great for me. Coffee is on me.

Peter: We'll see about that.

They both laugh.

Thomas is anxious. He and Peter are such close friends, but he is about to make Peter aware of some things that he has been wrestling with internally; uncertainties, doubts, and a journey that seems to be taking him to a very unexpected place. On the other hand, Peter has an intuition because Thomas has been acting a bit differently lately. Peter has noticed his anxious demeanor, and he has picked up on a deep sense of unsettlement within Thomas. Twenty minutes later, they arrive at The Shire. The Shire *is a small, quaint, coffee shop located a few minutes from a peaceful town in Maine. Right by The Shire is a forest trail leading to a calm and quiet lake. Lourdes, the owner and barista of* The Shire, *welcomes them both.*

Lourdes: *¡Míralos a los dos!* The same?

Peter: Yes, and it's on me.

Thomas sighs and rolls his eyes. Peter pushes Thomas playfully.

Peter: Oh, look! Our favorite table is free.

Their favorite table is next to a window with a view of the trail and the distant shimmering sun clothing the lake. There are trees on both sides of the trail, and whenever there is a breeze, all the leaves create a gentle melody that has soothed the burdened walks of many throughout the years. The two-mile walk is a metaphor for life, with its ups and downs along the smooth yet sometimes bumpy path that leads to the lake. There is no yelling, no arguing, and no pretending to be someone you are not. The Shire *is a place for good, deep, and vulnerable conversations where a challenge is always welcome. There is no drive-through because* The Shire *is a place for weekly reunions and lengthy stays. The small building is rectangular and decorated with a rustic cottage atmosphere. The wooden walls are painted in a gentle white that has lost its brightness over the years but has gained much wisdom because of all the conversations they have witnessed. If these walls could only speak . . . Sometimes, the coastal decorations at* The Shire *makes one feel as if he can hear the sea.*

Peter and Thomas sit down and get comfortable. A few minutes later, Lourdes brings two coffees to their table, still wondering after years of preparing cups like these whether she would choose coffee's aroma over its flavor if she had to pick one of the two. As she approaches their table, she still has time to wonder why she faces those internal dilemmas when no one tells her to do so.

Lourdes: Here you go.

Lourdes stops for a second, frowning while looking at Thomas.

Lourdes: Thomas, are you feeling OK?

Thomas: Yes, I'm fine.

Lourdes gently taps Thomas's shoulder. She and Peter exchange a quick and worried look before she goes back to attend to other customers.

Lourdes: Let me know if you need anything else.

Thomas: Thank you, Lourdes.

Peter and Thomas both try their coffee—knowing it will probably be hot—to give themselves a few seconds to settle, anticipating what they feel will be an unusual conversation.

Peter: Yes, this is terribly hot. As Lourdes would say—"Coffee needs to be served hot to warm up the blizzard we all are journeying within us."

Suddenly, everyone at the coffee shop hears Lourdes from behind the counter.

Lourdes: That's true!

Peter and Thomas seem to have forgotten Lourdes can do many things simultaneously: serving coffee, attending to customers, loving people, and always paying attention to comments about her favorite subject—coffee, of course. Peter and Thomas laugh at Lourdes' comment.

Peter: Well, Thomas, is everything going well? What is going on with you?

Thomas: Peter, I don't know how to say this . . .

Peter: Be sure I will need you one day, as you seem to need me today. Don't worry about me. Is it about Sofía?

Thomas: Kind of . . . ?

Thomas' eyes fill up with tears until one runs down his right cheek.

Peter: I am sorry, Thomas. What's going on?

Thomas: I don't know how to tell her.

Thomas sighs and wipes the tear off his face before gathering the strength to keep going.

Thomas: I don't know how to tell you either.

Peter: Just tell me.

Thomas leans forward to whisper something to Peter, but he needs to recompose before doing so.

Thomas: I don't think I believe Christianity is true anymore.[1]

Even though Peter can still hear people talking, Lourdes preparing coffee, and many other things around him, sometimes certain words or situations silence the world around you, making you feel incapable of hearing anything else. Peter worries for his friend, yet he maintains his soft smile.

Thomas: *(nervous as if expecting a sign of disappointment from Peter)* What are you thinking? How does this make you feel?

Peter: I am proud of you.

Thomas: What?!

Peter: I am proud of you.

Thomas: What do you mean?

Peter: I am proud of you because you care enough for truth that you are not afraid of asking questions.[2] You never stopped being inquisitive about the world around you. Also, I am honored you would share something as personal as this with me. I care for you, Thomas, and I will still care for you wherever your journey of doubting and questioning takes you.[3]

Thomas seems sad and emotional.

---

[1] Matthew 28:17: When they saw him, they worshiped him—but some of them doubted!

[2] Luke 2:46: Three days later they finally discovered him in the Temple, sitting among the religious teachers, listening to them and asking questions.

[3] 1 John 4:8: But anyone who does not love does not know God, for God is love.

Peter: Are you alright?

Thomas: Yes, I guess. I just didn't know how you were going to react. This is a harrowing process.

Peter: *(while carefully holding his coffee)* I am sure it must be. It was so for me 12 years ago when I became a follower of Jesus after being an atheist all my life. Ah! Sorry! This coffee is scalding!

Peter leans forward and, looking at Lourdes out of the corner of his eye, whispers to Thomas:

Peter: I don't know if "anyone's blizzard" needs a coffee as hot as this one.

Both Peter and Thomas smile.

Thomas: *(smiling while still emotional)* Did you lose any friends when you became a follower of Jesus?

Peter: Yes, I did.

Thomas: And how did that make you feel?

Peter: It wasn't fun at all. I miss them, but certainly, some of them changed their attitude toward me due to my faith in Jesus . . .

A sudden thought makes Peter change topics, almost interrupting himself.

Peter: Let me guess, are you afraid that Sofía might be disappointed when you tell her?

Thomas: Of course, I am. Her relationship with Jesus is everything to her,[4] *(his voice cracks a little)* and I love her.

Peter: There is no doubt about that.

Thomas doesn't feel as comfortable having to sit that long with his feelings, and Peter knows this about him, so he shakes it off by asking Peter a question he has never asked him before.

Thomas: Peter, do you ever doubt God's existence?

Peter: I would be lying to you if I said that I do not have doubts like that. However, when I doubt, I doubt toward Him, not away from him.

Thomas: What do you mean?

Peter: I mean that there will always be questions about God and His relationship with us that I will never have answers for on this side of eternity,[5] but my doubting has led to a discovery of a deeper love for Him. In your case, it seems that you have been doubting away from Him. Would you say that is the case?

Thomas: Yes.

Peter: When did you begin questioning your faith?

Thomas: I don't know if I can pinpoint an exact time when I began to doubt. However, a few months back, I realized my faith wasn't my own; it was my parents'. I feel like I came to believe Christianity was true because I had to, not because I needed to.

---

[4] 2 Corinthians 5:7: For we live by believing and not by seeing.

[5] Ecclesiastes 3:11: Yet God has made everything beautiful for its own time. He has planted eternity in the human heart, but even so, people cannot see the whole scope of God's work from beginning to end.

Peter: Huh . . . would you expound on that?

Thomas: You know? Growing up in a Christian family, the only worldview I experienced from childhood . . . I didn't come to believe in God out of necessity; or out of a personal experience with Him. I just accepted He was real from the very beginning, by default, without wrestling with it. As soon as I started asking questions about it, I realized I didn't have answers to many of my questions, making me very anxious.

Peter: *(pensively)* At the end of the day, I wonder if any of us have the answers to *all* the questions. What are some of your questions?

Thomas: I am on the fence about whether God is real or not, which in turn affects everything that many think is evidence of His existence: life, relationships, morality, big questions . . .

Peter: And what about *Jesus*?

Thomas: *(confused)* What about Him?

Peter: Because Jesus is Christianity. Jesus, God the Son, has always existed from eternity past,[6] but Christianity could not exist without Jesus[7]. Thomas, I respect your journey. So much. But would you allow me to share something with you about my journey?

Thomas: Of course.

---

[6] Hebrews 13:8: Jesus Christ is the same yesterday, today, and forever. See also Colossians 1:16–17; Revelation 10:5–6, which together affirm that Jesus is eternal.

[7] 1 Corinthians 15:3–4, 17: I passed on to you what was most important and what had also been passed on to me. Christ died for our sins, just as the Scriptures said. He was buried, and he was raised from the dead on the third day, just as the Scriptures said . . . And if Christ has not been raised, then your faith is useless and you are still guilty of your sins.

Peter: It's all about Jesus, Thomas. This sounds weird because I love Jesus so much that, at this point, my life only makes sense because of Him—but here it is: I think there are many reasons people say no to Christianity, but none of those reasons seem to provide sufficient answers for someone to say, "No" to the person of Jesus. After all, Jesus is the one who provides the structure and sustenance of the worldview you are doubting in the first place.[8] For example, have you ever heard about the problem of divine hiddenness?

Thomas: Yes, you mean that God is absent, hidden, or silent, and that causes many to doubt that He exists because He seems to be, well, remarkably absent from the world.

Peter: Exactly. This topic can be fascinating to explore as a thought experiment in philosophical and theological contexts. But in principle, the last thing God is doing is hiding from us because He became one of us in Jesus.[9] God did the opposite of hiding. Instead, He presented Himself to us so everyone could see Him. If God entered history in the person of Jesus, then saying no to Jesus is the most tangible way to say no to Christianity. Trust me, my friend, it is bizarre for me to invite the thought of rejecting Jesus, but the whole premise from God was and has always been that we have the freedom to choose Him or reject Him. Therefore, seeking the truth through the many questions that we may wrestle with is a really important part of our journey.[10] So, as your friend, I do not want

---

[8] Colossians 1:16: for through him God created everything in the heavenly realms and on earth. He made the things we can see and the things we can't see—such as thrones, kingdoms, rulers, and authorities in the unseen world. Everything was created through him and for him.

[9] John 1:14: So the Word became human and made his home among us. He was full of unfailing love and faithfulness. And we have seen his glory, the glory of the Father's one and only Son.

[10] James 1:5: If you need wisdom, ask our generous God, and he will give it to you. He will not rebuke you for asking.

to hinder your search for truth. The pursuit of truth is the greatest endeavor that any human being can devote themselves to. In my experience, it was and is my pursuit of truth that has been so life-changing, and discovering truth has brought so much freedom in my life. But all of that started with serious, honest questions about the most important things. A person's faith should be questioned, because it is often in the questioning that we can land on a sincere, justified belief. Thomas, if I hadn't asked any questions, perhaps I wouldn't be a follower of Jesus today.

Thomas: I can see that, Peter, and it makes sense from your perspective. The problem for me is that believing in Jesus entails both that God exists and that we can trust the Bible, and I am not sure about either anymore.

Peter: That makes sense . . .

Peter sighs to relieve some tension, trying to settle in Thomas' newfound journey, seemingly moving him away from God.

Peter: What about sacrificial love?

Thomas: What about it?

Peter: Have you ever felt the tension, nervousness, fear, and uncertainty that settles in your stomach when someone you love is suffering? Have you ever come to the point that you would do anything to stop it?

Thomas: *(confused)* Yes?

Peter: God feels just like that for you, me, and the entire world. It is a level of unconditional love that surpasses all understanding. Think about someone you love this way.

Thomas remains quiet. He knows who . . .

Peter: I know that I am humanizing God, but I wonder how it must "feel" to carry this intense concern in your "stomach," not for one person, but for the entire world. I guess Jesus, in His human nature, had to feel that too . . .[11]

Peter winces as if the mere thought of it had already begun hurting. Peter seems lost in his thoughts for a moment.

Peter: . . . A love so profound that became sacrificial in Jesus.

Peter and Thomas look out the window momentarily since words don't seem capable of filling the void Peter's comment just opened in their conversation.

Peter: Anyway, Thomas . . . So, at this point on your journey, would you say you are saying "no" to Christianity because of Jesus?

Thomas is taken aback.

Thomas: *(doubtful)* When you put it like that, I guess not.

Peter leans back in his chair, allowing the conversation to rest a little bit.

Peter: Is there anything I can do to help you? Going through something like this can be very unsettling.

Thomas: Thank you, Peter. Would you be open to exploring all my questions and doubts about Christianity with me?

---

[11] One example is Matthew 23:37, where Jesus lamented over the city of Jerusalem because they rejected Him.

Peter: Imagine me saying no to spending time with you, talking about the big questions in life! It's not happening!

Thomas: Wait, so you don't want to do it?

Peter: Haha! No! Sorry. I meant there isn't anything else I would rather do in this world than that.

Thomas feels more at ease.

Peter: I guess the only thing I'd like to say, Thomas, is that we need to care for each other and our friendship as we explore all these questions together. I don't want to lose you as a friend in the process. Let's make a deal.

Thomas: What is it?

Peter: Let's talk about everything without holding anything back. Let's also care for each other; I mean truly knowing that behind each of our opinions is a person full of wonder, awe, fears, and insecurities—someone who knows some things and doesn't know many things, etc.

Suddenly, Peter stops and frowns, looking directly at Thomas.

Thomas: *(bewildered)* What? What's wrong?

Peter: I just want to make sure . . . *(using a mocking, robotic tone)* Is there a person behind your opinions?

Thomas rolls his eyes and sighs. There is a hint of a smirk somewhere hidden in his face.

Thomas: Oh my. Was that supposed to be a joke?

Peter: You know it, mate.

Thomas: Your jokes are horrible, Peter.

Peter: I very much appreciate your subjective appreciation of my humor. However, it still doesn't deter you from wanting to be my friend, does it?

Thomas: That's true. I guess I *do* know what sacrificial love truly means after all.

Peter laughs. Thomas smiles for a second. In a way, Peter did at least make him smile, somehow.

Thomas: Yes, I want the same. One of my biggest fears through this process is losing many of the relationships I have with my family, at church, with you, and . . .

Peter knows where Thomas' list is going.

Peter: Sofía.

Thomas: Yes, Sofía.

Thomas begins feeling uncomfortable again.

Peter: Why are you afraid of Sofía's reaction?

Thomas: Well, I am not afraid of her reaction toward me, meaning that she would stop caring for me. My fear is hurting her because she and I have rooted our relationship in God, so I am afraid that if I question God, she might think I am questioning the love I feel for her. Besides, we are engaged at this point. This could be devastating for her.

Peter: The fact that you are worrying more for her than yourself, though, says so much about the motivations of your heart.

Thomas: She is the most important person in my life.

Peter: Then, if that is so, why should you be afraid of telling her? The most important person in your life wouldn't like to see you embark on this journey without her beside you.

Thomas: Peter, what if my doubts cause her to doubt too? How could I live with the thought that I could be the reason she lost her faith in God, too?

Thomas' fear becomes Peter's fear for a moment, weighing heavily in his heart. Suddenly, something seems to catch Peter's attention outside. Two little birds fly by and perch on a tree, oblivious to their conversation. Thomas notices Peter's body language becoming more serene as soon as he notices the birds outside. Internally, Jesus' words echo in Peter's heart: "What is the price of two sparrows—one copper coin? But not a single sparrow can fall to the ground without your Father knowing it."[12] *Peter looks at Thomas as he sits back, gathering the words he'd been holding onto for what felt like an eternity.*

Peter: "Love never gives up, never loses faith, is always hopeful, and endures through every circumstance."[13]

Thomas: *(smiles)* I still feel that's true. Do you think I should tell her?

Peter: I think so. Ultimately, neither you nor anyone is responsible for any other person's faith. Sofía's faith belongs to her. If your questions made Sofía doubt her faith, this would be a good thing for Sofía to face, an opportunity to grow closer to Jesus after those questions are answered.

---

[12] Matthew 10:29.

[13] 1 Corinthians 13:7.

Thomas: It almost sounds like you see doubting as something . . .*good*? It's tough on me.

Peter: Perhaps I wouldn't say "good." Instead, I would say doubts are a great "opportunity" to refine what we understand about truth so that we can act accordingly.

Thomas: But what if your doubts take you away from the belief you thought was true?

Peter remains quiet.

Thomas: You don't have an answer to that question?

Peter: No.

Thomas: Or is it that you don't want to answer it?

Peter: Neither.

Thomas: So?

Peter: *(lost in his thoughts)* Um . . . Sometimes, we believe getting an answer is the only way to move forward. But, sometimes, embracing the uncertainty of not having one is ultimately better for the person we aim to become.

Thomas: OK, man. Are you avoiding my question?

Peter: Are you avoiding my answer?

Thomas and Peter smile and let it rest for a few seconds.

Peter: Thomas, you should tell her. It is the right thing to do.

Thomas: It feels the right thing to do, but that doesn't make it easier.

Peter: I know.

Thomas: OK, I'll tell her tonight and tell you how it goes.

Peter: Would you like to meet next week at the same time here?

Thomas: I'd love that.

Peter: OK, Thomas. I hope it goes well. Please don't fear your questions because God doesn't either.

Thomas: I still feel some people at church would be afraid of my questions, though.

Peter: I know, but Thomas, perhaps you might have been afraid of other people's questions at some point in your life within different circumstances. Every person's journey is sacred. The questions we ask—and even those questions we don't ask—constantly wrestle in our hearts. I believe only God and the person who is asking know about them. Please, don't focus on others' opinions. Instead, focus on your questions and this faith journey, and of course, Sofía.

Thomas: I never thought I would have to go through this. This is not like changing your opinion about whether I like this coffee or not—please don't tell Lourdes I said that! Instead, this is something that can change the way I see the world and even the way others see me. Honestly, it feels very daunting.

Lourdes did hear it.

Peter: What do you mean by the way others see you?

Thomas: Sofía, you, the church—if I stopped believing in God, would you treat me the same way?

Peter: It depends on what you mean by belief. If you mean merely "ideas" that have no consequences on behavior, then nothing will change between us. But I don't think we are talking about that. In Jesus, we remain in Him,[14] we make Him the Lord of everything that we do,[15] and we live our lives on mission for Him.[16] So, if you stop following Him, your lifestyle will also change as a consequence of it. In that case, if you were to begin doing something that goes against God's will for your life and everyone's life, I wouldn't support it, but this wouldn't change the fact that I would care for you all the same.

Thomas: Why do I feel that this wouldn't be the case with all Christians? I feel that if they knew I was questioning my faith, some of them would start treating me differently.

Peter: I think you are right, unfortunately. But think about this: isn't that the case with all of us, no matter what we believe? This is what I mean. Some of my friends began seeing me and treating me differently when I became a follower of Jesus back in England. This has nothing to do with believing or not believing. Instead, this is the natural human response to something new or something we don't understand happening around us; we are all reticent at first. That's all true, but I know how you feel. This is not easy because we are talking about your life and the genuine relationships that are within it.

---

[14] John 15:4: Remain in me, and I will remain in you. For a branch cannot produce fruit if it is severed from the vine, and you cannot be fruitful unless you remain in me.

[15] Galatians 2:20: My old self has been crucified with Christ. It is no longer I who live, but Christ lives in me. So I live in this earthly body by trusting in the Son of God, who loved me and gave himself for me.

[16] John 17:18–19: Just as you sent me into the world, I am sending them into the world. And I give myself as a holy sacrifice for them so they can be made holy by your truth.

Thomas: Exactly. You know? You asked me a few minutes ago about when I began to have questions or when I began doubting my faith. Something I can tell you is this: As soon as I started having questions, I immediately felt I didn't have many friends who consider themselves Christians with whom I could openly have the conversation I am having with you right now. This doesn't help at all, and it makes me feel many people believe out of fear, not out of freedom and love for Jesus. If they are free in Christ,[17] they shouldn't be afraid to ask questions.

Peter: You have a point there, Thomas.

Thomas: So, why do you think that happens?

Peter: I think no one ever stops being afraid of something, not even Christians. Christ sets us free from the bondage of our sin, meaning that I keep sinning all the time, although I don't belong to sin anymore. I don't "serve" it as I used to. It doesn't control me. I am free in Christ in that sense. Now, what do I do with that freedom once I am free in Christ? That's a totally different question. Freedom entails having more than one option. Options entail consequences, and we rarely can control the consequences of our actions. Therefore, fear and uncertainty will always be there as we follow Jesus.

Thomas: So, your belief in Jesus doesn't comfort you or change your fears?

Peter: It does. It reduces them, to be sure, but I still feel them. There is at least one thing I am not afraid of: God's judgment when He responds to injustice—including mine—in the end, because

[17] John 8:36: So if the Son sets you free, you are truly free.

He has already accepted me as a member of His family through Jesus' sacrifice on the cross.[18] When I began to follow Jesus, my destination was set, but I still had to walk the journey. Christ never promised it would be an easy one.[19] All that to say: Thomas, if some Christians are afraid of your questions, it doesn't necessarily have to do with a "he is different, he is not like me" mentality, Perhaps your questions are tapping into their fears; fears that they are trying their best to not have, fears that could make them reminisce about the people they were before coming to Christ. Thomas, I have always believed that one question can be the first step toward absolutely anything. Therefore, it is expected to find people, Christians or not, who would rather live peaceful, quiet lives, and not worry about questioning how and why things are the way that they are. Who knows what is behind all the fears we have? I believe only God knows. We rarely know why people react or behave as they do; answers are usually more complicated than a simple yes or no. Therefore, I encourage you to focus on your journey for now and try to understand your reasons for doubting. And as much as we would love to, we cannot control what others think about anything, including what they think about us.

Thomas: You don't mind what others think or say about you?

Peter: Oh, yes, I do, but I know I cannot control it, so that brings me a sense of constant peace as I struggle with it. I focus on obeying Jesus and letting my actions speak of the faith I claim to carry within me. However, this is harder with people who are closer to us, like it is in the case of Sofía for you, for example.

---

[18] Romans 8:1 So now there is no condemnation for those who belong to Christ Jesus.

[19] John 16:33: I have told you all this so that you may have peace in me. Here on earth you will have many trials and sorrows. But take heart, because I have overcome the world.

Thomas: That's what I mean.

Peter: I know, Thomas.

Thomas looks around the coffee shop. People are having conversations, drinking coffee, and relaxing. Everything looks unsettlingly "perfect" around him. He had known this pain before, one that disconnected him from his surroundings and left him feeling stranded in a separate reality, even for a moment. Peter interrupts his moment of introspection.

Peter: Do you still pray?

Thomas holds his coffee and takes a slow sip, pretending Peter never asked him that. Unfortunately, after swallowing his coffee, the question is eagerly awaiting him.

Thomas: Praying hurts. It reminds me of all my doubts and makes me feel uncertain and confused, and the thought of having talked to a God who might not be real for so many years feels a little bit like a . . .

Peter: Like what?

Thomas: A failure?

Peter: A failure? Why?

Thomas: What if both of us have wasted our time on something that is actually not real? How would that make you feel?

Peter: It would make me feel horrible. That's how I felt when I stopped pursuing the world and began following Jesus. I felt as if I had wasted my life in some sense. Did I actually waste it? I don't think I did. My experience in the world and what it offers helped me know how to value what Jesus did for the world itself.[20]

Thomas, pensively, looks down at his empty cup of coffee, which for a moment reminds him that everything has an end. But even his faith in Jesus?

Peter: Thomas, take it easy. Why don't you take some time to think, give yourself time during the day when you don't think about this, and talk to Sofía. And then we meet in a week to talk about everything? You could also bring one of your questions, and we could explore it together.

Thomas: OK, sounds like a plan.

As both leave The Shire, *Lourdes gestures to Thomas, waving a small bag with something inside.*

Thomas: What is this?

Lourdes: *Llévate esto.*

Thomas: Lourdes, I don't know what that means.

Lourdes: It's your favorite muffin. Take it. I hope it makes you feel better. The more you think about whatever is burdening you, the more of a burden it will become.

Am I that obvious? *Thomas wonders. He is thankful for the muffin, which is Sofía's favorite, too, and it reminds him of the conversation he is bound to have in a few hours with her.*

Thomas: Thank you, Lourdes.

---

[20] Luke 15:11–32: The Parable of the Lost Son.

Lourdes smiles as she gets back to making coffee. Once outside, Thomas rolls his eyes in disbelief.

Thomas: They say God is omniscient . . . but, man, what about Lourdes? She is aware of everything that happens in her coffee shop. I guess I was too obvious.

Peter: We care for you, mate. I'll be . . .

Peter interrupts himself, feeling unsure.

Thomas: What?

Peter: It's OK. No worries, Thomas.

Both smile and hug each other as they walk to their cars in the parking lot. Lourdes also saw the hug through the window. Peter didn't say it to Thomas, but the first thing he was eager to do after leaving The Shire *was to find rest in the solitude of the trail. Another burdened walk on the trail that leads to the lake.*

Peter: *(whispering while seeing Thomas drive out of the parking lot)* I'll be praying for you, Thomas.

Thursday, September 21

As Peter approaches The Shire, *he sees Thomas sitting at their favorite table inside. Through the window, he notices Thomas holding something in his hands. A letter? Thoughts rush through Peter's mind as he tries to discern Thomas' emotions from a distance. However, the reflection of the trees and the sky on the window doesn't let him do it. As Peter opens the door of the coffee shop, he stops for a second; lost in his thoughts, he wonders:* Should I have called him? I don't think so. Pain needs room to breathe even more than the people who carry it. Remember, Peter, prayer is our greatest ministry. *The coffee shop is emptier than usual, with only one more person sitting on the corner of the coffee shop. An old man with a steaming coffee on the table writes something calmly but intently on a notepad. Lourdes has her back turned as she works on making coffee. Peter waves at Thomas. There is a hint of a smile on Thomas' face, but it rapidly dissipates.*

Peter: Hi, Thomas, do you want something?

Thomas: Hey, Peter, yes—Lourdes is making our coffee right now.

Lourdes is turned away and focused on her coffee-making, unaware that Peter is approaching the counter.

Peter: Oh, thank you, Thomas. *(to Lourdes)* Hi Lourdes. It's good to see your . . . back?

Peter's voice makes Lourdes jolt for a second.

Lourdes: Oh! *¡Qué susto, Peter!* Where have you been? The last time you stopped by was last Thursday when you came with Thomas. Is everything OK?

Peter: Oh yes, I couldn't come as much as I would have wanted. A couple of doctor visits messed up my schedule a bit.

As soon as Lourdes hears the word "doctor," she stops what she is doing and turns around as intently as a mother would do upon hearing her child crying.

Lourdes: Doctor? You are too young for doctors. *¿Qué te pasa*?

Peter: I guess that means . . . what's going on?

Lourdes: *Sí*. What's going on?

Peter: They are running some tests—nothing unusual. But it takes so much time to go to the doctor! It does mess up your entire day. I am thankful for medicine, though; understand me.

Lourdes notices Peter's voice shake a little bit. He is pretending to show a level of confidence he doesn't have. Peter realizes Lourdes can see through it but changes topics as fast as he can while thinking: Today is about Thomas. Don't let your fear stop you from caring for your friend. Trust and surrender.[21] Please, help me, Jesus. *Lourdes knows both Thomas and Peter well.* What is going on with these two? *She wonders.*

Peter: Let us know when our coffees are ready, Lourdes.

Lourdes: *(suspicious)* I will...

Thomas: Thank you, Lourdes.

As Peter heads to their table, curious, he says to himself, There is no question about it. That's a letter.

Peter: Hey, Thomas. How is it going?

Peter knows. Thomas knows that he knows.

Peter: *(after a few seconds)* Not OK?

Thomas: Not OK.

Peter: What's going on?

Thomas: It's Sofía.

Peter: Did you tell her?

---

[21] Proverbs 3:5–6: Trust in the LORD with all your heart; do not depend on your own understanding. Seek his will in all you do, and he will show you which path to take.

Thomas: Yes, the same night we had our conversation last week.

Peter: And how did she feel about it?

Thomas: She is . . . gone.

Peter: Gone?!

Thomas: No! No! Not in that way.

Peter: What do you mean then? Please don't scare me!

Thomas: We met to have dinner together, and as soon as she saw me, she knew something was wrong. She has worried about me for a while because I feel more evasive. Then she asked me: "Thomas, is there anything you need to tell me?" For a moment, I wished from the bottom of my heart that she hadn't asked me that question, but I knew I couldn't keep pretending anymore. So, I told her.

Peter: What did you tell her?

Thomas: I told her I don't know whether Christianity is true.

Peter: How did she react?

Thomas begins to feel agitated and nervous.

Thomas: I have never seen her like that, Peter. She began crying inconsolably, and she couldn't stop saying, "I cannot do this again—I cannot do this again."

Peter: *(confused)* I cannot do this again? What did she mean?

Thomas sighs, trying to calm himself down.

Thomas: Well, there is something I have never told you about Sofía's brother.

Peter: What is it?

Thomas: Once their father passed away, her brother fell into a deep depression, began questioning his faith, blamed God for the whole thing, and moved away, leaving Sofía and their mom all alone. She tried her best to help her brother as she was mourning the sudden loss of their father, feeling that, in a sense, she was losing her brother, too. And she did. He is bitter toward anything that relates to Christianity and repeatedly tells Sofía and their mom that they are living a lie. He has almost cut off all connection with them. They rarely talk to each other at this point.

Peter: And now she feels she might lose you too.

Suddenly, Lourdes turns around the counter, holding their coffees. In her mind, she concludes that she would choose coffee's aroma over its taste if she had to. But again, Why should I choose at all when I can have both? *She wonders.*

Lourdes: OK! Here are your coffees. Is there anything else I can do for you?

Peter: No, thank you, Lourdes.

Thomas: Thank you.

Lourdes wished they had told her there was something else she could help them with, but they didn't.

Peter: *(pointing at the envelope)* OK. What is that on the table?

Thomas: It's an envelope from Sofía. After we had our conversation, I told her that I loved her and that my feelings toward her were not going to change no matter what, but I don't think the memory of her pain allowed her to see through my words. She kept saying that suffering and doubts are part of her journey with Jesus to this day, too, but she was frustrated to see how her brother forgot about all the good things Jesus did in his life through their father before he passed. She said her brother was trying to fit Jesus into *his* lifestyle, not vice versa.[22] I told her I had doubts for months, and she didn't understand why I didn't tell her before. I didn't want to hurt her or make her feel afraid because I knew what happened to her brother.

Peter: So, what did she write in the letter?

Thomas: Nothing.

Peter: Nothing?

Thomas: Yes, it's not a letter, but a ring.

It takes Peter a few seconds to understand what's going on. When he does, he feels his stomach turning.

Peter: Did she break off the engagement?!

Thomas: She pulled a small envelope from her purse, took off the ring I bought for her, put it inside, and gave it to me. She said she was afraid of being abandoned once again, and the fear was too unbearable for her. She looked at me and said, "I am sorry, Thomas." She couldn't stop crying. She said: "I need some time to process this. It was so hard to lose my brother after my father's passing. No matter how much time I spent listening and caring for him, I felt insignificant to him. I believe he had already made up his mind about Jesus when he told us he was 'doubting.' Every conversation we had with him turned into an attempt to attack and

[22] Matthew 16:24: Then Jesus said to his disciples, "If any of you wants to be my follower, you must give up your own way, take up your cross, and follow me.

destroy our faith. There wasn't any doubt. Thomas, I wish I could be with you through this, but I physically can't for now."

Peter: Thomas, I am very sorry. I don't know what to say. What happened next?

Thomas: We hugged, and she left the restaurant.

For a few seconds neither one of them says anything. Then . . .

Thomas: Do I love her enough to put aside my doubts so that I can be with her? Yes, I do. But I don't think that would be sincere.

Peter: Have you guys talked since then?

Thomas: No, we haven't. Sofía wasn't doing well in general before that, and I know her; she is the type of person who needs time to think about things.

Peter: I am so sorry.

Thomas realizes Peter looks puzzled. Thomas doesn't say anything.

Peter: Thomas, is it OK if I make one comment about something Sofía said to you?

Thomas: Sure.

Peter: She said her brother wasn't doubting even though he said he was. I think I have found this to be the case sometimes. Some people say, "I am deconstructing," or "I am doubting," implying they are going through some questioning process, while in reality, they already know they don't *want* to believe for some reason or another. If the doubting or deconstruction process is rational and sincere, there should always be a possibility for the person who is doubting or deconstructing to remain a Christian through the whole journey. Might there be, in certain cases, some type of deeply emotional situation that precedes all the deconstructing or doubting, which makes people not want to be a Christian before sincerely exploring the questions they claim they don't have answers for?

Thomas hasn't thought about such an idea before.

Thomas: Was that your case before you became a Christian?

Peter: It's only fair that you asked me the same question. I don't know. I struggled quite a bit on my journey from thinking Christianity was utterly stupid to now thinking it is the actual reason my whole life makes sense at all. Many tend to see emotions as a weakness or a "not enough reason to believe or stop believing in something," but I don't see it that way. I find it curious how some say, "I am doubting" or "I am deconstructing," while what they really mean is, "I don't want to believe anymore, and for that reason, I am doubting or deconstructing." Those aren't quite the same starting point. What about you?

Thomas: What about me?

Peter: Is it your case that you, "don't want to believe anymore"?

Thomas: I . . . think it isn't. Actually, Sofía is a good enough reason for me to "want to believe." I think I began finding some of the arguments for Christianity unconvincing. But I am still open to be convinced of the contrary. It's interesting. When you put it like that, I highly doubt anyone would be open and vulnerable enough to recognize, if true, that their doubting or deconstructing is happening because they have already decided not to *want* to believe anymore due to some experience with suffering or emotional pain.

In fact, that would entail their doubts, even if sincere, and could primarily be fueled not as a rational or intellectual endeavor, but as sentimental or emotional ones.

Peter: I agree. I'm sorry, mate. I didn't want to interrupt you. I am still willing to hear your feelings about what happened with Sofía.

Thomas: No worries, man.

Thomas knows that having a conversation with Peter will constantly challenge him to be deeply introspective about his feelings (something he would rather avoid). His feelings are too wild to control, but he can do nothing about it because he has them too.

Thomas: Sofía *(he sighs her name while shaking his head).*

Suddenly, Thomas drops the envelope on the table in frustration, sits back in his chair, and looks away out the window.

Peter: Hey, Thomas, Thomas—What's going on?

Thomas: It bothers me that she would compare me with her brother.

Peter: I don't think she is intending to, but her fear of the possibility that the same thing could happen to you is at least understandable. Fear, pain, suffering—they are so overwhelming. Sometimes, it feels like someone else is taking control of you, and you can do nothing to avoid it. It is as if you want to escape from yourself, but you can't. She needs time to see through her emotions and see that you are not her brother.

Thomas: . . . and they say, "God is love."[23] Doesn't that sound like a bunch of . . .

Thomas does his best to hold his tongue while making a fist with one hand. It is heartbreaking for Peter to see his friend endure all of this.

Peter: Thomas, don't lose yourself in the frustration of the moment. Take a second.

Thomas: This is one of my biggest issues with Christianity. God is love? OK. But what about all the pain and suffering there is in the world? There is non-stop suffering everywhere, in every person's life. God is all-powerful[24], yet for some reason, he doesn't do anything to stop all the pain and suffering we see around us. This sounds to me like God isn't that loving.

Peter: Actually, it makes even less sense if we followed your train of thought there.

Thomas: What do you mean?

Peter: I believe God, in Jesus, experienced an incommensurable amount of pain and suffering. That doesn't make sense if you stop and think about it from our perspective as His created beings. He didn't have to do it that way, but He did it. He bled Himself out on a cross without having to do that at all. I have a question for you: Having the option to create any world He wanted, why would God choose to make one where He would have to suffer in the hands of His own creation in order to redeem it? Why would He create it that way?

---

[23] 1 John 4:16: We know how much God loves us, and we have put our trust in his love. God is love, and all who live in love live in God, and God lives in them.

[24] Psalm 115:3: Our God is in the heavens, and he does as he wishes.

Thomas: I don't know.

Peter: That's a courageous thing to say!

Thomas: I don't know?

Peter: Yes?

Thomas: Why?

Peter is thrilled. Thomas never knows what is coming next with Peter.

Peter: Because you are showing me you are honest regarding the limitation of your knowledge, and that's a straightforward way to know a person is willing to grow. There are so many things I don't know, and I love it because that means I still have room to grow. Sorry, mate, I got carried away a little bit.

Thomas is baffled, but he cannot contain a smile.

Thomas: Is there any other person besides you who gets that excited when realizing they don't know something? Who are you?

Peter: Haha! I don't know! See? Potential everywhere.

Thomas: Haha! So bad . . .

Peter: Let's go back to the question I asked you: Having the option to create any world He wanted, why would God choose to make one where He would have to suffer in the hands of His own creation in order to redeem it? Why would He create it that way?

Thomas: I am hesitant to say it, but here I go . . . I don't know?

Peter laughs.

Peter: Thomas, I believe it is—from my finite mind—the most brilliant way to show us how much He is willing to sacrifice for you and me. I believe He made you in awe; He knew about you from eternity past, more time than the time you have known yourself. He knows everything about you and loves you unconditionally, but He also wants to give you room to lovingly choose to love Him or reject Him. Real love is an act of freedom. When life gets hard, we mourn and realize that everything is finite and transient, and the world is not how it's supposed to be. When we feel lost, Jesus on the cross reminds us that the One who created us has the most unimaginable love for us. He wants us to know how he feels about us. Love cannot be love if it cannot be rejected. I believe true freedom is the reason God created a world with the possibility of evil. Without true freedom, there is no context for true love.

Thomas: So, are you suggesting people will also have the option to reject Him in Heaven? According to you, love cannot exist without the freedom to reject it.

Peter: That's a great observation! People who will inhabit the new Heaven and the new earth will be those who freely chose to love God when they had the freedom to do so on this side of eternity. However, when it comes to attempting to explain what our relationship with God will be like once everything is changed to last eternally, I don't know how to explain it because I have never experienced perfection in my life.

Thomas: OK. Let me understand something. Are you saying that pain and suffering are necessary for love to exist?

Peter: Yes, maybe for now. This is very paradoxical in nature, but both pain and suffering, probably unwillingly, help set up a stage where love can truly shine. For example, I remember years ago, when I didn't know Jesus, they found a tumor in my neck, and the pain was . . .

Peter must stop to recompose.

Peter: I couldn't swallow, I couldn't lie down in bed, I couldn't sleep. It was horrible. I remember thinking: "What is the purpose of all this suffering?" From my perspective, the idea of God didn't make sense at all, so I didn't even have the option to deal with the pain while having to reconcile that God was loving me through it. I wish I at least had had that. Instead, it felt like I was suffering in a vacuum, with no reasons, no explanations, nothing. And I thought: "That's it? This is life? Doing my best to avoid pain and suffering, doing some good for other people around me, and pursuing pleasurable things 'til one day I die?" As a follower of Jesus, I know He never promised happiness in this life, but joy through suffering as we wait for eternity.[25] If Jesus suffered and died for you and me, and we claim to follow Him, I shouldn't expect His followers to have an easy life either. Love, pain, and suffering are meant to coexist so that we can distinguish one from the other.

Thomas: I am sorry to hear that. That must have been horrible. What caused the tumor?

Peter: I don't know…

Thomas: I don't know? Well, at least there is room to grow in this.

Peter: Haha! Thomas, you might hate my jokes, but you sound more like me the more we spend time together.

---

[25] John 16:33: I have told you all this so that you may have peace in me. Here on earth you will have many trials and sorrows. But take heart, because I have overcome the world.

Thomas smiles.

Thomas: So, wait, you said you couldn't swallow at all?

The very memory of the pain he went through makes Peter wince.

Peter: No. I really couldn't. The tumor was located behind my neck and was exerting some pressure on my nerves back there. Any sudden motion would radiate sharp pains through my back and left arm and would even make my leg spasm involuntarily.

Thomas: I am so sorry, Peter.

Peter: Do you like cheese?

Thomas: *(baffled)* Do I like cheese?

Peter: Yes, do you like cheese?

Thomas: Why?

Peter: Because I believe, in God's providence, that everything happens for a reason, and I know you will think this is one of the cheesiest things to say.

Thomas: I like cheese, but that's a lot of it.

Peter and Thomas laugh.

Thomas: How can you be so profound and abstract and become a five-year-old from one second to another?

Peter looks around, worried that someone might hear what he is about to say to Thomas. He leans forward intently and whispers to him:

Peter: *(whispering)* I don't become a five-year-old. I *am* a five-year-old who sometimes pretends to be an adult. It's so much fun.

Thomas is drinking his coffee, and Peter almost makes him spit it all out.

Thomas: *(laughing)* OK. That was funny *and* scary because I think you are not lying.

Peter and Thomas laugh again.

Thomas: Going back to our conversation, though. There is just so much gratuitous suffering on earth, and we haven't even talked about the evil caused by nature.

Peter: What do you mean by "the evil caused by nature"?

Thomas: Earthquakes, tsunamis, diseases . . . the world is unbelievably cruel.

Peter: I don't think nature is evil, because there is intention and awareness behind evil, and nature doesn't have that since it only follows natural laws. However, you and I both recognize that the world is not how it should be. You raise a challenging point, Thomas. In the big picture, I don't know exactly how sin affected nature, this is something I cannot explain to you. But Paul wrote in the book of Romans that creation is groaning in pain, bringing attention to the point you are bringing up—that there is chaos in creation too.[26]

---

[26] Romans 8:19–21: For all creation is waiting eagerly for that future day when God will reveal who his children really are. Against its will, all creation was subjected to God's curse. But with eager hope, the creation looks forward to the day when it will join God's children in glorious freedom from death and decay.

Thomas: Sorry if this sounds too blunt, but Paul could say anything he wanted; the question is whether it's true or not. You see and understand the world through the perspective of Scripture, but I don't think I do anymore.

Peter doesn't say anything, but his heart sinks to his stomach when Thomas says that. Yet, his heart keeps loving Thomas the same way.

Peter: Thomas, how would you explain evil and suffering beyond a loving God and the nature of sin?

Thomas: I am not sure. Maybe when it comes to the evil we perpetrate as humans, after thousands of years on earth, we have figured out the things that work and those that don't by doing things and making mistakes. That's exactly how it happens in life with anything we do. When it comes to natural disasters, from the point of view of nature, it's not a disaster at all. Nature goes through specific cycles that, indirectly and unintentionally, affect us. Therefore, our objective should be to alleviate pain as much as possible rather than trying to understand why the world is the way it is. "Good" and "evil" might be only a way to name the things we do right and the things we do wrong, and we don't need a "God" to tell us which one is which because we simply need to experience the consequences of our actions to know.

Peter: So, why do we keep failing in the way we treat each other after thousands of years of trial and error? Doesn't that suggest there is something else going on underlying all this evil?

Thomas: We are imperfect, and I don't think anyone ever said the contrary. What could be underlying all this evil?

Peter: Sin, our broken relationship with God.

Thomas: Well, if we all restored our relationship with Jesus on this side of eternity, I think suffering would still exist because Christians keep sinning even though they have been saved. What kind of promise is that?

Peter: Yes, that is the mystery of God and the way He loves us because "the wages of sin is death."[27] For that reason, we all must die once, and because of our sin and the way we all broke our relationship with God, Jesus took on our sin[28] and died in our place to bring us back to Himself. Think of it like two people trading places. Jesus, who is perfect, willingly took the blame for all of humanity's wrongdoings. In return, humanity gets His perfect record. That "trade" is what makes people right with God. It was tough for me to understand this, even during my first years as a follower of Jesus. Jesus never sinned. Therefore, He shouldn't have died; but He did to bear the sins of the world—past, present, and future, yours and mine—to reconcile the world to Himself again. But then He resurrected, which put an end to humanity's greatest enemy—death itself. The promise is that if we follow and obey Jesus, we will also go through the process He had to go through: life, submission to God, death, and resurrection. Jesus suffered on our behalf, and because of His suffering on the cross, we can have the hope of eternal life. Thomas, I understand that many of the things I just said imply that all those things are true, and you are not sure of them anymore; but I was an atheist myself, so before believing all of it was true, I also had to struggle the way you are struggling now . . . I don't believe any of this "just because." But because I have

---

[27] Romans 6:23: For the wages of sin is death, but the free gift of God is eternal life through Christ Jesus our Lord.

[28] 2 Corinthians 5:21: For God made Christ, who never sinned, to be the offering for our sin, so that we could be made right with God through Christ.

experienced pain, suffering, hope, and things that don't make sense for the world, like joy in suffering or hope in despair . . .

Thomas: I am sorry, but none of it makes much sense to me anymore.

Peter: Don't be sorry. Instead, embrace your pursuit of truth as you work through your doubts because it is a brilliant way to arrive at sincere, justified belief. I don't want to convince you of anything; I am just trying to share my life with you and how Jesus changed it forever.

Thomas: But what if it's not true?

Peter: You know what, Thomas? If it is not true, it would be the evilest lie ever told to humanity. Think about it, Jesus is asking the world to stand up to the evil of the world by showing love to it, even to hope in suffering because of what He did. If He wasn't God, then He didn't die for our sins; if He wasn't God, then He never resurrected. Countless people will have died while having hope in something that was false. Now, that would be evil. Besides, what did Jesus or the apostles have to gain from any of this? The stakes are high, and that's why I personally believe there is no middle term with Jesus. His way of seeing the world is so revolutionary that, ultimately, Jesus is either "the Truth" or "the biggest lie" ever told to humanity.

Thomas: You seem very passionate about considering the possibility that Jesus was a liar.

Peter: How can I not be, Thomas? Think about this. I had to make countless decisions, some of them very hard, to come to terms with the reality of Jesus. It is not easy to empty myself of my ways to follow Him daily. I don't want to just believe in Him; I want to obey Him, and obeying Him entails sacrificing many things in this life.

Thomas: *(somewhat frustrated)* But wait a second, you don't believe in Jesus primarily because of love, but because of fear, remember? You told me a few months ago that your biggest fear is death, and that was one of the main reasons why you became a Christian. Isn't that true?

The word "death" travels deep into Peter's heart. Peter goes blank for a few seconds, almost as if he has left the coffee shop entirely.

Peter: *(unsure)* That's true, Thomas.

Peter sighs.

Peter: Would you excuse me for a second? I need to go to the loo.

Thomas: Are you OK?

Peter: Yes, I'll be right back.

As Thomas sees Peter getting up and heading for the bathroom (or the loo, as Peter says), he wonders if his questions might also make him lose Peter; but they agreed that they would be honest with each other. Thomas stares at the envelope on the table, a hint of the ring's shape textured against the thin paper. A few minutes later, Peter returns, and Thomas thinks he has been crying.

Thomas: Peter, what's going on? I am sorry if I said something that hurt you or offended you.

Peter: Thomas, you are fine. We had to be honest with each other; there is no other way to talk about the most essential things in life, and this is one of them.

Peter seems to be more nervous than usual.

Peter: I just . . . death is . . . I don't—it doesn't make sense to me. I have always been afraid of it. The resurrection of Jesus allows me to have hope for what'll come after it, but I still have to die and suffer, anticipate suffering, and live in uncertainty.

Thomas: Why are you so afraid of death?

Peter: I . . .

At that moment, Thomas' phone rings unexpectedly. His eyes don't seem to believe what they are seeing. The more the phone rings, the less he seems to move.

Peter: Are you alright, mate?

Thomas: No.

Peter: Who is it?

Thomas: It's Sofía's brother. I need to answer this. I'll see you next week, Peter.

Thomas grabs the envelope with the ring inside and leaves The Shire. *Before getting into his car, he looks at the trail and the lake for a second, already talking to Sofía's brother at this point. Peter remains at the table, insecure, wondering if showing his imperfections and weaknesses might move Thomas away from God. But, how could he not? To follow Jesus, one must do something extraordinary: learn to acknowledge one's weaknesses and depend on someone else.*[29] *Peter takes a few moments to pray silently. After that, he takes a long breath and lets it go, ready to talk to Lourdes.*

Peter: Lourdes, I heard bad storms are coming next week. Will you be open on Thursday?

Lourdes: My goodness! You will never learn! What is the best way to calm your nerves through a storm?

Peter: *(smiles)* Of course! Coffee!

Lourdes notices Peter is getting ready to leave.

Lourdes: Are you leaving?

Peter: Yes, I need to go back home.

Lourdes: Hey, I meant to ask you . . . how often do you see your family back in England?

Peter is from a small town in southern England. He moved to Maine several years ago after becoming a follower of Jesus.

Peter: Not as much as I'd like. But we talk a few times every week. My father's health is starting to decline. Sometimes, I wish to be there with him and help my mom. I miss them.

Lourdes: Peter, I have known you for a few years now. When did you start coming to our church again?

---

[29] 2 Corinthians 12:9–10: Each time he said, "My grace is all you need. My power works best in weakness." So now I am glad to boast about my weaknesses, so that the power of Christ can work through me. That's why I take pleasure in my weaknesses, and in the insults, hardships, persecutions, and troubles that I suffer for Christ. For when I am weak, then I am strong.

Thomas, Lourdes, and Sofía all go to church with Peter.

Peter: I think it's been four or five years now. Why are you asking?

Lourdes: Well, I don't know what is happening with you and Thomas. But remember, you need to take care of yourself as you care for others. I am here if you need me.

Lourdes sighs.

Lourdes: Richard was just like that.

Peter: You mean your husband?

Lourdes: Yes, *Richarcito*, who never learned how not to feel responsible for everyone's problems around him. He carried all the burdens he could, believing this would help people around him. But did he take care of himself in the meantime? Not as much as he should've.

Peter: I am sorry to hear that, Lourdes. Do you miss him?

Lourdes: *Mucho*. This coffee shop is here because my dream became his, and he did everything he could for me to have it. I still cannot believe I married someone who didn't like coffee.

Peter: *(laughs)* What?! He didn't like coffee!?

Lourdes: That's the same way I feel about myself marrying him! He was the first person in the world who introduced me to the idea that people can be good even if they don't like coffee.

Peter: *(laughs)* So, what did he do to convince you?

Lourdes: He bought me lots of coffee!

Lourdes has always been able to see the bright side of everything. Peter is a young Christian who yearns to be like her: joyful in Christ, no matter the circumstances.

Peter: Lourdes, everything is OK with me and Thomas. I guess it's difficult not to carry other people's burdens when you genuinely care for them.

Lourdes: I know. But . . . OK. For example, there will be a storm next Thursday, and I cannot control that. However, I can still make coffee through it. Do you get it?

Peter takes a few moments to think about it.

Peter: Yes, I do. Thank you, Lourdes. Will you be at church this Sunday?

Lourdes: No, I won't. I am planning to visit Richard's grave in the morning.

Peter: I'll be praying for you, Lourdes.

Lourdes: Pray for me, but don't worry about me. Deal?

Peter: Deal.

Lourdes can have a deep conversation with you while running an entire coffee shop, and she always seems to have a witty answer ready to outsmart you at every turn. Lourdes is a force to be reckoned with. As Peter leaves, he still sees the old man calmly writing something on his notepad. Has he even drunk from his cup at all? *Peter wonders. Peter heads for his car only after looking at the sun playing hide and seek as it sets on the horizon and the trees relish making shapes of the light piercing through them. If it were earlier, he would surely take another walk to the lake.*

Thursday, September 28

Yes, the weatherman was right; it is a stormy day. It's gray and cloudy, the wind rushes through the branches of the trees, and the lake is agitated. The Shire *is open, and Lourdes is making coffee through the storm—working, moving, and helping customers. Has she been here since last Thursday? It feels like it. It doesn't matter how bad or good the weather is, the trail always seems to be inviting, always wanting to share in people's burdens with its ups, downs, and turns. Peter has been praying and thinking about Thomas the whole week.* What other questions might he be struggling with? Has Thomas spoken with Sofia? *Peter is ready to have a good conversation with his best friend again.*

Lourdes: Hi, Peter! I'll bring your coffee right away.

A mother and her two sons are sitting at their favorite table. The boys' food is everywhere but the table. Peter enjoys seeing them play; such innocence and purity. Their mom is frustrated but enjoys seeing her two boys playing together. She is even trying her best not to laugh at the whole situation. Is it sometimes difficult to be a mother? Yes. Do mothers love their children? There is no doubt about it.

Where is Thomas? *Peter wonders.* Weren't we meeting at 3 pm? *The mom and her two sons are ready to leave. It is downpouring. Right before leaving, she grabs her umbrella, opens it, and tries to cover her boys as best as possible. The three of them begin laughing and teasing each other as they run toward her car. Peter knew it, the mom knew it—everyone was getting wet. But who cares? It'll dry eventually.*

The whole scene sparks some memories of Peter's mom back in England. Although we are not that scared about a couple of drops. *He smirks, feeling oddly proud of how bad the weather is at home.* I wonder what mom is doing right now. Please, Lord, take care of her and reveal Yourself in her life as You did in mine. *Peter's thoughts keep drifting away from* The Shire *toward his sweet mother.* Mom was never very expressive with her words, but her actions spoke volumes of her character. She worried so much about me all the time. Is that how our Father in Heaven feels about all of us continually? He commands us to, "Love your enemies." But how? *Peter gets comfortable at the table and checks his phone to text Thomas and make sure he is OK, when he realizes Thomas sent him a message a few seconds ago.*

Text conversation:

Thomas: Peter, Sofía's brother was visiting for a few days, and today was the only time we could spend together. Would it be OK if he joined us for the conversation?

Peter: Yes. Should we hold off on the big questions for another day?

Thomas: Actually, he told me he is more open to talk about the big questions now.

Peter: By all means. Are you OK?

Thomas: Yes, see you in a bit.

End of the text conversation.

Peter goes back into his thoughts: Well, I guess I am getting to meet Sofía's brother today. According to what Thomas said, he had a rough time after his father passed. What would I have done if I had lost my father so unexpectedly? Life is so hard sometimes. Maybe he is bitter about Christianity because of it? *Peter knows how bitterness festers because he was also bitter in the past. When he wasn't a follower of Jesus, he too was bitter toward Christianity and anything that had to do with it. But he grew to understand that where there is bitterness, there is pain. Where there is pain, there is fear, and fear is bitterness's favorite meal.* If Sofía's brother is bitter toward Christianity, *Peter wonders,* what is he fearing?

Jesus treats everyone alike, so Peter always puts an effort into seeing everyone around him as a potential follower of Jesus.[30] *Yes, the mother and her sons are soaking wet. Peter sees their car leaving the parking*

---

[30] Romans 3:22: We are made right with God by placing our faith in Jesus Christ. And this is true for everyone who believes, no matter who we are.

lot, wondering what their life looks like, who they are, and who those kids will one day become. Another car pulls up at The Shire. *It seems Sofía's brother is the one driving. Thomas gets out of the car and shares a quick look with Peter, who is already sitting at their favorite table.* Is he OK? He seems a bit uncomfortable, perhaps? *They both dash to the door to avoid getting wet (unsuccessfully) and approach Peter's table.*

Thomas: Hi, Peter, this is Landon.

Landon: Hey.

Peter: Nice to meet you, Landon.

Thomas: Peter, I told Landon we meet weekly to talk about Christianity, God, and the big questions. He already knows I am not sure about my faith anymore.

Peter: Oh, he does?

Landon: Yes, I called my mom, and she told me Sofía wasn't engaged to Thomas anymore because he was "questioning his faith." Pretty pathetic of her, don't you think?

Oh, boy. *Peter and Thomas share a look. Both feel what is coming. This is going to be a hard one.*

Peter: Why do you think it's pathetic, if you don't mind me asking?

Landon: Because she judges his character according to her beliefs, without letting his actions speak of his character. Who cares if God exists or not? The issue here is whether he treats her well or not.

Thomas doesn't usually show his emotions as much. However, a few seconds into the conversation, Landon is already stirring them.

Thomas: I don't know if I feel comfortable talking about Sofía like this. Could you stop saying that about her?

Landon: Didn't you tell me you guys had conversations about the big questions in life "in all sincerity"? What do you want me to do, not share what I really think about something?

Landon's tone is full of mockery. Yes, he is bitter toward Christianity. But I wonder why?

Peter: It's OK, Thomas. I think Landon wants to have this conversation more than we both do.

Landon: You don't even know me. Stop assuming things about me. See, Thomas? All Christians are the same.

Peter and Thomas know this whole thing might have been a mistake already. Conversations are crucial to understanding one another, trying to discover wisdom, and land on truth; however, the kinds of comments that Landon is making can also be traps. Peter knows that if he retaliates to Landon, Peter will give Landon a reason to confirm what he seems to have already thought about him. Peter has seen this type of bitterness before, which has nothing to do with atheism or Christianity, with belief or disbelief. Peter himself has even been bitter about other things while claiming to follow Jesus, so he is no one to judge. Carrying one's cross hurts sometimes. It is like deliberately choosing to experience pain because you know it is the only way to experience true peace. Indeed, the pathway to peace found in Jesus Christ is not pain free. Beyond all the emotional chaos and all the combativeness, a person is crying out for help. Peter tries to slow down briefly by bringing attention to Landon's needs.

Peter: My apologies, Landon. Would you like to eat or drink something?

Thomas: I'll get it for you, what do you want?

Landon sighs in frustration and asks for a chocolate muffin and a coffee. Thomas realizes Landon and Sofía still have some things in common. Chocolate muffins always remind him of her, and her brother likes them too. Thomas leaves the table but not without sharing a quick look with Peter to make sure they are going to be OK.

Peter: Landon, you know the last thing I want is to fight with you, don't you?

Landon: Then stop assuming things about me.

Peter: Do you know why I said you want to have this conversation more than us?

Landon remains quiet, but he is still eager to hear what Peter is about to say.

Peter: Because it didn't even take us one minute to get into the conversation, and you quickly began to question your sister's character. I think you want to have this conversation for some reason. I don't claim to know why. And, please, you can correct me if I am wrong.

However, Peter believes he knows why: Landon is afraid of something. That said, Peter is always open to be proven wrong.

Landon: My sister doesn't want to be with Thomas because Thomas is asking questions. Because Thomas is *asking questions*?! That is ridiculous!

It's not Peter's business, but he realizes Landon doesn't know yet that the reason Sofía is afraid of Thomas asking questions is the person Landon became—especially toward her and her mom—when he started asking questions. His questions didn't come out of a curious mind but from a desire to undermine what he already believed was false in the first place. It's not about the questions but why *we begin to ask them.*

Peter: I understand.

Peter feels talking about it would make things worse, no matter what he says at this point.

Peter: Anyway, did you get to spend time with your family? What are you doing in town?

Landon tries to calm himself down for a second.

Landon: Yes, we went to a restaurant last night. I came for work, and I am leaving tonight.

Thomas gets back to their table.

Thomas: OK, Lourdes is working on the coffee. Here is a chocolate muffin for you, Landon.

Landon: Thanks, man.

As Landon opens the bag, his demeanor changes. He is excited about the muffin. Thomas sees Sofía all over her brother in how he moves and reacts to things.

Thomas: What were you guys talking about?

Peter: Not much. We just relaxed, waiting for you, and he told me he was leaving tonight.

Landon: Yes, Thomas. I'll take you home and then head for the airport. But I still have a few hours before I must check in.

OK, let's start all over again with this. *Thomas thinks.*

Thomas: So, Landon, did you want to meet with both of us to talk about God?

Landon: Yeah. I have heard a few things about you, Peter. Were you an atheist in the past?

Peter senses his questions feel more like quick judgements. Thomas has little interest in hearing Peter's answers.

Peter: Yes, I was.

Landon: What made you change your mind?

Peter: That's a good question. For me, the journey went from my brain to my heart. I started asking questions about philosophy, science, theology, and history and was convinced about some evidence for God. All that matters to me, but nothing like the personal experience of having a relationship with Jesus and realizing I needed Him to make sense of my life.

Landon: "Evidence" you said? I'd die to hear that. I have never seen any evidence for God.

Peter: You were a Christian once, weren't you?

Landon: I guess so, but because of culture and my family forcing it down my throat, not out of my own will. When I started asking questions, all my beliefs were gone.

Peter: What prompted you to begin asking questions?

Thomas knows where Peter is trying to lead the discussion.

Landon: *(avoiding it)* At one point, none of this made sense to me; it doesn't stand to scrutiny. It's all wishful thinking. I am glad Thomas is getting out of this nonsense.

Thomas: Well, I haven't gone that far yet. I don't think it's nonsense. Something could be ultimately false, but there could still be value in it.

Landon: Oh, really? What value do you see in Christianity?

Thomas: Christians are prone to living in a community, supporting each other, and looking after each other; and there are some good moral lessons we can learn from Scripture.

Landon: Like having slaves?[31] Like committing genocide?[32] Like hating gay people?[33] Like burning in Hell for eternity?[34]

Peter: Discussing all those topics would be so much fun, Landon. But asking questions like that one after the other is not an argument in itself. We might not have time to talk about all of those; but Thomas, you and I can talk about these if you want to, anytime.

Landon: What? Are you afraid of facing a few facts about your worldview?

Peter is starting to lose his patience but is doing his best not to.

---

[31] Ephesians 6:5: Slaves, obey your earthly masters with deep respect and fear. Serve them sincerely as you would serve Christ.

[32] Joshua 6:21: They completely destroyed everything in it with their swords—men and women, young and old, cattle, sheep, goats, and donkeys.

[33] Leviticus 18:22: Do not practice homosexuality, having sex with another man as with a woman. It is a detestable sin.

[34] Matthew 25:46: And they will go away into eternal punishment, but the righteous will go into eternal life.

Peter: Remember when you said I was assuming things about you, mate? You just asked me a "question" stating I am afraid of facing a few facts about Christianity that I myself don't understand. That's a bit impertinent, isn't it?

Thomas interrupts.

Thomas: You know what, guys? This wasn't a good idea. Landon, let's just talk about something else—the weather, football, or whatever.

Landon: No, no, no, no. I have been training for this trash, unless your friend here is a coward.

Thomas looks down and sighs. Peter has been holding his coffee this whole time, and he gently leaves it on the table.

Peter: *(smiling, containing his frustration)* Landon, think about me whatever you'd like. Let's try this again. Is there anything of value for you in the Bible?

Landon: The Bible is horrible.

Peter: I agree.

Landon smirks. Thomas seems confused.

Landon: Oh, you do?

Peter: Of course I do! The Bible is horrible in that it doesn't shy away from all the evil and suffering there is in the world. The main people God chose to communicate His messages were fallible people who made countless mistakes. Jesus also knew that even His followers would keep sinning while following Him.[35] God does a fantastic job in the Bible laying out why we all need Jesus. That's the whole point. There isn't even one person who is good in the Bible—only Jesus, who is both human and God. If I had opened the Bible and saw that everything and everyone was perfect, then God wouldn't have done a good job describing what humanity is capable of, including me. That's the whole point of God showing us all the suffering and struggles in the Bible. That's what I meant by "horrible." Ultimately, I believe the Bible is awe-inspiring. In fact, Jesus Himself suffered for you and me so that, one day, if we believe and obey Him, no one else will have to suffer anymore.

Landon: That sounds to me like a bunch of bull that you tell yourself to have an excuse for the problematic passages.

Peter: Well, that's unfortunate you see it that way because there is much to unpack there.

Suddenly, Thomas becomes more direct with Landon.

Thomas: Hey man, could you not talk like that to him? We don't have to disrespect each other like that. You could just say, "I believe it's false," "wrong," or even, "You are lying, and here are the reasons why . . . "

Landon: I have heard these types of arguments for many years, and Christians intentionally make them sound vague to distract you. There is a twist at every corner, something else you should know, another reason everyone is wrong except them.

---

[35] Romans 7:21–23: I have discovered this principle of life—that when I want to do what is right, I inevitably do what is wrong. I love God's law with all of my heart. But there is another power within me that is at war with my mind. This power makes me a slave to the sin that is still within me.

Peter: But I have been wrong many times.

Landon: Could you be wrong about God?

Peter: Yes, I could.

Landon: How?

Peter: Instead of criticizing me, Christians, and Christianity, you could show me evidence or arguments against it. But, so far, you are doing a horrible job at it.

Thomas looks at Peter, a bit surprised. He never saw Peter answering a question like this. Is this the rebellious side he sometimes has hinted at? On the other side, Peter regrets saying that even though he still thinks it's true. Time and time again, Jesus has been patient with him through countless sins and never stopped loving him. How could he not be patient with others in the name of Jesus? Jesus died for Landon, too. Suddenly, Lourdes interrupts.

Lourdes: Here are your coffees! I think it's going to stop raining soon. Is there anything else I can do for you? Oh! Thomas, who is your friend?

Thomas: This is Landon.

Lourdes: Landon? Sofia's brother? Oh, nice to see you! It's been a long time! The last time I saw you, you were so young! You look just like your father. Oh! You know? I saw your mom and your sister visiting your father's grave last Sunday on my way to visit my husband's. How are you? Where are you living now? What church do you go to?

Thomas doesn't even know where to begin. Lourdes has unknowingly dropped a few atomic bombs in their conversation. First, he just heard something about Sofía after two weeks without hearing anything from her. Secondly, she mentioned Landon's father to him. Thirdly, she still assumes he is a Christian. Landon is speechless.

Thomas: *(nervously)* He is just visiting for a few days and leaving tonight.

Lourdes: Well, I hope you are enjoying this good weather!

Lourdes—completely unaware—goes back to her routine, humming the happiest of tunes.

Thomas: Hey, man, sorry about that, she doesn't know.

Landon: It's OK, she seems to be as nosy as always though.

Thomas: She just doesn't know. She means well.

Landon: Yeah, all Christians do, but you see what happens.

Landon is trying to regain his usual "confidence," but something has changed. Lourdes has unknowingly struck an emotional chord somewhere in his heart.

Landon: So, what's the evidence you found for God?

This is a pretty hard turn for Peter because he adores Lourdes and wants to defend her; but he loves Jesus and, yet, sometimes still behaves like Landon. He tries to recompose and leave his anger behind, answering the question as if nothing had happened.

Peter: Well, I guess it all began with me exploring "god" as a general concept. Is it even rational to entertain an idea like this? To my surprise, humanity has always had a sense of the divine, so it is rational in the sense that it has always been a part of us. When I was an atheist, I judged the "god" concept as mere nonsense without exploring it first. In fact, when I began researching it, it was overwhelming to realize how unread and uneducated I was about it. From before the time of Socrates to today, both theistic and atheistic philosophers have entertained the idea in many ways for centuries. Many scientists, both theists and atheists, also delved into the metaphysics of everything they were discovering with wonder and openness about the concept of a potential agency behind it, even if some did not believe there was a god. All these philosophers, scientists, and thinkers in general became pretty much the bedrock of our civilization: Plato, Aristotle, Averroes, Descartes, Hume, Nietzsche, Kierkegaard, Kepler, Newton, Maxwell, etc. Whether they believed in a god or not, they took their time to explore it, something I never did, and they were—without a hint of doubt—more intelligent than I'll ever be. However, the fact that they were all intelligent and some were believers doesn't entail that God exists. But all in all, this was humbling and an adequate first step for my potential faith.

Thomas: When did you go from "a god" to God?

Peter: Well, once I was open to the idea of a god, I realized some religions or systems of thought conceptualize god as an ethereal reality you can only contemplate and reflect upon, almost like an ideal. However, Jesus wants to have a personal relationship with us, and I think that is more "human," more in tune with who we are. Within me, there are emotions, feelings, hope, intellect, sadness, brokenness, talents, failures, awe. If "a god" exists, I expect this God would consider everything we are as humans—because He supposedly created us—as He communicates and interacts with us. Long story short, in Jesus, I found the most unimaginable compassion,[36] the most outstanding mercy[37], awe-inspiring love[38], and a way of living that matched my inner being's yearning for how I always supposed the world should have been. Besides, the most fascinating thing was that Jesus is rooted in actual history, meaning you can falsify Him. It's not all big ideas and philosophy, but a real person who lived, died, and was resurrected. God and man in one. Metaphysics and physics united, and all based simply on sacrificial love and relationship, something anyone can understand without having to be intellectual or unique in any respect. For me, "a god" became "God" when I began to truly know and trust in the person of Jesus. He loved me even when I despised Him. I know I haven't given you specific details about what arguments or what personal experiences pushed me to consider following Jesus; I was only trying to give you both a general idea of how my heart began to be open about the idea of the divine.

Landon has been biting into his muffin this whole time and showing a careless attitude toward Peter's comments.

Thomas: Hmm . . .

Peter: What are you thinking?

Thomas: We can conceptualize so many ideas, but that doesn't entail that those concepts are necessarily true. In other words, there is a big jump from conceptualizing an idea to believing the final concept to be real. At this point I would need to hear specific evidence for God. What if we talked about whether there is evidence

---

[36] Matthew 9:36: When he saw the crowds, he had compassion on them because they were confused and helpless, like sheep without a shepherd.

[37] Matthew 5:7: God blesses those who are merciful, for they will be shown mercy.

[38] John 3:16: For this is how God loved the world: He gave his one and only Son, so that everyone who believes in him will not perish but have eternal life.

for the existence of God or not? This is the one question that bleeds into everything else. If God doesn't exist, then anything we say or claim to know about Him is automatically not true.

Landon just finished his muffin.

Landon: So, Thomas, you still believe "a god" exists?

Landon's tone sounds mocking. He is not asking a question but affirming his own beliefs through a question.

Thomas: I don't know what to think at this point. On one hand, the concept of God is so prevalent for so many people. Prevalence doesn't entail truthfulness; I am aware of that. But people's lives change radically because of it. Actually, some would say that many people's lives change radically, for good, when they also stop believing God exists. There is something about the idea of God that has enormous consequences on people's behavior, whether you think He is real or not. I find that very . . . puzzling.

Peter: There is another way to ask this question that could take us to the heart of it, perhaps. Landon, would you *like* for God to be real?

Landon: Why would I like for a vindictive hypocrite who doesn't care about anything to be real?

Peter sighs in frustration.

Peter: Why is he a "vindictive hypocrite"?

Landon: He just is. It is just one of His attributes, but theologians always forget about that one.

Peter is running out of patience. Unfortunately, sometimes, there is just no way to have a conversation. But Peter knows others might have wanted to talk with him in the past, even though he was acting like "a Landon" toward them. Again, Peter is no one to judge.[39]

Thomas: Landon, we don't have to talk about this if you don't want to. What's the point of spending our time throwing dirt at each other's worldviews?

Landon: I thought you were questioning this crap as well. Why are you trying to defend him?

Thomas: See? Right there. Why do you have to talk to me like that?

Peter cannot take it anymore. A rush of adrenaline goes through him like fire. Landon first questioned his sister's character, then mocked Lourdes, and now he is disrespecting Thomas' questioning and doubting process. Peter could always learn things about people without anyone telling him about them. It is not some superpower; he listens and observes, and in his anger, he sometimes confronts people with information about them they didn't know he was aware of. For one moment, Peter becomes the person he fights so hard not to be anymore, raising his voice slightly.

Peter: This has nothing to do with atheism, God, or anything else. You are just afraid since your father died. You are just trying to blame everything and everyone around you because you are scared out of your mind.

---

[39] Romans 2:1: You may think you can condemn such people, but you are just as bad, and you have no excuse! When you say they are wicked and should be punished, you are condemning yourself, for you who judge others do these very same things.

Thomas' jaw drops on the ground. Peter appears calm and firm, but was actually feeling sorry for saying all of that in the midst of saying it. Landon becomes furious and gets up, ready to jump on Peter and hit him. Landon knocks over their table, spilling all the cups of coffee. Thomas sees everything happening, as if in slow motion, and stops him with an arm right before he gets to Peter. Everyone stops what they are doing and turns, startled. Something is not going well at The Shire, *where everything is supposed to always be OK.*

Thomas: *(while holding Landon)* Stop!

Landon: *(raging against Peter)* Who do you think you are, talking about me that way!

Thomas: Enough!

Thomas pushes Landon toward the entrance, looking intently at him.

Thomas: This is not OK. Please leave. Go away. I'll find a ride home myself.

Peter: I can take you home, Thomas.

Landon: *(yelling)* Of course you can, you idiot. You just want to take advantage of every opportunity to indoctrinate everyone around you.

Landon looks at Thomas while grabbing his jacket from his chair.

Landon: I am disappointed in you. You don't deserve to be with my sister either. This town is exactly the way it was when I left it. What a waste of time!

Peter is holding his tongue, although it is a little late at this point. One simple word can become a spark that ignites an entire forest,[40] *and at this point, anything he could say could damage Thomas' relationship with Sofía even more. Landon leaves the coffee shop, slamming the door on his way out. Everyone remains silent, not knowing what to do for a few seconds. And then, a voice rises from behind the counter, breaking the eerie silence . . .*

Lourdes: He didn't like my coffee or what?

She definitely has a talent for telling the most unexpected jokes at the worst possible moments. A few guests laugh, and others crack a smile. Peter and Thomas don't know what to do because the joke is funny, but it doesn't feel like a moment to laugh.

Peter: Everything is OK. There is no reason to worry. Please get back to your coffees and conversations. We are fine.

Peter and Thomas begin cleaning up everything that fell on the floor, including Lourdes' coffee.

Lourdes: Even on the ground, the best in town.

As Lourdes finishes picking up the cups (one of them actually broke) and cleaning up all the coffee, she gets closer to Peter and Thomas.

Lourdes: *(whispering with a sad tone)* He has never been the same since his father passed away.

Peter and Thomas try calming down briefly as Lourdes returns to the counter.

---

[40] James 3:6: And among all the parts of the body, the tongue is a flame of fire. It is a whole world of wickedness, corrupting your entire body. It can set your whole life on fire, for it is set on fire by hell itself.

Peter: Thomas, I am so sorry.

Thomas: No, I am sorry. I should have read the room better. I don't think bringing him into our conversation was a good idea. He picked me up at home and didn't say nice things about his family on our way here. He was also mocking Christianity in an attempt to try to connect with me, but it wasn't working either. I feel so bad for him. He was never this way. I wonder what he will tell Sofía and her mom about this. I don't even want to know.

Peter: I am sorry, Thomas. He made fun of my beliefs—which is fine—Lourdes—which is not— and your doubting—which is horrible. I wasn't trying to create a problem between you two.

Thomas: Being around him is hard, but he has no one. On his way here, he told me he sometimes feels alone.

Peter: It doesn't surprise me. When you let resentment go wild without leaving room for forgiveness in your heart, however hard the situation might be, it can alienate you quickly from everyone around you. By the way, Thomas, if you allow me to say something, this attitude and bitterness has nothing to do with him believing or not believing in God, but only with his personal story and how he chooses to assimilate it. Some people don't believe in God, but having conversations about the big questions with them is a delight. As I said before, this type of bitterness also affects some people who claim to follow Jesus but choose not to surrender all their fear and resentment to Him. Sin does treat everyone alike. It makes no distinctions between people, no matter who you are. Its focus is to devalue humanity and bring it down to self-destruction.

Peter grabs his phone to check the time.

Peter: It's been 20 minutes since we got here. Are we looking forward to the next three hours?

They both sigh in disbelief.

Thomas: I need to go out to get some air. I'll be back in a second.

Thomas leaves The Shire *and walks toward the trail, lost in his thoughts.* What just happened? How in the world. . .? *Sigh.* This is just perfect. This could make things even colder with Sofía. I didn't do anything, though. Is this a natural consequence of questioning one's views on life? Having fights and fallouts with everyone around you? *At that moment, Thomas looks back at* The Shire *and can still see Peter through the window in the distance.* But Peter is not like that; Sofía is not like that either. Could we not just live and let others live? Why does everything have to be so complicated? Then, you go out there, and people have the same problems or worse, for reasons that have nothing to do with God or anything like that. What's wrong with us? Should I text Sofía about this? *Thomas leans on one of the trees on the side of the trail, looking up at all the branches spreading from the main trunk.* Why am I questioning my faith all of a sudden? Why is this happening to me? Am I being fair? I am; I know I am. If Christianity is true and God is real, then my questions shouldn't undermine a truth like that. Yet, somehow, I feel like my questions are undermining it. What does this all mean for my life, family, friends, and future? If You are there, God, why won't You show yourself to someone sincerely searching for You? Or are You just letting me go? *Thomas breathes deeply a few times to relax before returning to* The Shire. *As he approaches the main door, he can see Peter inside. His eyes are closed, and he leans back in his chair, gently rubbing his face with both hands, hoping to relax too.* Is he actually doing OK? *Thomas wonders. Thomas gets back to his chair, and he and Peter shake their heads in disbelief once again, shocked that everything happened so quickly.*

Peter: Are you alright, mate?

Thomas: I don't know.

Thomas seems exhausted.

Thomas: Should we leave and try another time?

Peter: Whatever you want to do.

Thomas: I don't know. I still want to talk, though.

Peter: We can if you want to. I worry about you and Sofía.

Thomas: There is nothing I can do. I might text her to tell her what happened, but I don't know. Anyway, are *you* OK?

Peter: Thomas, in the past, I would have been worrying about this for days. Now, I worry about the things I have some control over. Maybe I wasn't patient enough? I might need to work on that.

Thomas: *(skeptical)* Pff, I don't think it was that.

Peter and Thomas say nothing to each other for a few seconds.

Thomas: I know it doesn't feel organic. But, at this point, there is nothing else we can do. Let's try to get back to where we left the conversation. Could we discuss the evidence you see for God's existence outside the Bible?

Peter: Yes. But first, let me know your thoughts.

Thomas tries his best to get back into "search for truth" mode. However, it still feels uncomfortable at first.

Thomas: Well, in principle, I don't see God anywhere. I don't hear His voice; I don't see Him in nature. If we spend enough time looking, there seems to be empirical explanations for many of the questions we ask about the world. I only hear about God through people, through Scripture, but I cannot go out there alone and tangibly find God on my own. Sounds to me that God is an idea or a filter through which you can choose to see the world, but you can never experience God firsthand in an empirical way.

Peter: Yes, that's very well put. You cannot meet with God and have a conversation like you can have with me. That's true. I struggled with this idea as well. Where do you think the concept of the divine or "a god" or "gods" came from?

Thomas: Civilizations have always been prone to believe in some divine interventionism, and most of their beliefs have been disproven once the scientific method came about. Much of their religious claims and theology were based on natural principles for which they still didn't have explanations. Once those explanations began to arrive—such as in the cases of how gravity works, when and why lightning happens, what the sun is and isn't, etc.—all those claims were falsified, consequently falsifying the religious assumptions that supposedly sustained them.

Peter: I have nothing to say to you; I wholeheartedly agree.

Thomas: Well, if you do, how is it that you still believe in God?

Peter: There is a simple reason why I do: Because once we get to explain what gravity is, when and why lightning happens, what the sun is and isn't, etc., we are explaining everything in terms of its function—descriptively—but we still don't know what any of those things are because we didn't create them—we didn't put them there. Humanity doesn't create anything; we can only discover and describe how everything functions. For something to be discovered and described, however, it must first exist. But why does it exist? And why does existence look the way it does? Those are the two main questions for me when it comes to evidence for the existence of God outside of Scripture.

Thomas: I'd like to hear more about this. I don't know why anything exists or why everything looks like it does. I just say: "I don't know." On the other hand, you seem to believe why, but to get to your explanation, you need to go out of the universe to explain the universe itself. Isn't it more probable to expect the reason we exist to be *inside* the universe instead of beyond it? We don't even know if there is a "beyond" after all.

Peter: This is all very interesting to me. Let's look around and start with the obvious. "There is something." That alone is extraordinary. OK, what's next? What does this "something" look like? We can see there is order. Furthermore, to discern order in nature, we first need an entity to discern and describe that order. Is there anything like it in the universe? Yes: us—you and me. What else? To discern and describe this order, we need to be aware of it to make conclusions and behave according to them. In other words, we need to be conscious. Until now, as you can see, science must accept all these brute facts of existence because, without them, science itself couldn't be possible.

Thomas: So, you see evidence, not on *how* things work, but *why* things are.

Peter: Exactly. The universe could have possibly been any way "it" wanted, but it happens to be *the way it is*—a place that allows for the existence of conscious minds with the capacity to discern and describe the patterns and the structure that form it. But why is it that way? Does that question even make sense? From the very beginning, the "ingredients" of the universe, all space, energy, and matter—and I would venture to say there are still "ingredients" yet to be discovered—allowed for the existence of life; and not only life but life that is aware that it is alive. Why would the universe begin to exist with the necessary "ingredients" to "bake" conscious life in it? Sorry for the cooking analogy. Actually, you might not like it because you are an atrocious cook.

Thomas: Hey!

Peter: Hey, what? Some things are factually true, no matter how we feel about them.

Thomas shakes his head with a smirk.

Peter: As far as we know, minds are the only thing in the known universe capable of discerning the patterns of our intelligible universe. Minds can also be creative with their surroundings and cause certain things to exist—although not out of nothing. The universe doesn't create things like planes, satellites, or movies on its own, though the universe does offer the possibility for their existence due to the matter contained within it and its laws. Only minds can be creative enough to use that matter to "create" things like a plane, a satellite, or a movie. So, what is the meaning of all of this?

Thomas: What is it?

Peter: From my perspective, as a chocolate cake is a possibility to bake only when you have the right ingredients, minds are a possibility only because the universe had the right "ingredients" to make them possible from the beginning. Once we know all the ingredients to bake a chocolate cake are on the kitchen counter, we can ask the baker: "Why do you want to make a chocolate cake?" Don't you think asking the universe the same question would be reasonable? "Universe: Why do you make minds?" The main difference between galaxies and minds is that galaxies exist to only "be," but minds exist to be and *to will.*

A mind wills things, hopes for things, orders things, and is creative with its surroundings, even to the point of doing things the universe on its own cannot do. A mind lives in the present but is aware of the past and future; it has intuition and can even wonder about its existence. A mind can analyze itself and challenge the laws that came together to form it. A mind can love. A mind is the most extraordinary thing in the known universe. It is humbling to realize that we are the only ones who possess a mind. If we, finite human beings, can do all these extraordinary things with our minds, perhaps you can better understand *why* I believe—as all Christians do—that there is a Mind behind, beyond, and even sustaining the universe. A mind is the only thing we know that can be creative and has a will. Extrapolate this to the universe with all its laws, order, space, matter, energy . . . After learning what a mind is capable of and realizing that it is the only thing that can understand the universe itself, is it far-off to suggest and even believe that a Mind created it? I don't think so. I think it is very rational to believe the universe has been created by Someone, a conscious will who willed it into existence, without having to use Scripture to support this belief. The conversation that takes us from a conscious will to Jesus is different. For now, I am just sharing why believing God exists, without using Scripture, is rational.

Thomas: When it comes to thinking about God as an idea or concept, I am OK with exploring it and being open to the possibility of its existence. However, there is an obvious problem with this. People have been determined to discover who this god or gods are from their sociocultural backgrounds and the knowledge limitations they faced in their historical times. This has resulted in thousands of religions and ideas of what the divine is or should be, and most of them don't even come close to being similar to one another. If the divine is something we can discern somehow, and the divine is "one thing" waiting to be discovered, why don't we all come to the same conclusion as we all do when we study the world through the scientific method? Shouldn't we all expect to find the same?

Peter: Wow, Thomas, that's so good.

Suddenly, Lourdes shows up with two coffees and a smile.

Lourdes: Here they are! Two more coffees. They are burning hot, as they should be.

Peter and Thomas smile.

Thomas: So, if I want to get an iced coffee one day, you wouldn't prepare it for me?

Lourdes: Oh yeah, I would! But I would do it in such a way that you would not want to return to my coffee shop anymore.

Peter and Thomas laugh. Lourdes returns to the counter, and Peter and Thomas resume their conversation.

Peter: Going back to your fantastic insight. Yes, there are thousands of religions in the world. But I don't see that as a problem in one sense. The yearning for the divine has always been a part of the human psyche, giving me more reasons to believe there must be something out there because of it. I am not saying that because many believe there must be something out there since that conclusion doesn't follow. However, it highlights the brilliant fact that we have always had a sense of the divine. Therefore, I don't think it is reasonable to say that because there are many religions, they all must be false—because that conclusion doesn't follow either. At that point, the only thing I can do is to experience them. Human beings are not machines who merely describe the world around them without being a part of the world they are describing. We are living; we have emotions; we make decisions; we are moral beings; we hope; we fear; we love; we die. I think when you look at our human experience as a whole, then it makes sense, at least to me, to talk about Jesus as the one who can make sense of it all.

Thomas remains quiet. Too quiet.

Peter: What are you thinking about?

Thomas: I have never heard the idea that people can believe in any god or gods without having their own "holy scriptures" to tell them so. At the same time, I struggle to believe something can be real beyond the material world we can sense, observe, or deduce because of how it functions.

Peter: A fair way to summarize my view is this: why is there a world we can sense, observe, or deduce at all? I doubt science—or at least the way we do science right now—will ever get to answer a question like this. This pertains to the realm of metaphysics, theology, philosophy, and, most importantly, human experience.

Thomas: Hmm. Science and faith would be an exciting topic to discuss next Thursday. Would you be open to doing that?

Peter: I would love to. Wait a second . . . Oh yeah, *(disappointed)* unfortunately, I won't be able to meet next Thursday. What do you think about Friday at the same time?

Thomas: Sure. What's going on?

Peter: Oh, nothing. It's just a doctor's appointment to go over some results. Nothing important.

Thomas: OK, then Friday it is.

Peter: I'll take you home.

Thomas: You know what? I would rather walk; I need some fresh air.

Peter: It's a 30-minute walk, are you sure?

Thomas: Yeah. Actually, it stopped raining!

It has. The sun shows up timidly between a blanket of clouds as it sets, bathing the trail with light as if it were dawning instead. The Shire *has served its purpose another day, giving people a place to be honest, authentic, and vulnerable about the big questions in life.*

Peter: Will you text Sofía about what happened with her brother?

Thomas: I don't know what to do. Everything seems to be falling apart around me, and everything worsens when I try to fix it. Peter, you might be the only stable thing I have right now. I appreciate you, my friend.

Peter: I am very tempted to quote a Scripture passage right now.

Thomas: *(smiles)* Do it.

Peter: "Then Jesus wept."[41] If he did, those who follow Him should also expect some crying along the path to eternity.

Thomas: Eternity . . .

Thomas seems unsure and doubtful.

Thomas: Bye, Peter.

Peter: Bye, Thomas.

As Peter heads to his car, Thomas begins his walk back home. For a moment, Thomas stands still in front of the trail, staring at the distant lake bathed by the timid light of the sunset. He used to see these events as reminders of hope. However, it might only be a set of fortuitous events that just happens to be beautiful, but nothing else. A few minutes later, he notices there is something on the ground. It seems like a small, rounded, orange bottle with a soft green cap lying on the ground right where Peter had pulled up. What is that? *Thomas picks it up. It's medicine. Peter's name is on it.* Depression medicine!? What? What aren't you telling me, Peter?

---

[41] John 11:35.

Chapter 4

Truth Is a Journey

Friday, October 5

Peter cannot wait to talk about science and faith with Thomas. He had always wanted to be a scientist and explore the universe. As he arrives at the parking lot of The Shire, *he sees a familiar face, someone capable of changing Thomas' life with only one word, one gesture, one conversation. It's Sofía. She and her best friend, Linda, are about to start their walk on the trail. Both are holding a cup of coffee from* The Shire, *and Sofía is holding a muffin. It's a chocolate muffin, for sure.* Yes, that's Sofía, *Peter thinks to himself. Thomas doesn't seem to have arrived yet. Peter wonders if Lourdes might have said something to Sofía about everything that happened last Thursday. Something is always brewing at* The Shire, *not only Lourdes' coffee. Peter parks near* The Shire *and begins walking to the entrance. Lourdes has been busy; everything is decorated with fall paraphernalia.*

Peter: Hi, Lourdes! It looks beautiful. Are you hosting your pumpkin carving party this year?

Lourdes: *Por supuesto*! On Saturday, October 28. Are you coming?

Peter: I want to!

Lourdes leans over the counter to whisper something to Peter.

Lourdes: *(whispering)* I don't think Sofía and Thomas are coming, at least not together.

Of course, she knows, *Peter says to himself.* But how does she know? *He wonders.*

Lourdes: Oh! Don't act as if you don't know it! She came to talk to me about what happened with her brother last Thursday and apologized to me.

Peter: Oh, good . . . *(hesitant),* but how do you know about Thomas and Sofía?

Lourdes: We shook hands and hugged, and that's when I noticed she was not wearing her engagement ring anymore.

Peter: Lourdes, please, don't say anything about it. Thomas is about to arrive.

Lourdes: Oh, you guys are about to talk away all the world's problems again?

Peter: *(smiles)* Yes. By the way, I have always wanted to ask you something.

Lourdes doesn't stop doing ten things simultaneously as she listens to Peter.

Peter: I like all your muffins, but I fancy some bickies now and then. Do you have any?

Lourdes suddenly stops what she is doing.

Lourdes: *(puzzled) ¿Qué dices*? What language are you talking to me?

Peter: Well, clearly not English by your reaction.

Lourdes: Haha. What did you say to me—you fancy some *what*?

Peter: Oh! I see what happened. Bickies! Biscuits! Cookies! Or *(with a thick Spanish accent) Galletas*!

Lourdes: Oh! Hahaha. Look at you! Do you still practice your Spanish sometimes?

Peter: Here and there, yes.

Lourdes: Maybe I should consider adding some "bickies" to the menu.

Out of nowhere, Peter begins singing a song and doing a silly dance.

"Bickies, bickies, bickies…

choccy, choccy, bickies…

gimme, gimme, gimme…

with milky, milky, milky…"

Peter ends the song with a huge smile on his face, looking intently at Lourdes. Lourdes is speechless and stands like a statue.

Peter: Hahaha! *(Lourdes' reaction makes him laugh hard.)*

Lourdes: I am glad *someone* enjoyed . . . that.

Peter: *(Peter keeps laughing.)* Oh, Lourdes, please don't be so hard on me! This is the song I used to sing to my mom to make me some biscuits when I was a child. Sorry, I got carried away just by the thought of it.

Lourdes: You are one of a kind, Peter.

Peter keeps humming the "bickies song" as he heads to his usual table, unaware that Lourdes is still speechless after his performance. What a great talent to have to know how to make oneself laugh. I need more of that, actually. *Peter's sudden thought makes his joy vanish at once. From joy to melancholy and pensiveness in one second.* Help me, Jesus. *Through the window, he still can see Sofía and Linda walking over to the lake in the distance. At that moment, he sees Thomas' car in the parking lot. Both Sofía and Thomas are in Peter's field of vision. This is his first time seeing them "together" in weeks. They, however, are unaware they are so close to each other.*

Thomas gets out of the car, bringing the antidepressant bottle in his pocket. Peter is utterly unaware of it, while Thomas is worried about Peter. What's going on with him? *Thomas doesn't know if it's a good idea to show it to him because he wasn't meant to see it. As Thomas enters* The Shire, *Peter gets up, and they hug each other.*

Thomas: Peter! It's good to see you! How are you?

Knowing something is going on with Peter, Thomas looks at him to greet him and quickly examines him. He seems fine to me, *Thomas thinks.*

Peter: Same here, Thomas.

Thomas: I saw Linda's car parked outside. Did you happen to see her?

Peter notices Thomas is asking about Linda while thinking about someone else.

Peter: Umm . . . no, well, yes.

Thomas: Peter, the law of non-contradiction, remember? Nothing can both be and not be.

Peter: *(smiles nervously)* Well, then, yes.

Thomas: Why are you so nervous?

Peter: I think I saw her with Sofía.

Upon hearing her name, a rush of adrenaline stirs Thomas from within.

Thomas: They are walking the trail together?

Peter: I think so. Have you talked to her at all?

Thomas: *(leaning over to look out the window, trying to see her)* I haven't. I wanted to text her to apologize for the Landon debacle, but I feel anything can potentially become a problem at this point. I want her to have her space, and I probably need mine.

Peter: I understand.

Thomas: Peter, how are you doing?

Peter: I am fine.

Thomas: How was your doctor's appointment yesterday?

Peter: It went well. Better than expected!

Thomas wonders why Peter has never told him about the depression medicine. His words seem to say one thing, but his body language appears to be saying something else.

Lourdes shows up with their coffee.

Lourdes: OK, here are your coffees. Hey, Thomas, I haven't seen you at church lately. Is everything OK?

Peter is starting to fear any word that comes out of Lourdes' mouth.

Thomas: I am giving myself time to think about my life and what I want from it.

Lourdes looks around to ensure no clients are waiting for her. She grabs a chair and sits down next to Thomas, gesturing with her hand, suggesting that she has something important to say to Thomas.

Lourdes: Don't be afraid of whatever is happening to you, Thomas. Everything in this life has an end, even life itself.

Peter: But not forever.

Lourdes: Yes. Sometimes, we must get lost to find the path we should have been walking all along. Pain hurts, but pain teaches. Just keep walking through whatever valley is in front of you. The key is to never stop moving.

And just like that, Lourdes gets back to her coffee-making. Also, the same old man who a few weeks back was sitting at a table in the corner of the coffee shop is back with a pad and a pen, ready to order some coffee and keep writing. Lourdes' words have traveled deep into Peter's heart; he cannot take it and tears up a little bit.

Thomas: Peter, are you OK?

Peter: You never know with Lourdes, do you? This woman is unbelievable.

Thomas: She truly is. Actually, I meant to ask you. I know her husband passed away years ago, but I never knew how it happened. Do you know how she lost her husband?

Peter: Yeah, Lourdes had two main dreams in life: becoming a mother and owning a coffee shop. She and Richard could never conceive, which made Lourdes feel depressed. Richard couldn't take seeing Lourdes mourning that she could never be a mother, so he began working hours and hours extra, even on the weekends, to gather enough money to buy this property; but he never told Lourdes he was doing this.

Thomas: *The Shire*?

Peter: Yes, the land where they built this coffee shop. He was a car mechanic. One day, a few weeks before they planned to open the coffee shop, he was working on a car whose support failed, fell on him, and he instantly passed.

Thomas: *(horrified)* What!?

Peter: Yes . . . He planned to stop fixing cars because of the physical toll it takes and help Lourdes run the coffee shop. But it couldn't be.

Richard died while working on fulfilling Lourdes' dream of owning a coffee shop. I remember Lourdes sharing her story, saying that the day she saw Richard the happiest was when he took her for a date, bought some coffee for her—of course—and brought her to see this land. As soon as they arrived, she told him: "Richard, if it weren't for the coffee, this would probably be the worst date ever! What is this?" Then Richard told her he would build her a coffee shop there. "I am sorry we never got to have a child together." He showed her all the documents and papers already signed, and Richard later told some people that all the extra work had been worth it when he saw Lourdes smiling for real again after she got the news that she would never be a mom. He was dedicated entirely to loving his wife to the best of his ability.

Thomas: Man . . .

Thomas looks at Lourdes for a second, both sad and proud of her. Listening to someone's story suddenly makes people look so different.

Thomas: Why is it called *The Shire*?

Peter: Richard loved *The Lord of the Rings* novels, and in the story, *The Shire* is a place where time doesn't seem to pass, everything remains the same; a place where people from different journeys in life could find some rest away from the darkness of the world. He was always talking about it and seeing its connection with Heaven. Actually, Richard wanted this coffee shop to be named "Lourdes' coffee shop." But when he passed, Lourdes decided to call it *The Shire*. When she shared her story, she also said that every coffee she makes "feels like a step closer to seeing Richard again." Have you never heard Lourdes' story?

Thomas: No, I never did.

Lourdes' story makes Thomas feel uneasy, and unaware he is doing anything, he leans over to look outside the window, hoping to see Sofía.

Peter: Do you want me to tell you if I see her from here?

Thomas: No, it's OK.

After a few seconds of a deafening silence . . .

Peter: Well, are you ready for some science and faith?

Thomas: Yes.

Thomas gets comfortable in his chair and ready to have a conversation he has also been looking forward to.

Thomas: OK. Here is my first question. Is there a conflict between science and faith to you?

Peter: No, there isn't. I think they are two aspects of the same reality, which I believe God created as a whole.[42]

Thomas: However, as we said last week, many times, beliefs in the metaphysical or divine were given as explanations for material occurrences, and then science demonstrated they were false. For example, the Greeks attributed lightning to the god Zeus.

Peter: You know? While searching for the divine, we all have made inevitable mistakes because we lack knowledge of the world surrounding us. This is known as the "God of the gaps" argument, the belief that God is always the answer for the gaps of knowledge we cannot explain. I think 400 years of science have taught us that,

---

[42] Genesis 1:1: In the beginning, God created the heavens and the earth.

when it comes to the material world, it is very reasonable to expect a materialistic explanation for how the world functions rather than a metaphysical one.

Thomas: So, where does your faith come into place?

Peter: Well, the crucial word here is "function." Here is an important distinction I find very helpful. Functionality is a very different characteristic of matter than simple *existence*. Therefore, if I explain how gravity works, I am not explaining why it exists, just how it *functions*. We get to "know" things in terms of what they do, not what they are intrinsically. I don't think science can answer the question "Why is there something rather than nothing?" nor "Why does this "something" look the way it does?"

Thomas: Peter, that sounds like an extension of the "God of the gaps" argument. What if one day we get to know things, not only because of how they function but because of what they intrinsically are? Would that make you doubt God's existence?

Peter: That's a great point. Let me ask you a question, Thomas. Do you think one day we'll find a materialistic explanation to explain why matter exists?

Thomas: Well, as you said, functionality and existence are two different things. We don't know at this point.

Peter: From a materialistic point of view, you are right; we don't know. However, if what explains the existence of matter is also material matter, we could also ask why matter comes from matter, and why matter came from matter that came from matter. This will lead us to an infinite regress of events. If this were so, we would have to conclude that matter is eternal.

Thomas: What's the problem with matter being eternal?

Peter: If matter is eternal, the question would remain: Why is there something eternal rather than nothing?

Thomas: You can keep asking questions like that, but I wonder if they are even necessary.

Peter: What do you mean?

Thomas: Regarding the universe, the question "why" makes sense within a cause-and-effect relationship. For example, why does a ball fall? Well, because that object feels a force, the strength with which the Earth pulls on it in the form of gravity. However, asking why there is a law of gravity at all is a question that science cannot answer.

Peter: So, what should we do with those types of questions?

Thomas: If we never get to actual answers, we should stop asking them.

Peter: What is an "actual answer" for you?

Thomas: One that can be verified, tested, and predicted.

Peter: Oh, I see. Thomas, I promise you, I am not trying to be funny or difficult. I hope this doesn't sound to you like a cop-out answer either, because it isn't for me at least. But why are there answers that can be verified, tested, and predictable rather than nothing?

Thomas: Ha! I don't know, and I feel that you will give me an answer for it that cannot be verified or tested and isn't predictable, either. Therefore, in principle, your answer to that should also be "I don't know."

Peter: Well, my answer can be verified, tested, and predicted. The fact that the world can be studied entails the universe is ordered, and order usually emerges from intelligence because only conscious minds can recognize it. My answer is the universe is intelligible; it can be understood. This is a bedrock of existence; in fact, without it, science couldn't even be possible.

Thomas: And?

Peter: If the universe can be understood, there would need to be conscious beings like us who are aware of their existence and can discern those patterns within it. Therefore, it is very rational for me to believe that the universe was created by some intelligence. The universe can be understood because of the way it functions, which means it is intelligible, which means the explanation for its own existence lies beyond the characteristics it exhibits. If there is matter, then the explanation cannot be material. We see space, so the explanation cannot be space. We see time, so the explanation cannot be time, and so on. Our mind is non-material, spaceless, and timeless, even if it solely emerges from the neurological interactions within our brains. That's why I believe it is rational to believe reality was created by "a mind" or something similar to a mind. God fits that explanation perfectly. If God, who I believe is omniscient,[43] created the universe, it is reasonable to expect that the universe would exhibit intelligible, discernable patterns that other minds can also describe. That is precisely what we see and do.

Thomas: So, let me try to understand what you are saying. The universe is intelligible. To understand it, you need a mind that is not bound by matter, space, or time. Therefore, a mind could have

---

[43] 1 John 3:20: Even if we feel guilty, God is greater than our feelings, and he knows everything.

created the universe because it exhibits features only minds can understand.

Peter: That's one way to say it.

Thomas: Well, as you said, minds emerge from matter—our brains.

Peter: Thomas, that is true. But even if we conceded that point, the question remains: How could matter create something non-material, in this case, consciousness? I am OK with the idea that our form of consciousness emerges from physical interactions in the brain, but the result remains non-material. So, since matter is one of the main features of the universe, there is no problem with consciousness being related to matter at some level.

Thomas: But, God, or this supposed conscious mind who created the universe, is non-material; so it is still conscious but doesn't have a material brain?

Peter: Thomas, your questions are so good! I don't have an answer to your question at this point. I think consciousness is intertwined with matter in the universe because only things with brains have it. This is the case within the universe. But I don't think existence necessarily requires matter. Consciousness might not need a brain to exist outside of this system.

Thomas: You choose to believe this, but you don't know it.

Peter: Well, up to this point, I have been trying to figure out whether it is reasonable from a scientific, philosophical point of view to believe that God exists. And we are not far from it at all. However, I am a follower of Jesus. I believe God exists. So, in Jesus, I find a way to rest in all metaphysical and material questions, even the ones I still don't have answers to. I don't mean I have answers in the cause-and-effect, empirical sense, but a conceptual framework from which we could expect an ordered universe like this to exist.

Thomas: You can find rest in questions you have no answers to?

Peter: What I mean by this is even when I don't know the answer to a question I might have about the universe, I know that at least part of the answer will have to entail two things: one, that the universe is intelligible, and two, that conscious beings are necessary to understand it. So, in other words, the functionality of all that exists "rests" in the assumption that intelligence is a crucial aspect of it. Intelligence entails agency. Agency entails will. Will entails mind, and God seems to fit this description very well.

Thomas: From your perspective? Perhaps.

Peter: OK. Phew! Let me ask you a few questions. Did I survive yours?

Thomas: Meh!

Both Peter and Thomas laugh.

Peter: Great questions, by the way.

Thomas: Thank you.

Peter: Taking God out of the picture, how would you answer the question: Why is there something rather than nothing?

Thomas: I would say we still don't know.

Peter: That's fair. But don't the things we do know suggest something about why they exist?

Thomas: What do we know?

Peter: We know there is *something* rather than nothing. That this "something" is intelligible. That the universe allows for the existence of minds like ours.

Thomas: I see what you mean. However, a suggestion is not a hypothesis we can test.

Peter: Wait, Thomas, but reality's existence, the way it is ordered, and our minds are not a "suggestion"; they are here; they are inevitable facts of our reality. The whole scientific enterprise rests on the assumption that those things exist first.

Thomas: But wait, I said we "still" don't know. We cannot be closed to the idea that one day, we'll answer those questions without having to posit some non-physical explanation.

Peter: That's true. However, whatever answer we find in the future, there will always be another "why" question waiting to be uncovered behind the "why" question that was just answered. I think Paul was right when he said: "Now we see things imperfectly, like puzzling reflections in a mirror, but then we will see everything with perfect clarity. All that I know now is partial and incomplete, but then I will know everything completely, just as God now knows me completely."[44] The question "Why is there something rather than nothing," and "Why does 'something' look the way it does" will always remain—that's my belief. Since I believe God created reality, I also believe that those answers cannot be discovered; they must be revealed.

Lourdes approaches the table.

---

[44] 1 Corinthians 13:12.

Lourdes: I'm sorry it took me some time to prepare your coffee. One of my coffee machines is broken, and I can only go so fast. Here you go.

The steam rising from the coffee is blinding.

Thomas: You want us to believe you can drink coffee as hot as these?

Lourdes: It's the only way.

Thomas: There is always another way.

Lourdes: But it's not *my* way, dear.

Thomas, Lourdes, and Peter laugh. As Thomas maneuvers to sip his coffee, his eyes move nervously toward the window, hoping to see Sofía, but without success. A few seconds later, he returns to his conversation with Peter.

Thomas: My other question is about what some Christians think about science.

Peter: Keep going.

Thomas: Many scientists believe the universe is close to 14 billion years old and that life came together through evolution. This is where we are. However, some Christians use Scriptures to make scientific assertions about the world around them, like the earth is young, or that we were created "*ex nihilo*," out of nothing in our actual state. These beliefs contradict the current scientific consensus. But you say that faith and science don't contradict themselves. How is that?

Peter: Some believe science will ultimately answer all our questions, but that's clearly misguided. Science describes reality but has nothing to say about why there is a reality that can be described to start with. Science is contingent upon reality for its existence. Besides, Scripture was never intended to be a scientific book, but a unified story, rooted in history, that leads us to Jesus. Within the Christian tradition, 2000 years of faithful, yet imperfect pursuits of Jesus, there have been many views about many things. Indeed, some Christians wouldn't believe those things are true; but there is room in the Christian faith for disagreement on these topics. However, the central belief is that God created, and everyone agrees with that. Now, what is the purpose of the Bible? Is it teaching us how God has moved throughout history to bring humanity to Himself? Or to show us the cause-and-effect process through which He created everything? You are right; there are many views about this, but most importantly, they all share the core belief that God created. Now, each view has strengths and weaknesses at the scientific and theological level.

Thomas: What is your view on this?

Peter: God created the universe, became a human being in Jesus—the second person of the Trinity—and communicated His will to us through Scripture. This means that, ultimately, they cannot contradict each other. If we see a contradiction, then this means there is still work to do to understand them both well. I know this question is vital for both believers and nonbelievers, but ultimately, what unites the world is that we need Jesus for reasons that are not scientific but reasons of the heart.[45] Could some of us be making a mistake expecting Scripture to say things about the world that it may or may not be saying, for example, how young or how old the earth is? Or are some of us making mistakes because we are expecting Scripture to be reconciled with the scientific consensus of today?

---

[45] Romans 3:23: For everyone has sinned; we all fall short of God's glorious standard.

Yes, it is possible. Now, some things are way more essential than those: God is the creator,[46] God is love[47], our need for repentance,[48] Jesus' sacrifice for humanity,[49] Jesus' resurrection,[50] God's final judgment of our character,[51] the intrinsic value of human life,[52] etc. Those are the things that unite Christians all over the world. There is room for disagreement regarding secondary issues. I don't know about other Christians, but I know I am open to being wrong about the secondary issues of the faith. My favorite verse in Scripture, Ecclesiastes 3:11, puts it this way: "Yet God has made everything beautiful for its own time. He has planted eternity in the human heart, but even so, people cannot see the whole scope of God's work from beginning to end."

Thomas: I mean, I respect that. But think about this: What if an ancient book is causing people to believe things that aren't true? That's an actual possibility.

Peter: I don't think God's ultimate message in Scripture was to tell us the truth about how the world works mechanistically. If so, we could have expected to learn algebra, calculus, engineering, and physics in it, but we don't. To know those things, we need to study the

---

[46] Genesis 1:1: In the beginning, God created the heavens and the earth.

[47] 1 John 4:16: We know how much God loves us, and we have put our trust in his love. God is love, and all who live in love live in God, and God lives in them.

[48] Acts 3:19: Now repent of your sins and turn to God, so that your sins may be wiped away.

[49] 1 John 4:10: This is real love—not that we loved God, but that he loved us and sent his Son as a sacrifice to take away our sins.

[50] 1 Peter 1:3: All praise to God, the Father of our Lord Jesus Christ. It is by his great mercy that we have been born again, because God raised Jesus Christ from the dead. Now we live with great expectation.

[51] 2 Corinthians 5:10: For we must all stand before Christ to be judged. We will each receive whatever we deserve for the good or evil we have done in this earthly body.

[52] Genesis 1:27: So God created human beings in his own image. In the image of God he created them; male and female he created them.

world *He* created. Instead, the Bible clarifies that Jesus is the truth.[53] This means that Jesus is the truth from which the rest emerges. The focus of Scripture is the Truth of what God is accomplishing in this world, and history shows us that He has and He will accomplish it through Jesus. Jesus is the truth through which we can make sense of the world we live in. The more I seek truth, the closer I find myself to Jesus. We could still have unanswered questions about things Scripture does not tell us, even things about the universe itself, but that should be expected. Therefore, when it comes to secondary issues of the faith, many Christians, including me, can be wrong. If you read different Christian thinkers throughout history, you can see that some of them were wrong while making assertions about the world when figuring out how the world functions, but the essential beliefs have always remained the same.

Thomas: Science, however, solves actual problems that make people suffer here and now, like diseases or accidents. What does God do about those things?

Peter: Thomas, it sounds like you see science as separated from God, but I don't see it that way. God has created the world with discernible patterns through which we can solve problems that make people suffer here and now. See? When I get sick, thanks to God's grace, I have several options: pray and go to the doctor, and both are options within God's world. Besides, Jesus has changed countless people's lives with His teachings, and many stopped suffering because of them. God does solve problems for numerous people every day. Have you ever considered that God provides solutions in this broken world by allowing humanity to discover

[53] John 14:6: Jesus told him: "I am the way, the truth, and the life. No one can come to the Father except through me.

them through the field of science? I believe that the discipline of good science is also divinely providential.

Peter's opinion makes sense, but Thomas still needs clarification.

Peter: OK. I'll give you some time to think and digest what I said. Thomas, when you talk about science, you seem to talk about science as the ultimate boundary for humanity, as if science is the reason for everything, but science cannot explain itself.

Thomas: Science is making tangible steps toward people's well-being. Science is conceptual, as we hypothesize, but it is tangible in terms of the answers it offers. However, Scripture stays on the conceptual and never seems to give us actual, tangible answers about the world.

Peter: Haha, Thomas! I am walking proof of the opposite.

Thomas: How so?

Peter: OK. May I share a Scripture passage with you?

Thomas: Yes, go ahead.

Peter begins to look up a Scripture passage on his phone.

Peter: This is Romans 12:9–18:

Don't just pretend to love others. Really love them. Hate what is wrong. Hold tightly to what is good. Love each other with genuine affection, and take delight in honoring each other. Never be lazy, but work hard and serve the Lord enthusiastically. Rejoice in our confident hope. Be patient in trouble, and keep on praying. When God's people are in need, be ready to help them. Always be eager to practice hospitality. Bless those who persecute you. Don't curse them; pray that God will bless them. Be happy with those who are happy, and weep with those who weep. Live in harmony with each other. Don't be too proud to enjoy the company of ordinary people. And don't think you know it all! Never pay back evil with more evil. Do things in such a way that everyone can see you are honorable. Do all that you can live in peace with everyone.

Thomas: OK . . . What's your point?

Peter: Now, all of this becomes tangible if I obey it, *only* if I obey it. Countless lives have been changed tangibly because of following Jesus. The Bible's knowledge and assertions of reality can be tangible, too. My life has not been the same at all since I began following Jesus; even the way I think of myself and others, *everything* has changed. That is tangible change. Using the analogy you brought up, I could say that as a follower of Jesus, I have hypothesized about what He says for years without actually obeying it. Yes, I never saw any tangible changes in my life. The same happens with the hypothesis in science—at some point you must test them. And you can do the same with Jesus.

Thomas: Huh, I have never heard it said that way before.

Suddenly, Peter gets distracted by something happening outside the coffee shop.

Thomas: What—are you OK?

Peter is looking out the window, eyes fixated on something or someone that seems to be moving. Thomas's heart sinks to the floor, and he looks out immediately. Yes, it's Sofía and Linda returning from their walk to the lake. They are heading to Linda's car. Sofía is still holding her cup of coffee, and Thomas is not surprised because she always likes sipping slowly through it.

Thomas: Man . . .

Peter doesn't say anything.

Thomas: Part of me wants to go out and tell her how much I need and love her. But this other side tells me that doing that would make things worse.

Peter: You could just go and say "hi?"

Thomas agrees, but his emotions don't allow him to do it. It feels so weird. He could talk to Sofía about anything just a couple of weeks ago, and now saying a simple "hi" to her feels like an insurmountable mountain for him. Suddenly, Lourdes stops what she is doing, turns around the counter, opens the door, and begins talking to Sofía.

Lourdes: Sofía! I checked with the supplier; I'll have your order of 20 chocolate muffins ready in the morning for your mom's birthday! By the way, Thomas and Peter are here!

Thomas: *(whispering, embarrassed)* Please, earth, swallow me right now . . .

Peter: *(same)* What in the world, Lourdes?

Sofía waves both to Thomas and Peter. Linda waves at them too. The situation is awkward, except for Lourdes, of course. Sofía gets in the car with Linda, and Thomas and Sofía stare at each other until Linda leaves the parking lot. Thomas sits back in his chair, releasing a big sigh.

Thomas: It's just so frustrating.

Peter: What is frustrating?

Thomas: That Sofía doesn't want to be with me through this.

Peter: I think she said she can't, not that she doesn't want to.

Peter's comment bothers Thomas, and in a small burst of anger and frustration, Thomas takes the empty antidepressant bottle with Peter's name on it out of his pocket and puts it on the table, making a loud noise. Seeing Sofía brings the best and the worst out of Thomas right now.

Thomas: *(angry)* Man . . . it seems that the people I care for the most have decided to plot against me by not telling me what's going on in their lives. What the heck is this, Peter? Are we not friends or what?

Peter blushes, not knowing what to say; he cannot believe what he is seeing.

Peter: *(hesitant)* Where did you find this?

Thomas: In the parking lot after our last conversation. What is this? Are you OK?

Even while frustrated by everything happening to him, Thomas cares deeply for Peter.

Peter: Thomas . . . first, I am sorry about you and Sofía. I know you love and miss her, and I don't doubt she does too. I just didn't want to tell anyone, especially you, because of everything you are going through.

Thomas: Sorry. Seeing her is difficult enough, and I forgot it was her mom's birthday tomorrow. Anyway, what's going on with you?

Peter: *(whispering)* Would it be OK if I told you after we finish this conversation? I wouldn't want Lourdes to hear this.

Thomas: That's fine. I also noticed you felt very emotional after you went to the bathroom the other day, but I decided not to say anything about it.

Peter makes a gesture to Thomas, implying it is better to wait.

Peter: *(whispering)* Let's wait 'til we leave. Is that OK?

Thomas: That's OK.

They spend a few seconds in silence. Thomas is worried about Peter, and Peter is shocked he wasn't careful enough to hide his medicine from others. Thomas makes an effort to keep talking to Peter about the big questions despite how he feels right now.

Thomas: Well, the last thing I'd like to hear your thoughts about is miracles.

Thomas and Peter feel that the conversation won't flow the same because of what just happened, but they try their best to keep going.

Peter: What do you think about miracles?

Thomas: I have heard some people say that miracles transgress the natural order in the world, that the evidence for them should be as strong or even stronger than the miracle itself; and since they cannot be studied empirically, they are probably false.

Peter: And what do you think about that?

Thomas: I am not that old, but as far as I am concerned, everything that has happened around me so far can be explained empirically. Besides, scientists have demonstrated they can find answers to the most challenging questions about the world in due time. Four hundred years of science have given us reasons to expect that things we don't understand right now will eventually be explained in terms of matter, energy, space, and time. Miracles seem to override the natural laws that govern the universe . . . um . . .

Thomas seems unsure.

Peter: What?

Thomas: I don't know. Sometimes, it feels so strange to be the one doubting after being a Christian for so many years.

Peter: Thomas, I know it might feel strange, but asking questions is the key to knowing anything. You might feel weird, but sometimes, the intensity of our emotions doesn't let us see the world as it is. I know it isn't easy to separate feelings and thoughts, but asking questions is the right thing to do.

Thomas: Thank you, Peter. What about you? What do you think about miracles?

Peter: Well, it'll start with, as always, my belief in God. I believe God exists, allowing miracles to be real too. Do you know of the fallacy of equivocation?

Thomas: I think so. The fallacy of equivocation occurs when a key term or phrase in an argument is used ambiguously, with one meaning in one portion of the argument and then another meaning in another portion of the argument.

Peter: Exactly. Yes. Well, I want to do just that right now.

Both Thomas and Peter laugh.

Thomas: And you let me know as if you are even proud of it!

Both Thomas and Peter laugh again.

Peter: Well, not quite, I am just joking here. What I want to do is to share my best attempt to show the word *miracle* can be applied to other categories of existence beyond your suggested definition: "miracles defy the laws of nature."

Thomas: *(unsure)* OK . . .

Peter: Isn't reality a miracle in itself? I mean this: reality itself cannot be proven through a process of trial and error, but you have a process of trial and error because reality exists. As far as we know, reality has only happened once. I think that's, in a sense, an actual miracle.

Thomas: Oh, I see what you mean.

Peter: The laws of nature are a miracle because they allow us to study the world around us. The world could have been made in so many ways, but it is made exactly in a way that allows us, conscious creatures, to study it. The odds of the universe forming exactly as it has merely by chance are truly astounding. The universe is an incredibly complex and intricate system comprised of countless galaxies, stars, planets, and life. The precise arrangement and interplay of all these elements, from the formation of galaxies and the laws of physics to the appearance of life on Earth, point to a remarkable level of fine-tuning. This could also be seen as a miracle. What I mean by this is that if you pay attention, you can see miracles everywhere. But let's be fair, that's not the "type" of miracle you were talking about.

Thomas: By the way, when you say that to have a process of trial and error, you first need existence for it to happen, it sounds like you are saying that for existence to exist, you need existence. That's circular reasoning in all its glory.

Peter: *(smiles)* The way I express myself might not be ideal, but what I am trying to say is that we don't have an explanation for the actual system that allows us to find explanations of how the system itself functions within it. That's not circular reasoning; it is more like getting out of your circular reasoning to wonder why there is reason and a circle in the first place.

After listening to Peter's last phrase, Thomas remains quiet for a few seconds. He smirks and frowns at Peter.

Thomas: I think you need more friends.

Peter didn't expect that answer from Thomas. He begins laughing so hard that he falls back in his chair. This sudden, out-of-the-blue sense of humor always breaks Peter apart. Thomas cannot stop laughing as he tries to help Peter get up from the floor. Everyone at the coffee shop laughs after realizing that Peter is OK and laughing too. The old man sitting on the corner mysteriously writing whatever he is writing also shares a sincere laugh with them. Suddenly, Lourdes raises her voice to say something to everyone in the coffee shop.

Lourdes: Only my coffee can make you feel this way!

The whole coffee shop begins laughing now. After Lourdes' comment, it takes a few minutes for everyone to settle down and return to their conversations.

Peter: I am OK! I am OK!

Peter looks at Thomas, red but smiling.

Peter: *(repeating Thomas)* "You need more friends" . . . Man, Thomas, you don't even know how much I needed to laugh this way again.

Thomas: I am glad you found it funny. I didn't know it was going to be that funny. Well, haha!

Thomas looks at his phone for a second.

Thomas: I need to go soon, but let's finish the conversation we started. What do you think about miracles when defined as "occurrences that defy the laws of nature?

Peter: OK . . .

Peter needs a few seconds to get back into his train of thought. Internally, he is in awe of how friendship is just the absolute best, from depth to fun, from sadness to joy. No pretensions. Just two "blokes" bragging about how vulnerable they can be with each other.

Peter: OK, to know that a miracle is happening, you need the laws of nature to identify something extraordinary is happening. Without the regularities of the world, we wouldn't be able to recognize potential "irregularities." Therefore, I don't think miracles defy the laws of nature because we need the laws of nature to know that a miracle is happening. When it comes to the evidence needed to demonstrate that a miracle happened, let's focus our attention, for instance, on the resurrection of Jesus. Paul says that if the resurrection of Jesus never happened, our faith would make no sense whatsoever. That's how high the stakes are.[54] As far as we know, people don't come back to life after they die, so if one would come back to life, the evidence for it should be enormous. I believe that is exactly what we have: the empty tomb, Jesus' appearances to His disciples, the disciples' willingness to die with nothing to gain beyond the belief of the resurrection itself, how Christianity spread through uneducated fishermen overcoming the highly "educated" and philosophical worldview of the Greco-Roman world, and around 2 billion Christians all over the world with countless lives changed from desperation to living hope—including mine. I think that's enough evidence to believe that a miracle happened.

Thomas: You forget that the spread of Christianity didn't happen without "countless" people dying in the name of Christ too.

Peter: You are absolutely right. The people who first followed Jesus were the ones being persecuted, but everything changed centuries ago when the belief of Christianity—not Christ—became a state religion. I remember this was a hard pill to swallow in my journey from atheism to Jesus. However, Jesus says: "Love your enemies."[55] If someone who claims to follow Jesus ends up killing people to spread His teachings, something He Himself never did, then he or she is not a follower of Jesus, but something else. Jesus explained to Pilate that His kingdom was "not of this world." [56] Jesus did not die to set up a state religion. That was the Roman practice. Jesus died so people could actually *live* as God intended it in the first place.

---

[54] 1 Corinthians 15:17: And if Christ has not been raised, then your faith is useless and you are still guilty of your sins!

[55] Matthew 5:44: But I say, love your enemies! Pray for those who persecute you!

[56] John 18:36.

Thomas: I think we should talk about the difficult passages of Scripture next time. God commanded the Israelites to destroy the Canaanites. That is the opposite of "loving your enemy."

Peter: Yes, I would love to hear what you think about it. Let's do that next time. For now, going back to the topic of miracles, if God exists and created the universe, He can interact with it in whatever way He pleases. Now, miracles are interesting if we look at them through the lens of Jesus. In Matthew 13, Jesus returned to His town, Nazareth, and in verse 58, Matthew says: "And so he did only a few miracles there because of their unbelief." Earlier in Matthew 9:27–28 we read: " . . . After Jesus left the girl's home, two blind men followed along behind him, shouting, 'Son of David, have mercy on us!' They went right into the house where he was staying, and Jesus asked them, 'Do you believe I can make you see?' 'Yes, Lord,' they told him, 'we do.'" As you can see, miracles don't happen when we want them to happen, and Jesus never did miracles to show how amazing He was, but they have a purpose: to make us believe in Jesus and to repent from our sins. Miracles are not for show; they have a purpose and require belief.

Thomas: So, do you think miracles happen all the time?

Peter: Yes, I just think I lack the faith to see them all around me since God is always at work.[57]

Thomas: People don't resurrect all the time. People don't suddenly start flying. Many people are not healed, even if others pray for them. There are things God cannot do, like making a person's limb grow back. What do you mean by God working all the time?

---

[57] John 5:17: But Jesus replied, "My Father is always working, and so am I."

Peter: The whole premise of Jesus is exactly that: if you need all these things to happen around you so that you can believe, your belief is based on show or arrogance, not on love. Jesus dying on the cross for you and me is enough for us to believe in Him, but only if we truly love Him. But to love Him, we first must realize that we *need* Him. Jesus said this to the Pharisees in Matthew 12:38–40 *(it takes a few seconds for Peter to find the passage)*:

One day some teachers of religious law and Pharisees came to Jesus and said, "Teacher, we want you to show us a miraculous sign to prove your authority." But Jesus replied, "Only an evil, adulterous generation would demand a miraculous sign; but the only sign I will give them is the sign of the prophet Jonah. For as Jonah was in the belly of the great fish for three days and three nights, so will the Son of Man be in the heart of the earth for three days and three nights.

Thomas, Jesus was talking about the resurrection. Some people wouldn't believe and obey Jesus even if they saw Him appear in front of them and had a conversation with Him. It's not about evidence; it's about repentance and love. When repentance and love happen, you can see Jesus' miracles everywhere. For instance, you don't see people's limbs growing back, but you can see people who lose a limb doing good things for others in the name of Jesus. I don't think the point is to grow the limb you have lost, but to wonder what to do with the one you have left. The miracle is a change of heart and everything that happens afterward.

Thomas: It feels strange to have a conversation about miracles and talk about repentance and love. I would rather not make conclusions about the real world with theological assumptions I cannot prove.

Peter: Physics and Metaphysics became one in Jesus, so I can't talk about the world without talking about repentance and love. God, the sustainer of reality, is love. Love is the basis of everything. If that is true, then "love" must show up continually in the conversations about the big questions in life.

Lourdes interrupts them.

Lourdes: Hey guys, I *love* you, but I need to go home soon.

Thomas and Peter didn't realize that it was so late. Everyone had left, and it was getting dark outside.

Peter: Oh wow! I didn't realize it was this late. Do you need us to help you put things away?

Lourdes: Oh, no, no, no . . . I said I needed to go home *soon*, not in a few hours.

Thomas and Peter laugh.

Thomas: Got it! Leaving now. Good night, Lourdes.

Lourdes: *Buenas noches.*

Once they are outside the coffee shop, the conversation turns more somber.

Peter: About the pills . . .

Thomas: Yes?

Peter: It's getting late. Would you mind me telling you about it next week? I don't want to tell you quickly and then leave.

Thomas: Really? That's so mean! Man . . . OK. You need to let me know, though, if you need my help at any time. You hear me?

Peter: I do. Thank you, Thomas. Please, don't worry about me. I hope you can find a way to talk to Sofía soon.

Thomas: Me too.

Thomas and Peter hug each other. Thomas is holding Peter tighter than usual to let him know, without words, that he is there for him.

Chapter 5
For the Bible Tells Me So

Thursday, October 12

It's a calm, crisp afternoon. Temperatures are going down day after day. The sun shines brightly, giving a light sense of warmth despite the cold air that freely moves in the atmosphere. The trees on the trail are ready to let go, letting the color of their leaves change gradually from green to beautiful shades of red, orange, and yellow. Just like Jesus said about fasting, "don't let anyone know you are fasting," but "comb your hair and wash your face," nature also shows us its most intrinsic beauty when it seasonally fasts from its own beauty.

Thomas wants to have a conversation about the difficult passages of the Bible, but first, he is wondering what is going on with his friend.

Thomas gets to The Shire *first. He wants to talk with Peter, but not at* The Shire *this time. Lourdes is there, helping clients and serving coffee. Sometimes, it feels like Lourdes lives in her coffee shop. It's very encouraging to see people doing what they have been born to do. There are a couple of people there. One of them is the old man in the corner, who keeps writing intently on a notepad. Thomas is becoming curious about this man.*

Peter's jokes are starting to rub off on Thomas. How is this even possible? *Thomas wonders. He has been wondering for a few days what Lourdes' reaction would be if he ordered an iced coffee.* Would Lourdes implode and cease to exist? Oh, man. I need to stop hanging out with you, Peter. OK. I am doing this. *Thomas enters the coffee shop decisively, eager to explore the dark side of Lourdes.*

Thomas: Hi, Lourdes, how are you?

Lourdes: Hi, Thomas, I am doing fine.

Thomas: May I have an iced coffee?

Lourdes: Of course; how much poison would you like in it?

Thomas: Enough to taste it but not die.

Both laugh.

Thomas: For real, Lourdes, what's the problem with an iced coffee? I want to hear a serious answer from you.

Lourdes: The problem is those who like it.

Lourdes makes herself giggle uncontrollably; Thomas finds it funny but not as much as Lourdes.

Lourdes: OK, here is the serious answer. It is the water. When ice mixes up with coffee, its taste dilutes as the ice melts, and you lose the essence of it, both in smell and taste. It's like asking someone to be someone they are not. The same happens, in my opinion, when you add ice to coffee.

Thomas: And why do you serve coffee so hot?

Lourdes: *(smiles)* I am so honored for this interview.

Thomas: According to Peter, I am good at asking questions.

Lourdes: It's about Richard.

Thomas: Your husband?

Lourdes: Yes. *The Shire* represents peace and quietness. I serve coffee "burning hot," as you boys say it, because it forces people to slow down, learn how to wait, and be patient. These values were very important for Richard. It is a way to make him a part of everything I do, even if he is not here anymore.

Thomas nods while reflecting on what Lourdes said. Every person has a wealth of knowledge, experiences, and emotions behind them, and Thomas is just a few questions away from discovering them. Talking about Richard has made Lourdes put down her "witty wall," Thomas can even feel her tone becoming softer.

Lourdes: Would you like me to prepare an iced coffee for you, Thomas? I don't mind.

Thomas: You know what, Lourdes? No. I want to learn to slow down, wait, and be patient. I need that more than ever. Richard seemed to be a very wise man.

Lourdes shares a sincere smile with Thomas.

Thomas: Actually, could you make two coffees to go?

Lourdes: You guys are not having a conversation here today?

Thomas: I think we are taking a walk to the lake today.

Lourdes: I need to do that soon myself. I'll have your coffee ready in a second.

Thomas looks at his phone to make sure Peter didn't text him. He is usually punctual.

Old man: Excuse me, Thomas?

Thomas: Yes?

The old man who always sits in the corner waves at him, inviting him to join him at his table. What a curious feeling this is, to hear your name from the lips of a person you don't know, *Thomas ruminates as he approaches the man with a mixture of curiosity and hesitancy.*

Old man: Do you have a second to talk?

Thomas: Sure. But first of all, do we know each other?

Old man: I have heard you and your friend saying each other's names a few times. This place is small. I don't mean to pry, but sometimes, hearing what you guys are talking about is unavoidable. By the way, my name is Jim.

Thomas: Hi Jim. Nice to meet you. How can I help you?

The man has a firm shake, and his smile looks way younger than the rest of his body.

Jim: Well, I hear you have doubts about your Christian faith. I am aware that asking a stranger about this can be strange.

Thomas wonders if other people know about this. The Shire *is certainly a place where you can hear people's conversation fairly well if you pay attention.*

Thomas: *(doubtful)* I guess so. Why do you ask?

Jim: Well, I am a former pastor myself. I left the Christian faith 18 years ago, and I believe that it was one the best decisions I ever made. I don't know who this other friend of yours was that day when there were three of you here, but he was very . . .

Thomas knows he is talking about Landon. He wishes he could still say he is his future brother-in-law.

Thomas: Passionate?

Jim: I guess that's a way to say it. He was very frustrated about Christianity. I am an atheist, but I still value certain aspects of Christianity, even though I don't think it is true anymore. I have been in town for a few weeks, caring for my mother, and my sister told me this is a good place to disconnect. Would both you and . . . Peter, is it?

Thomas: Yes.

Jim: Would you both like to meet next week here to discuss my experience as an atheist? I'd like to hear your thoughts too.

You never know what's behind any person you encounter. A former pastor, now atheist . . . I wonder what he is writing? *Thomas cannot contain his curiosity anymore.*

Thomas: I'll talk to Peter, but I think he would be thrilled if you were to join us. By the way, what are you writing there? Peter and I have noticed you are always writing.

Jim: Oh, this?

Jim holds the notepad up, showing it to Thomas.

Jim: I am actually not writing anything. I am just drawing. I make sketches of people, places, anything around me. It relaxes me.

Thomas: Oh! Let me guess, have Peter and I become one of your art pieces at this point?

Jim laughs.

Jim: You have. I hope you don't mind. Do you want to see it?

It takes Jim a few seconds to get to the drawing. Jim drew a picture of Peter talking to Thomas while Thomas was looking out the window. It was probably last week when Thomas was waiting to see Sofía and Linda at the end of their walk.

Thomas: I know exactly when that happened.

Jim: Did you end up seeing whatever you wanted to see outside the window?

Man, Jim seems to be mindful of all the nuances of people around him, *Thomas wonders.*

Thomas: *(looking down)* You could say so . . .

Jim: Well, if you and your friend Peter would like to meet here next week at the same time, we could all talk together.

Thomas: OK, Jim. Let's plan on it. I know Peter, and he'd love it. Do you know he was an atheist for many years?

Jim: I did not know that. Yes, that will make the conversation way more interesting then.

Thomas: See you then, Jim, and nice to meet you.

Jim: Nice to meet you, too.

As Thomas returns to the counter, he sees that the coffee is ready and steaming hot. That's not a bad thing anymore; it's a reminder to be more patient.

Suddenly, the door opens, it's Peter.

Peter: Hey, Thomas! I'm sorry I'm so late. Someone showed up at church asking for food and clothes, and I lost track of time as I helped her and listened to her story.

Thomas: No worries, Peter. Here is your coffee. Let's go. Was everything OK with her?

Peter: I don't know. She showed up asking for money to buy some gas for her car. She did not look very healthy. One of my cousins back in England was a drug addict and ended up passing away because of it. I could see some of the same physical deterioration in her face and body. I gave her some money and asked her if there was anything else I could do for her besides giving her money. But she got very . . . defensive, one could say? Who knows?

Thomas: You seem sad. Are you OK?

Peter: It's just . . . following Jesus is so difficult sometimes.

Thomas: What do you mean?

Peter: I don't know. I wish I knew what she was "really" going to do with the money I gave her. It's difficult because Jesus taught us something very inspiring, though very difficult to put into practice.

Thomas: I am curious now. What is it?

Peter: Let me get my phone and read it. I don't feel like butchering Scripture today.

They both smile.

Peter: Here it is. This is Matthew 25:37–40. Jesus is talking about those who will inherit the kingdom of God: "Then the good people will answer me, Lord, when did we see you? When did we feed you when you were hungry? When did we give you something to drink when you were thirsty? When did we see you as a stranger and take you into our homes? When did you need clothes, and we gave you some clothes? When did we see you when you were sick or in jail? When did we come to you? I will answer them, 'I am telling you the truth: Since you treated some of my so-called "unimportant" brothers this way, you did it to me!'" Thomas, anything that we do for the *least of these*, we are in a sense doing it for Jesus.

At times, Thomas feels Peter doesn't read the same Bible he has been reading all his life. I wonder if I ever felt a passion for it like him . . . like ever? *Thomas wonders. Peter interrupts his train of thought.*

Peter: I mean, do you know how much dignity and value Jesus' statement about people brings to those on the fringe of society?[58] In some way, they "represent" Jesus.

---

[58] Proverbs 14:31: Those who oppress the poor insult their Maker, but helping the poor honors him. Proverbs 19:17: If you help the poor, you are lending to the Lord—and he will repay you!

Thomas doesn't say anything for a few seconds, letting the thought settle with a mixture of inspiration and confusion.

Thomas: That is . . .

Thomas seems to be out of words.

Thomas: That is . . .

Peter: Exactly. There are no words to describe such a revolutionary statement. How can I not love God, in Jesus, knowing this is how much He cares for any person no matter who they are?

Thomas: But why did you say it is difficult to follow Jesus again?

Peter: Ah, yes. In the past, when I saw a person like this woman I just spent time with, I tended to see them as "someone who needs a job," or "someone who needs to be more responsible." I did not see them as a person who is deeply valued by the God who created them and deserves to be loved, sacrificially, just like God loves me. It is difficult because Jesus' love had no boundaries. I mean, he died for people who hated him. But when I desire to love this way, I realize how much I can get hurt or taken advantage of in the process. My fears, insecurities, and weaknesses refrain me from loving people the way He did, but I still desire to love the way He did. At least I find some comfort in thinking that my salvation doesn't depend on my actions, but instead it is on God's grace and love for us. However, it is still challenging to obey Him and to become more like Him every day.

Suddenly, Peter realizes Thomas is holding two coffees and is heading out.

Peter: Hey, Thomas, wait—where are you going?

Thomas: We are going to take a walk to the lake.

Peter knows why.

Peter: That's a great idea.

Thomas: By the way, Peter, come here for a second.

Peter: What?

Thomas takes Peter to Jim's table.

Thomas: Peter, this is Jim. Jim, this is Peter. I'll tell you about Jim during our walk, but next week, Jim would like to join us if that's OK with you. He is a former pastor and now an atheist.

Peter: Oh, wow. It's nice to meet you, Jim. It would be great to spend time with you and hear your story.

Thomas: See? I told you. OK, see you next week, Jim.

Jim: OK, nice to meet you, Peter. See you both next week.

As Peter leaves the coffee shop, he waves at Lourdes and Lourdes back at him. Thomas tells Peter about his two conversations with Lourdes and Jim before he arrived.

Peter: Aaaww! That's why she likes serving coffee so hot? You never know with Lourdes.

Thomas: Not only that, but she was also willing to make me an iced coffee today.

Peter: I am telling you: " . . . continue asking, and it will be given to you. Keep on searching, and you will find. Be knocking, and the door will open for you."[59]

Thomas laughs. They both begin walking on the trail, heading to the lake.

Peter: Hey, how are you?

Thomas: I feel . . . better. I still miss Sofía. By the way, her mom texted me the day after we met last week.

Peter: Really?

Thomas: Yes, she was sorry because she thought Sofía had invited me to her birthday, but then she realized she didn't. I don't know if she should have told me this or not, but she said she talked to Sofía.

Peter: And?

Thomas: She misses me but is afraid that being around me in a moment like this could make me not want to be with her anymore, just as it happened to her with her brother because of her faith. She doesn't know what to do about it. Her mom is sorry all of this is happening.

Peter: Wow . . . sorry, mate.

Thomas: But that's not all.

Peter: It isn't?

Thomas: Sofía texted me on Sunday.

---

[59] Matthew 7:7.

Eyes wide open, Peter gasps.

Peter: What did she say?!

Thomas pulls up his phone. At one point, he notices his hand shaking slightly as he looks up at Sofía's text. Peter feels sorry for his friend.

Thomas: She said . . . here it is: "I am not afraid of your questions, I am afraid to lose you because of them."

Peter sighs as if some tension is suddenly relieved.

Peter: . . . Love is so beautiful and complicated at the same time. You know what? I wonder if Sofía also wants to give you space to ask your questions so that you do not feel your relationship with her could play a role in your process of getting answers for them?

Thomas: It could be. She was there for her brother, and look what happened. It wouldn't surprise me if that were a part of it.

Peter: Did you answer her back?

Thomas: Yes, I did. I thanked her and said that I missed her too.

Thomas and Peter keep walking through the trail. There are trees on both sides, squirrels playing around, a few birds singing songs or saying things Thomas and Peter wish they could understand. The trail curves left and right and goes up and down, much like life itself. They haven't been able to sip from their burning coffee yet, but at least now they know why.

Thomas: OK. Peter, no more secrets. What's going on with you?

Peter breathes in deep and sighs, anticipating the heaviness of what he is about to say.

Peter: I haven't been feeling well lately.

Thomas: Why?

Peter: I just . . .

Peter needs to stop to gather enough strength to say it. Thomas also stops and turns around to look at him.

Peter: My tumor is back.

Thomas' heart sinks to the floor for his friend.

Peter: I have been going to the doctor for a few months. Tests here, tests there. It's back.

They both resume walking, although the ground doesn't feel as firm as a few seconds before. Thomas knows he is moving but feels his mind is paralyzed.

Thomas: I don't know what to say. I am sorry, Peter . . . is that the reason you are taking anti-depressants?

Peter: Yes and no. I needed them because I didn't tell anyone for a while, and dealing with this alone was challenging. I cannot tell my parents because they are not doing well back home, and I don't want to worry them. I didn't want to tell you because, for a few months, I noticed you were not doing well either, so I didn't want to worry you. But it's difficult because I am afraid. Not of death itself, but of the process of dying.

Thomas leaves space for Peter to expound upon it.

Peter: My first tumor came out of nowhere, as it were, and it forced me to face my mortality without being ready to do so. Also, I wasn't a follower of Jesus then, so I didn't know how to find peace in the suffering or joy in the struggle. As a matter of fact, I didn't even know that that was a thing at all. I was focused on getting better, but all of my energy was fueled by fear, not hope. For a very long time, I fought for life because of my fear of death. In Jesus, I have found peace in the thought of not being here anymore one day, but I still remember the process of almost dying, and it is very difficult to shake that specific fear. I tend to be the type of person who yearns to understand everything around me, but Jesus has the tendency to tell me that I need to trust Him and let things go.

Thomas: Wait a second, is there no cure?

Peter: My surgery is in a few weeks. It's not going to be an easy surgery, so anything can happen. That's where the fear is for me, Thomas—living through the total uncertainty that I may survive the surgery or that I may not.

Thomas stops walking and tightly embraces Peter for a few seconds—a few seconds that feel like hours. Both break into tears.

Thomas: I am here for you, Peter. You should have told me before.

Peter: I am sorry. I don't want to worry anyone, especially those who care for me. This is why I didn't want to tell you at *The Shire*. Lourdes would ask the whole church to pray for me, which is not bad. However, what if these are my last few weeks on earth? I don't want to bring this type of attention to me. I don't want people to be sad for me. I want to live my life as normal as possible. I might tell people a few days before the surgery, whenever it's scheduled, so that people can pray for me, but not before. Please, don't tell anyone about this for now.

Thomas: I won't. Do you have any of the symptoms you experienced the first time?

Peter: Not yet. We caught it before the tumor began pressing on all the nerves around it. I am thankful for that. The problem is where the tumor is located and how dangerous it is to remove it.

Thomas: Man. I just don't know what to say . . . OK, give me a second.

Peter: What?

Thomas: If the first surgery went well, why wouldn't the second? Is your fear not letting you be hopeful about it?

Peter: Maybe you are right . . . There is no reason for my surgery not to go well again.[60] You know? Even though I have the tendency to worry, I also know that Jesus is with me through it.[61] Nothing will be perfect in this life, but I am OK with it. It is just that all of this reminds me of all the fear I went through the first time, which caused me all the stress I feel right now. Memories are so ingrained in us. I wish I could forget some of them, but I can't; and sometimes I don't want to. My first tumor was a big step for me to consider the meaning of life, and because of it, I ended up surrendering my life to Jesus. It almost feels like suffering and pain are pointers to better things if we know how to interpret them well.

Thomas: Doesn't prayer help you with it?

---

[60] Matthew 6:34: So don't worry about tomorrow, for tomorrow will bring its own worries. Today's trouble is enough for today.

[61] John 16:33: I have told you all this so that you may have peace in me. Here on earth you will have many trials and sorrows. But take heart, because I have overcome the world.

Peter: It really does. I don't really pray for God to take away the tumor; but instead, for His will to be done in my life. A few years ago, I realized that I was praying for God to take away all the problems of my life. I didn't realize it then, but my prayers were fueled primarily by fear. Years later, as my faith in Jesus began moving from my brain to my heart, I realized that I wanted my prayers to be fueled by how much I love Him, and that's when I began to pray with a deeper trust that God is in control and He is always good. Once I began to really understand that I can trust Him, it changed how I prayed. I only need to know that God loves me, and He demonstrated it in Jesus.[62] Jesus suffered, yet He still trusted in the Father. With Jesus as my example, I want to learn to do that too, and—just as Jesus did as well—I want to love others through all of it, but it is so . . .difficult.

Thomas: Now that you say that, I have noticed throughout the years that some people praise God in seasons of happiness, but they blame Him in seasons of pain.

Peter: That was me! It takes time to have the courage to carry my cross every day[63], which isn't about simply enduring life's general hardships but a complete reorientation of my life around the person and work of Jesus—a radical commitment to self-denial, absolute allegiance to Christ, and willing participation in His suffering and mission, which is the only path to true life. And, sometimes, I have to drop it because of how much it weighs. But, as time passes, when I carry it for a long time, it begins to weigh less and less, only because I am learning to trust in Him more and more. It is true

[62] John 3:16: For this is how God loved the world: He gave his one and only Son, so that everyone who believes in him will not perish but have eternal life.

[63] Matthew 16:24: Then Jesus said to his disciples, "If any of you wants to be my follower, you must give up your own way, take up your cross, and follow me.

what Jesus says: "Come to me, all of you who are weary and carry heavy burdens, and I will give you rest." The key is never to let go of it. Sometimes, it's difficult to wrap my mind around it, but while I don't enjoy suffering or sorrow, I know that in the end, no matter what, eternal life awaits if I trust and obey Jesus.

Thomas: I wish I were as sure as you are about it.

Peter: *(singing, poorly)* Trust and obey, for there is no other way . . .

Thomas: Anything, Peter, but your singing . . .

Peter smirks and jokingly raises his hand, pretending to hit Thomas, but Thomas moves away, making fun of him.

Peter: Hey, Thomas, I think Lourdes's coffee is drinkable now.

They both take a sip from it. Thomas tries first but still burns.

Thomas: Ah! Not quite!

Thomas spills some of it on the ground as the hot sensation meets his lips.

Peter: Is it still burning?!

Thomas: Fire in a cup.

They both laugh.

The path that goes to the lake is made of fine gravel. The sound their sneakers make reminds Peter of his walks in his small town in England. From time to time, you can see a tree blown down by the storm, deer running around the trail and the forest, and the sound of small branches falling due to the wind. The air is fresh, and plenty of leaves cover the path. One can see the lake in the distance throughout the route, giving a sense of purpose to everyone who dares to explore it. The sound of the lake's waves is shy and gentle, as if the lake is lamenting not being an ocean; but the sound grows louder and louder, from nothing to a soothing whisper, the closer one gets to the lake.

Peter: OK. Enough of it for now. I think we planned to talk about . . . what was it? Oh yeah, some of the difficult passages in the Bible. Thank you for listening and caring for me like you do, mate. I'll keep you updated, and even though you are doubting and questioning your Christian faith, if you ever feel like praying again, please do so. Prayer is our greatest ministry.

Thomas: *(doubtful, but willing)* I will.

Peter: If you had to define where you are right now on the faith and non-faith spectrum, where would you place yourself?

Thomas: I cannot say, "I don't believe in God," Or "God doesn't exist." I feel more like an agnostic at this point. I never got to explore life beyond the Christian faith, so I am curious. However, there are some things about the Bible that, the more I explore them, the more skeptical I feel about them.

Peter: OK, let's give it a go.

Thomas: OK, one thing that I find quite . . . quite . . .

Peter: Quite. I get it.

Thomas: Well, there are certain passages in the Bible, both in the Old Testament and New Testament, where God doesn't seem to be worried about slavery. Moreover, he seems to be OK with it.[64] You said it's all about love, but how is something like this love?

Peter: That was tough for me, 'til it wasn't. To understand it, I consider these passages not as God's timeless, perfect moral ideals but as legal and social regulations given to a specific people group in the Ancient Near East over 3,000 years ago. God didn't create the world like this; slavery is a consequence of our sin. God wasn't trying to bring about a timeless moral ideal, but a system of *regulation* for a deeply flawed, pre-existing culture. God was meeting the Israelites where they were. While the law did not abolish the institution of slavery, it placed limits on it that were often more humane than those of surrounding nations. Seeing the word *slavery* in the Bible can be incredibly jarring, especially when we picture the horrors of the race-based slavery from more recent centuries. It's a tough thing to wrestle with. But I can tell you that the forms of servitude in the ancient world, which the biblical texts address, operated in a different context. For instance, the Old Testament discusses indentured servitude, often a way for people in dire economic straits to survive, with legal protections and prescribed limits on service. They key point here is this: the Old Testament explicitly condemns *manstealing*—kidnapping someone to sell them into slavery, as stated in Exodus 21:16—which was and is a foundational evil of the slavery we know of today.

It's also vital to remember that everyone is made in God's image—a profound truth that fundamentally undermines the idea of one person owning another as mere property. In those days, being sold as property, as horrible as it sounds to us today, in many cases

[64] Ephesians 6:5: Slaves, obey your earthly masters with deep respect and fear. Serve them sincerely as you would serve Christ.

was the only way to survive, since there weren't organizations, hospitals, orphanages, charities, and governmental organisms fully dedicated to care for people, which in turn are direct consequences of Christ coming to the world and Christian values extending all of the world! It's kind of ironic when you think about it. We assume all of those are a given today, but in fact they are a direct consequence of what God has been trying to bring about as He has been working through humanity right after we sinned. The Mosaic Law regulated servitude to prevent worse abuses in that ancient culture; it also contained seeds of liberation and justice. Then, in the New Testament, while existing within a Roman empire deeply immersed into slavery, the apostles urged masters to act with justice and fairness, recognizing their accountability to God, and taught radical concepts like spiritual equality in Christ where there is "neither slave nor free" (Galatians 3:28). Paul's letter to Philemon, urging him to receive Onesimus back "no longer as a slave, but as a beloved brother," is a powerful example of how Christian principles were meant to transform such relationships from the inside out, pointing toward a redemptive trajectory that ultimately fueled abolitionist movements. It wasn't endorsing the brutal system we rightly condemn, but rather working within a fallen world to affirm dignity and steer humanity toward God's heart for justice and love.

Thomas: So, people had to "sell" themselves and become property in order to survive?

Peter: Yes, at least they would for a time, until debts were cleared. Thomas, slavery existed *before* the Bible was written, *while* it was being written, and *after* it was written. Neither the Israelites nor the Christians invented slavery. Unfortunately, it has been and continues to be a part of society nowadays, and it is still not God's vision for humanity.

Thomas seems lost in his thoughts . . .

Peter: Thomas, slavery wasn't part of God's plan for creation, but another consequence of our disobedience. Remember when I said God is working His plan of redemption through the mess we have created? In the end, Jesus—who is God—became a "slave" for the world He Himself created.[65] Jesus revealed a capital Truth concerning slavery, a case closed once and for all. Paul says it this way: "There is no longer Jew or Gentile, slave or free, male and female. For you are all one in Christ Jesus."[66] That was God's will all along. Jesus didn't come to set up a new socio-political-economic system; He came to fulfill the law, to save souls, to die for us, and ultimately, to defeat sin—including slavery, which is one of the thousands of consequences of sin. He came to establish the kingdom of God, whose purpose is to change the heart of humankind to free us from sin. If you defeat slavery in the world, you will still have plenty of evils to face. However, if you defeat sin, all evils will cease to exist. That's what Jesus came to do.[67] So, in a very direct way, He did talk about slavery more than anyone because he brought attention to the actual root of it: our sinful nature, the one "place" from where all evil emerges.

Thomas: Then why didn't He reveal this in the Old Testament era?

Peter: Actually, He did, during creation, when He said that every human being, male or female, is created in the image of God.[68] It was sin, again, that ruined it all. God has been placing pointers to

---

[65] Philippians 2:7: Instead, he gave up his divine privileges; he took the humble position of a slave and was born as a human being. When he appeared in human form.

[66] Galatians 3:28.

[67] 2 Corinthians 5:21: For God made Christ, who never sinned, to be the offering for our sin, so that we could be made right with God through Christ.

[68] Genesis 1:27: So God created human beings in his own image. In the image of God he created them; male and female he created them.

His absolute goodness from the beginning, and we were the ones supposed to follow them. The problem is that we are all sinners. Sin is the problem, Thomas. Slavery, sexual immorality, pride, jealousy, violence, and countless things we deem as evil are just consequences of it.

Thomas gets impatient.

Thomas: And what about the "Christians" throughout history using the Bible to claim it is OK to own slaves while having the option not to do it?

Peter: And what about those Christians who fought against it? Out of those two, I believe you know who did right and who did not do right because God Himself helps us know the difference. It is God's moral standards in motion that cause you to be bothered in the first place. Thomas, the Bible doesn't deny that there is something wrong with the world, and God has been patient and loving enough to walk us through it from the beginning. Sin is the problem; every evil emerges from it. Christians are sinners, too, but they found forgiveness in Jesus. The only difference there is between a Christian and a non-Christian is that the Christian knows he or she is a sinner, and the non-Christian doesn't. Jesus said, "I have come to call not those who think they are righteous, but those who know they are sinners and need to repent."[69] That's me.

Thomas: Well, we are told that "God is love," yet He commanded the Israelites to exterminate the Amalekites, including women and children.[70] God committed genocide. There is something inside of

---

[69] Luke 5:32.

[70] 1 Samuel 15:3: Now go and completely destroy the entire Amalekite nation—men, women, children, babies, cattle, sheep, goats, camels, and donkeys.

me that tells me that's inherently wrong, and you don't need the Bible to know it.

Suddenly, Thomas seems hesitant, not knowing what to say or do.

Peter: Are you OK, Thomas?

Thomas: Peter, I don't know, man. I don't think it's a good idea to discuss this after what you told me about your health. We don't have to.

Peter: Oh, but we have to! Thomas, I remember the first time I read this passage in the Bible after becoming a follower of Jesus; it was so challenging. You look around the world and within yourself, and you think, "Man, there is something wrong with life." Then, I opened the Bible thinking: "Here is where I'll find how the world should be. No questions about it." However, what did I see? Killing, murdering, sexual immorality, jealousy, violence, blood, death . . . What in the world?!

Thomas: Yeah! That's almost the feeling I am having now. I was quite selective with the way I read the Bible. But once you try to digest it all, it is sour and sometimes . . . disgusting.

Peter: You might have lost some of the passion you had for the Bible, but you do have passion when it comes to describing the things you don't like about it!

Thomas: Haha.

Peter: At one point, though, something struck me: if I opened the Bible and the only thing I found was perfection in all its pages, would it describe the world the way it actually is? I don't think so. If that were so, I would be wary of trusting it because it would describe a world that doesn't represent the real world.

Thomas: I just feel you are going to do your best to justify genocide by taking me through a journey of beliefs and assumptions you yourself are not sure about. Sorry if that sounded harsh.

Peter: It sounded just the way it must sound—no worries about my feelings or putting into question my beliefs, Thomas. If we are trying to figure out the answer to a difficult question, I don't expect the path to be an easy one.

Thomas: You are right. Well, continue.

Peter: So, the Bible describes the world as it is. Jews and Christians didn't invent murder, violence, sexual immorality, etc. Instead, all of this was part of the world before they all existed, and they also participated in it. Unfortunately, God had to use the evil we caused to bring about His will for us. God gave us the liberty to choose; but when that liberty led to evil, He was moved to act, redeeming our choice to fit His greater purpose.

Thomas: So, are you saying that it is just "unfortunate" that God had to commit genocide? Isn't His will perfect?

Peter: I don't think God committed genocide.

Thomas: That's exactly what he did.

Peter: Genocide, as far as I understand it, is the premeditated killing of a particular nation or ethnic group. But God didn't do that.

Thomas: What did He do then?

Peter: God was responding to injustice. Let me explain. Whenever we look at a passage from Scripture, we cannot just take it out of its context and scrutinize it as a singularity. We must always look at every passage within the whole story or history that the book tells us. So, let me ask you a question. What was the Bible written for?

Thomas: There are many ways to answer that question. However, a believer would say it is God's story of redemption and what He has done throughout history to reconcile humanity to Himself.

Peter: I guess that's a way to answer the question and beautifully put. Let me ask you differently. What caused the Bible to be written?

Thomas: I don't know where you are going with this.

Peter: Sin. It was sin. The Bible wouldn't have been written if we hadn't sinned. God created the world, and everything was good.[71] We were in communion with God in the beginning. Then, our sin broke that communion—our sin fractured everything. If we hadn't sinned, we would still be in perfect friendship with Him to this day. But unfortunately, we really did sin, and due to that sin, we are all in desperate need of God's story of redemption for humanity. So, if we take this into consideration and stay faithful to the story, it wasn't God's will for us to reject Him. The Bible we read today is what it is because of sin; it is what it is because of *us*.

Thomas seems unsure.

Thomas: OK . . .

---

[71] Genesis 1:31: Then God looked over all he had made, and he saw that it was very good! And evening passed and morning came, marking the sixth day.

Peter: Now, let's think about this command from God to destroy the Amalekites within that context. Whether you believe or not, God did not create the world to be filled with war and death and bloodshed. Therefore, in principle, the main culprit for all the horrible things that we can see in the Bible is ultimately people, not God. God is the one who is trying to reconcile the world back to Himself; He is the only one who is helping the world as a whole.

Thomas: Helping people by killing us?

Peter: No, no. God has to reconcile the world through the mess that we ourselves have created. Now, think about what happened after what God did within this context. God, in Jesus, sacrificed Himself for the entire world to free us from the sin we ourselves started, saying things like "love your enemies." Now, let me ask you a question: How do you reconcile the order to kill the Amalekites with Jesus' statement: "Love your enemies"?

Thomas: I don't know if that is even possible. Either these books have nothing to do with themselves, or God's personality changes through them; or to be fair, there is something about God's character I still don't understand.

Peter: That's fair. In the story, God created everything good, and Jesus sacrificed Himself for humanity. And along the way in the redemptive story, we read moments like you are referring to—commands from God that will bring judgement upon certain groups of people. However, I would point our attention to the fact that God is very consistent in how He responds to rebellion and sin. God chose Israel, and their history reveals how much they rebelled against God, even as His people. Think about it: If the Israelites had come up with these stories themselves, why would they show their own God bringing judgement upon them several times, instead of just exalting their behavior no matter what they did? However, the Bible reveals that God judged Israel when they refused to repent from sinful rebellion. So, even though I can admit that some passages are indeed difficult to process, I can also acknowledge that in all of those passages, God is consistent: His holiness requires judgment of sin.

Thomas: So, God committed genocide, no matter how you look at it and regarding the context.

Peter: No, I do not believe that God committed genocide. There are a few more aspects of the context that are important to keep in mind. God commanded the Israelites to respond to the injustice the Amalekites were causing at a specific time in history. But why? That's the question. Why?

Thomas: I appreciate your sincerity, but doesn't it bother you?

Peter: Yes, it does, but not in the way that it used to. Now, I am more bothered about the heart of God being broken by the destruction that sin has brought into this world. Scripture says that God desires that none perish, but that everyone be saved. God gave humanity the wonderful gift of free will, but it does come with the liability of freely rejecting Him instead of freely choosing him. Even still, God has always been patient to provide opportunities for people to repent and follow him.

Thomas: OK. What did you want to say about the context of this passage?

Peter: Oh yeah. Thomas, let me pull up . . . let me see . . . Genesis 15:16, God says this: "After four generations your descendants will return here to this land, for the sins of the Amorites do not yet warrant their destruction." Here is an example showing that God gives opportunities to people, and He said this over 630 years before it happened. What sins were they committing? Some pre-Israelite culture studies have revealed that the Canaanites were known for very wild rituals and practices revolving around their objects of worship. Historical documentation, as well as archeological findings, reveal that the Canaanites would engage in terrible sexual actions with young children and then sacrifice those children to their pagan idols by burning them alive. Another component of their worship would often include sexual engagements with animals. And that is just a couple of grotesque things that the people would participate in. When we have a fuller picture of the actions and pursuits of some of these various groups that God was bringing judgement upon, it becomes clearer that this is not a simple decision to kill them out of God's capricious will, but a judgment for their evils.

Thomas: So, ultimately, what you're saying is this: God gave time to the Canaanites to change their attitude for centuries; the Canaanites practiced all kinds of evils in their religious practices; if we hadn't sinned, none of this would have happened. Therefore, all of this helps you justify genocide.

Thomas seems to be bothered by it and keeps choosing to say the word "genocide" to emphasize what, for him, cannot be denied.

Thomas: What about the animals and the children? Why did they have to be killed too?

Peter: That's a good one . . . I don't know.

Thomas: You don't know?

Peter: Yes. I don't know. I struggle with it myself. I can logically understand why He judged the people for the gross evil that was being done by them, but it is not as simple to logically understand why God included the animals and children. However, that is one that I choose to trust that God saw things that we cannot see; He knew things that we just cannot know. Could it be that He could see the potential consequences for His people generations later if those children became men and women? Could it be that He knew the ripple effect of leaving remnants of those evil practices if they were left unchecked?

Thomas: It just doesn't sit well with me. I find it so . . .

Peter: Disturbing.

Thomas: Yes.

Peter: Thomas, do you find abortion disturbing?

Thomas looks puzzled.

Thomas: What does that have to with it?

Peter: Do you?

Thomas: *(doubtful)* Well . . .

Peter: Thomas, the world has normalized the killing of thousands of human beings every day, they just found a technical, neutral term for it: "Abortion." However, we still get appalled that the Creator of the universe might choose to end the life of a specific group of children within a specific time and clearly "disturbing" context, for a clear purpose; even after He gave them hundreds of years to change their ways.

Thomas is speechless.

Peter: The most important thing is this: Jesus had to die on the cross for all of this. Ultimately, God provides the way to solve the problem for all of this kind of evil. He provided the solution in Jesus. It's all about Jesus; the answer is always in Him. Remember the question I asked the first time we met?

Thomas: Umm, which one?

Peter: Are you doubting because of Jesus?

Thomas: I . . .

Thomas looks down and remains quiet for a few seconds while they keep walking together toward the lake.

Peter: It's OK. I want to make sure that that question is very present during your doubting and questioning process.

Thomas tries to forget about the question for now.

Thomas: Well, going back to what we were talking about. The God of the Old Testament certainly feels very different from Jesus in the New Testament. What if they have nothing to do with each other?

Peter: Thomas, do you know that was one of the first questions I asked myself?

Thomas: Oh really?

Peter: Absolutely. At first, I thought they didn't seem like the same God. But there are a few times during the Old Testament when God shares His will with the Israelites, and He says things like: "I want you to show love, not offer sacrifices. I want you to know me more than I want burnt offerings."[72] Let me read another passage to you. I remember this one being longer, so be as patient with me as you are with your coffee.

Thomas smirks while Peter tries to find the passage he is referring to.

Peter: Here it is. God was also bothered by Israel because of their persistent disobedience:

"Every leader in Israel who lives within your walls is bent on murder. Fathers and mothers are treated with contempt. Foreigners are forced to pay for protection. Orphans and widows are wronged and oppressed among you. You despise my holy things and violate my Sabbath days of rest. People accuse others falsely and send them to their death. You are filled with idol worshipers and people who do obscene things. Men sleep with their fathers' wives and force themselves on women who are menstruating. Within your walls live men who commit adultery with their neighbors' wives, who defile their daughters-in-law, or who rape their own sisters. There are hired murderers, loan racketeers, and extortioners everywhere. They never even think of me and my commands, says the Sovereign LORD.[73]

Thomas: Is that the Old Testament?

Peter: Yes, it is. All these things were against the will of God for His people and are against people's will for the world today; in fact, they are mostly against the will of people who have grown under the influence of Judeo-Christian values. I believe God is God and has never changed. We are the ones that change constantly, and

[72] Hosea 6:6

[73] Ezekiel 22:6–12.

He—because He loves us—has been patient throughout history and given us the freedom to choose Him or not to choose Him.

Thomas: Would you stop believing in God if you heard Him telling you to kill someone?

Peter: His will was to die for the world, not to kill it for His glory. That wasn't the purpose for which He created us. He created us to be in a relationship with Him and to worship Him out of love,[74] because He first loved us.[75]

Thomas: OK, Peter, I don't want to hurt your feelings.

Peter: Why do you say that?

Thomas: I just feel . . .

Peter: What?

Thomas: I just feel all you have to do to end up "justifying God's genocide" is kind of . . . ridiculous . . .

Peter: Oh, Thomas! You scared me! You don't hurt my feelings! This is exactly why we are having this conversation. I do feel at peace with God's order for the Israelites to kill the Amalekites because of everything I just said and especially because of Jesus. But, please, no worries at all.

Thomas: OK.

---

[74] Isaiah 43:7: Bring all who claim me as their God, for I have made them for my glory. It was I who created them.

[75] 1 John 4:19: We love each other because he loved us first.

Peter: Let me ask you a question: When we kill people here on earth—criminals, enemies at war, people who are doing evil according to our morals—are we killing them or murdering them?

Thomas: If someone is committing a horrible crime, we are not killing him capriciously and without a good reason to do so. Sometimes, we even need to kill people solely to defend ourselves, unfortunately. That's not murder, however.

Peter: Well, in a real sense, that's what God did at times throughout history, not to murder, but to respond to injustice. Something many are still compelled to do today in our supposed advanced, modern world.

Thomas: Oh . . . I see what you mean. Still . . .

Peter: I know . . . The world is not the way it was supposed to be. Don't be so hard on yourself in the sense of not finding a good answer to your questions. These are hard questions, and knowledge is not the only thing required to answer them; emotions, experiences, and even the hardships of life are involved in them too.

Thomas: The things we choose to talk about!

Peter: Indeed!

After walking for around 20 minutes, Peter and Thomas arrive at the lake. A gentle breeze combs the water as waves splash timidly against the rocks on the shore. A trail goes around the lake, and several rest points have benches along the path. There is a small island in the middle of it, which certainly brings some memories to both of them. Peter and Thomas sit down on one of the benches, but not after picking up some stones to throw at the lake while talking. Some things never change.

Thomas: OK, I think we can start drinking our coffee now.

Peter laughs. Thomas looks at the small island in the middle of the lake, willingly reliving an old memory that causes him to smile. Thomas elbows Peter.

Thomas: Do you remember?

Peter: Oh yes, I do.

Thomas: I remember when you first came to our church and asked us to baptize you on the small island. Why did you want that?

Peter: Well, I never got baptized back in England when I surrendered my life to Jesus. I came here a few days after I landed, and when I saw this lake with the island in the middle, I couldn't resist the urge to do it here. I don't know why. It's not a long swim at all, but I guess it would be more comfortable to go there on a small boat or something.

Peter teases Thomas and playfully taps on his arm a few times.

Peter: Although, you didn't want to miss the opportunity either . . . did you?

Both laugh, Thomas harder than Peter; and he is also blushing a little bit.

Thomas: *(while laughing)* What can I say? When Pastor John told us you asked him to be baptized on the island, I thought it was the perfect time and location to ask Sofía for a date. I was excited about your baptism, though . . .

Peter: Haha! I am sure you were! On our way to the island, I remember you asking me, "What if she says no?" seventy times seven.

Thomas: Haha! Yes, I did. I was so nervous.

Peter: I even forgot I was going to be baptized! At one point, I thought, "What did we come to do here?"

Thomas and Peter keep laughing. Suddenly, Thomas' tone grows somber.

Thomas: . . . and then she said no.

Peter cannot hold it and laughs even harder.

Thomas: *(laughing)* She said, "Seriously, you are asking me during Peter's baptism?"

Peter: I remember seeing your face right before I was going to be immersed and thought, "Oh no, she said no . . ."

Both keep laughing.

Thomas: When we were back at church to celebrate, she said, "Context, Thomas, context!" And then she said yes.

Peter's demeanor changes suddenly.

Peter: My friends and family back in England thought I was just joking about Jesus, but when I went back to visit and told them I had been baptized, everything changed.

Thomas: What happened?

Peter: Well, my friends and I always made fun of Christianity and thought it was pure nonsense. When they saw I became a follower of Jesus, and they thought I was serious, they started alienating me; some members of my extended family ended up doing the same thing.

Thomas: But did you do something to them, you weirdo?

Peter: Haha! No! I just stopped feeling comfortable with some things we used to do. For example, we used to objectify women, looking at them like they were just bodies. My relationship with Jesus changed that completely, and now I see them as whole people—sorry if that sounds too harsh—but that was the way we all were, as sad as this sounds. Sometimes, I drank alcohol, smoked, and tried some drugs with my friends to feel a part of something. Then I stopped cursing too. Everything sounds very legalistic, but I wasn't going to any church or anything. I was alone. So, I was only doing it because I loved Jesus and what He did for me, that's it. I didn't think I was a better person than my friends because of not doing those things though. I still wanted to be friends with all of them; but bit by bit, things got colder between us. They began hanging out together and "forgot" to call me a few times. I loved my friends. I didn't want that to happen. Also, my friends were very apathetic about the big questions in life.

Thomas: You mean atheists?

Peter: No, no. *Apatheists*. Apathetic about the big questions in life. I wasn't. My interest in the big questions made me feel a bit weird among them sometimes.

Thomas: So, you were weird in England too?

Peter: You know it, mate.

Both laugh.

Peter: Like, for example, I would be drinking at someone's home, having conversations with some girls, pretending that talking is everything we wanted to do with them.

Thomas: Very common.

Peter: Exactly. And then, suddenly, I would ask a girl something like, "Why do we exist?"

Thomas: . . . Seriously?

Peter: When I say it, then I mean it. And I meant the question too. But of course, my friends thought it was the cigarettes and the alcohol, but it truly wasn't. I wanted to find some type of depth and share it with others.

Thomas: Imagine the questions you would ask if you were high.

Peter: I guess we would never know.

Both laugh again.

Peter: That's when I went to a small church in my town and got connected to a Christian who told me about our church here in Maine.

Thomas: What about your family?

Peter: My family was reticent at first, mostly when they learned I wanted to come here to learn more about how to serve Jesus. The name "Jesus" sounds to many people like "church of England," "Catholicism," or simply "religion"—things that unfortunately bring some unnecessary sociopolitical connotations to the conversation. But I just wanted to focus on Jesus, the core foundation of Christianity. They didn't understand me at first, but we were all very independent in my family, so I worked for an entire year to gather money to visit our church. After a few months of being here, I decided to stay. What is interesting to me is that the isolation that an atheist might feel in a predominantly Christian town is the same isolation a Christian feels in a secular one. If we only judged people by their actions and not only by what they say they believe in . . . Actually, if we only stopped judging people . . . [76]

Thomas: How is everyone doing at home?

Peter: They are not doing that well. My father's health is declining slightly, but he is in good spirits. That's why I don't want to tell them about my tumor; it was horrible for them when it happened to me the first time. From England, the only thing they can do is worry, and I don't want them to worry unnecessarily for me.

Thomas: I understand. Would you like to go back to England?

Peter: That was the idea. I wanted to go back and love on people and talk to them about Jesus, but who knows anymore . . .

Thomas: We need to wait and see what happens.

Thomas notices Peter is getting sad and changes topics immediately.

Thomas: OK, it's rocks time. The one who throws them the farthest wins!

---

[76] Matthew 7:1: Do not judge others, and you will not be judged.

Peter realizes Thomas is worrying about him and plays along with him.

Peter: You go first.

Thomas throws the first rock. It's not a bad throw, but he has done better in the past. Then, Peter throws another one and throws farther than Thomas.

Thomas: Look at you, Peter! You'll see now . . .

Thomas gets ready to throw another rock. He looks around to find the best type of rock, one whose weight and shape are perfect. Once he finds it, he steps backward, gets ready for the throw, and throws the stone with such strength that it reaches the island in the middle of the lake.

Peter: Wow! What in the world, Thomas! You did it!

Thomas: I did it! I did it! How many years have we tried to do this?!

Peter: I don't even know! That's amazing! No one is going to believe us!

They both laugh and jump around, celebrating fulfilling a long-awaited dream. Dreams become way more complicated as we age, don't they?

Peter: I cannot believe you reached the island, mate.

Thomas: OK. You can do it, Peter. You can!

Peter gets excited at the idea of doing it too. Thomas finds another perfect stone and gives it to Peter.

Thomas: Peter, use this one! You can do it!

Peter holds the rock, gets ready for the throw, and suddenly—

Peter: Ah! Ah!

Peter is wincing in pain.

Thomas: What's going on?!

Peter: Oh, man, it hurts so bad! I think I should stop for now. Ah!

Peter seems stiff, as if he were afraid to move his neck.

Thomas: Are you OK!?

Peter: Would you help me lie down for a second?

Thomas: Yes.

Peter seems to be in a lot of pain. He manages to lie down with Thomas' help.

Thomas: Why do you need to lie down?

Peter: *(in pain)* Oh no . . . I think it's the tumor. I think it's starting to reach my nerves, just as it happened the first time.

Peter's face goes white.

Thomas: Hey, man, I am here. Don't be afraid. What do you need me to do?

Peter: Any sudden move is going to cause me to have a lot of pain in my shoulder, my upper trap, and my arm. I think it will get better if I stay here for a second.

Thomas: OK.

Thomas observes Peter lying on the ground, showing his pain by the gestures of his face, but without making any noises. It is the first time he considers what it would mean to lose him. However, Thomas doesn't say anything, just thinks a sudden and almost uninvited, Please God, don't . . . *within the confinements of his heart* . . .Oh, man. Did I just pray? *He wonders, confused.*

Thomas: Do you want me to call an ambulance?

Peter: No, no worries. I know I am going to get better. I need to wait until my nerves relax so that I can move again without feeling any pain.

Peter is lying on his back. The pain seems to fade, and he gets fixated on the sky. As the sun slowly but steadily goes away, he can see some stars appearing here and there. Thomas decides to sit next to him and practice what a Christian friend taught him once: "The ministry of presence"—being next to a person who is hurting without feeling the need to say anything.[77] *Peter's breathing begins to regulate, and his body calms down.*

Peter: Do you think that one day we'll explore them all?

Thomas: What?

Peter: The stars.

Peter tears up, placing his hand on his face. He is embarrassed to show this side of himself to Thomas.

Thomas: Peter, what's going on?

---

[77] Job 2:12–13: When they saw Job from a distance, they scarcely recognized him. Wailing loudly, they tore their robes and threw dust into the air over their heads to show their grief. Then they sat on the ground with him for seven days and nights. No one said a word to Job, for they saw that his suffering was too great for words.

Peter: I just . . . don't want to die.

Thomas: You are not going to. Your surgery went well once, and it will go well again.

Peter: Remember when I told you about the process of dying?

Thomas: Yes.

Peter's voice cracks as sorrow overwhelms his soul.

Peter: This pain reminds me so much of the desperation I felt when I first experienced it. It's very counterintuitive, because internally I am at peace, but externally I am not. Paul said it well when he talked about God's peace, "which goes far beyond all human understanding."[78] I am crying because of the pain, but I am at peace because of where it will ultimately take me.[79] What Jesus did for the world is so counterintuitive. Nothing makes sense about Christianity if Jesus doesn't make sense first.

Thomas remains silent.

Peter: Still, there is something in me that desperately wants to yell to God and ask Him why. But when I think about the cross, I also feel the need to ask why because I don't understand that type of love either. It took me years to realize, Thomas, that all our questions are good and necessary, but ultimately, belief must turn into surrender. There is no other way. It is what Jesus had to do as well. These are

---

[78] Philippians 4:5-7: Let everyone see that you are considerate in all you do. Remember, the Lord is coming soon. Don't worry about anything; instead, pray about everything. Tell God what you need, and thank him for all he has done. Then you will experience God's peace, which exceeds anything we can understand. His peace will guard your hearts and minds as you live in Christ Jesus.

[79] John 3:16: For this is how God loved the world: He gave his one and only Son, so that everyone who believes in him will not perish but have eternal life.

the moments you don't hear many people talking about; moments where you feel pain, fear, insecurity, desperation, and loss . . . that's when Jesus' light shines the brightest, though everything around you is darkness.[80] There is no rationality in pain, death, suffering . . . All our intellectual endeavors dissipate instantly when we feel grief, rage, anger, anxiousness, or fear. Those are the things the world does its best to run away from, while Jesus confronted them all at once so we didn't have to one day. He died for our sins[81] and was resurrected[82] so that everyone's death could be the beginning of something better. That's why I think, in a sense, death doesn't make any sense.

Peter keeps tearing up.

Peter: As you keep asking all the great questions you are asking, always remember that Jesus came as the ultimate message from God to tell the world that He loves us unconditionally. It's not about figuring everything out intellectually because no one does, ultimately. Instead, it's all about love.

Peter sits up and wipes the tears off his face. He breathes in and out a few times to recompose.

Peter: I think I am feeling better. But this was a warning to me. I need to move slowly from here on out since any sudden motion could make my nerves spasm again. Let's go back.

---

[80] John 1:4-5: The Word gave life to everything that was created, and his life brought light to everyone. The light shines in the darkness, and the darkness can never extinguish it.

[81] Isaiah 53:5: But he was pierced for our rebellion, crushed for our sins. He was beaten so we could be whole. He was whipped so we could be healed

[82] John 11:25: Jesus told her, "I am the resurrection and the life. Anyone who believes in me will live, even after dying.

As Peter starts moving slowly, he loses his grasp on his coffee, and some of it spills onto the ground. Luckily, it is not as hot anymore.

Peter: Well, today keeps getting better and better, doesn't it?

Thomas: But do you have enough energy to go back?

Peter: Yes, I just need to take it slowly.

They walk without saying anything to each other for a long time. The island and the lake fall behind, perhaps wondering about the next time they'll enjoy Peter's and Thomas's presence. Thomas is uncertain about Peter's health, Sofía's relationship, and his faith. Peter is uncertain about life itself. It's too much to take in, but nothing that a walk through nature cannot alleviate.

Peter: Thomas, I need to apologize.

Thomas: Why?

Peter: Well, when I talk to you about my deepest fears and Jesus simultaneously, it's not my intention for you to feel inclined to believe based on our friendship and how much we care for each other. You shouldn't believe in Jesus because of me. You should believe in Jesus because of Jesus. I encourage you to keep asking as many questions as you need. There isn't one Christian on earth who believes in Jesus and knows everything there is to know about God and the universe. At one point, we all believe in something or someone despite our doubts and questions about them.

Thomas: No worries, I know that's not your intention. I am glad we can be vulnerable with each other.

Peter: Thomas, don't tell anyone about my tumor please. And even more important than that, don't tell Lourdes I dropped her coffee.

Thomas: I won't tell anyone about your tumor, Peter, but . . .

From the distance, Lourdes opens the door of the coffee shop.

Lourdes: Hey, guys!

Peter and **Thomas:** Hey, Lourdes!

Lourdes: How was the walk and the coffee?

Thomas: The walk was fantastic, but Peter spilled some of your coffee on the ground!

Peter gives Thomas a look that could kill..

Peter: *(whispering)* Thomas, what in the world?!

Thomas: *(whispering)* I am not telling anyone about your health, but you dropping Lourdes' coffee wasn't a part of the deal.

Peter: *(laughing while feeling some frustration)* That's so bad.

Lourdes: What happened?!

Thomas: He didn't like it!

Peter is speechless.

Peter: *(whispering)* Thomas, what's going on? *(louder)* Lourdes! He is just joking!

Thomas: Yes, I am! But he did drop it, and he was pretty sad about it.

Lourdes: Did you fall or trip over something?

Peter doesn't know what to say, but Thomas comes to the rescue.

Thomas: Yes, that storm broke many branches from the trees a few days ago, and he tripped over one of them.

Peter wishes Thomas didn't have to lie.

Lourdes: Peter, Peter, Peter . . . Your mind is in the clouds, but your feet are on the ground! I'll prepare another one for you.

Peter: Thank you. Hey, Thomas, by the way . . .

Thomas: What?

Peter: You reached the island with that rock today. That was mind-blowing.

Thomas: Haha! No one is going to believe us. OK, man. I need to do some errands. I'll see you next week, and we'll talk with Jim!

Peter: I cannot wait to hear his story.

Thomas: If you need me for anything, please call me.

Peter: I will.

Peter enters The Shire *to get his coffee while Thomas heads toward his car. Thomas gets into his car, sits down, closes the door, and releases a big sigh. It has been a long evening.* I don't even know what to say or think about, *Thomas contemplates.* Peter said it's not about knowing many things but realizing that we cannot know everything. According to him, faith is about grace, trust, a relationship, sacrifice, and love. That's what Jesus is all about. However, the Bible is rough at times . . . What if all of this is not true after all? What a horrible way to give false hope to people. It seems there is no middle term with Jesus. In that, Peter is right.

Thursday, October 19

Thomas and Peter are curious about what Jim might have to say about the big questions in life and his experience with all of them. Every person's story is sacred, and any moment we hear someone's story, we are invited to see reality through another human being's perspective, including what gives them hope, what makes them tremble, what inspires them, what breaks them, and so much more. Jim is already sitting at their usual table, waiting for Peter and Thomas to arrive. What would a former pastor have to say about Christianity? *Thomas wonders.* What would a former pastor say about Jesus? *Peter wonders.*

Peter and Thomas arrive almost simultaneously, but just before getting inside the coffee shop, Thomas has something urgent to ask him.

Thomas: Hey, Peter!

Peter: Thomas, *¿qué pasa*?

Thomas: *(laughs)* Please, don't try your Spanish on me; we know how horrible it is.

Peter: *(with a thick British accent) No tienes ni idea de lo que estás hablando.*

Thomas: Wow! Have you been practicing more lately? What does that even mean?

Peter: "You have no idea what you are talking about."

Peter is so proud of himself.

Peter: What do you think?

Thomas: I think you are right! I have no idea what I am talking about!

They both hug.

Thomas: Peter, has your surgery been scheduled?

Peter: Not yet. They haven't called me yet, but I think it will happen soon.

Thomas: OK. How are you feeling?

Peter: I am OK as long as I move slowly, so no more rock-throwing until after the surgery. I need to reach the island myself; I have to!

They begin walking toward the coffee shop.

Peter: What about you? How are you feeling?

Thomas: I am holding on. I am just very curious to hear what Jim has to say. I have never met a *former* pastor before.

Peter: Me neither. I cannot wait.

They open the door and get inside the coffee shop. But something catches both their eyes immediately.

Thomas: Oh! What is this?!

Thomas asks the question out loud and with quite a bit of emotion, which causes Lourdes to get scared since she is focused on her coffee-making.

Lourdes: Ah! Thomas! You scared the grounds of coffee out of me!

Thomas: Oh no! I'm sorry, I didn't mean to.

Peter is doing his best to contain his laugh.

Thomas: What is this?!

Thomas is pointing at a dog resting in his bed near the counter.

Lourdes: Come on, Thomas! You know what this is! It's a dog!

Thomas: I know it's a dog, Lourdes. I mean, what is a dog doing here?

Lourdes: Well, meet Truman.

Truman is a stunning blue merle Australian shepherd with one blue eye and one brown eye.

Peter: He is gorgeous, Lourdes. Whose dog is it?

Lourdes: Mine.

Peter and **Thomas:** Yours?!

Lourdes: Yes, mine! It gets lonely in the morning and at night when I am preparing everything for the next day, and Truman will give me some company here and welcome all the clients. Say hi, Truman!

Truman barks one time and looks back at Lourdes.

Thomas: He is very well trained.

Lourdes: Apparently, he has been trained by a well-known dog trainer in the area. However, his owners had to move overseas, so he needed to find a new home. Someone at church told me about it, and I contacted them last week.

Peter: I am sure it was very sad for them to leave Truman behind.

Lourdes: It was. But they were happy that Truman would spend his last few years near the trail and the lake. You should have seen how his family cried and hugged him the day they dropped him off at my house. We don't know . . . but I hope they'll see him again in Heaven.

Peter elbows Thomas when they both hear the word "Heaven."

Peter: *(whispering)* That's something we should talk about soon.

Thomas: And Hell . . .

Lourdes: Oh, you guys and your light conversations! Two coffees?

Lourdes gets back to serving other clients.

Thomas: Yes. Can we pet him?

Lourdes: Ask him, not me.

Thomas plays along.

Thomas: Truman, can we pet you?

Peter and Thomas feel the dog understands them. Truman jumps out of his bed and cuddles excitedly, leaning all his weight into them.

Peter: Oh, man, he is amazing!

Truman is panting in excitement. The whole coffee shop is in awe of him.

Lourdes: OK, Truman! Go to your bed! I'll bring the coffee to you in a second.

Truman returns to his bed, and Thomas looks around to see if Jim is there.

Jim: I am here, guys!

Jim is sitting at their usual table.

Thomas: Oh great! You got "our" table.

Jim: Haha. Hi. How are you doing?

Peter: Good. You?

Jim: I am a bit tired. I told Thomas the other day I am taking care of my mom because she cannot physically move anymore. I am not that young either; but other than that, I cannot complain.

Thomas: How old is she?

Jim: 97.

Peter: 97? If you don't mind me asking, how old are you?

Jim: I am 68.

Peter: Unbelievable. I wouldn't have guessed that.

Jim: Oh, thank you. I try to care for myself.

Thomas: What is your secret?

Jim: I don't know . . . I mean, we don't eat much food. We are "light-eaters." But I have no idea if that's the reason, or genetics, or a mixture of the two, or something else.

Thomas: Well, if eating too much food is the problem, then I'll probably die tomorrow.

Everyone laughs.

Thomas: Have you been drawing these past few days?

Jim: Oh, yes. I draw something every day. It helps me calm down and disconnect. I was here yesterday and made a few drawings.

Peter: I am sure you did one of Truman, didn't you?

Jim: How can I not? Have you seen that dog? Here, take a look at all my drawings from yesterday.

Thomas and Peter flip through the pages.

Peter: Oh, here it is! Truman . . . a cup of coffee . . . the mom with her two kids I saw the other day!

Thomas: Who?

Peter: Oh, no worries. I just saw them once here.

Suddenly, Thomas goes speechless as he flips through the pages. Peter knows why. One of the drawings shows two girls drinking coffee, and one of them looks a whole lot like Sofía.

Thomas: When did you draw this?

Jim: This? Oh, it was yesterday. These two girls were reading the Bible together, specifically a verse I know very well—Jude 1:22: "And you must show mercy to those whose faith is wavering . . . "

Peter looks at Thomas to see how he is taking everything in. It sounds like Sofía was here the day before.

Jim: It was quite a profound conversation. Do you know her?

Thomas: Yes, we know each other . . . it's like I can actually feel people's emotions through your drawings. That's so difficult to accomplish.

Peter notices Thomas is making a 180° to avoid talking about it.

Jim: Well, thank you.

Jim places his notepad back on the table, and his demeanor suddenly changes, with a mixture of curiosity and confusion.

Jim: Oh! I didn't want to forget. I have a question for you if you don't mind.

Jim leans forward and softens his tone almost to a whisper.

Jim: Do you know why she serves her coffee sooooooooo hot?

Peter: Who, Lourdes?

Jim: Lourdes is the owner's name?

Peter: Yes.

Thomas cannot let this opportunity go.

Thomas: Jim, you should order one of her iced coffees one day. She loves making them.

Thomas looks at Peter, and they both laugh. Meanwhile, Lourdes is unaware that all of this is happening.

Peter: There is a very personal and meaningful story behind why she serves them this way. It involves her husband.

Jim: Oh really? It's OK, I don't have to know. But how interesting . . . Her coffee is delicious and burning hot.

All three laugh and get comfortable for a conversation they have all been looking forward to.

Thomas: OK, Jim, so why don't you tell us your story? I think you told me you were a pastor at some point, but you are not anymore. Is that right?

Jim: It is.

Thomas: Peter and I are conversing about the big questions in life concerning God, relationships, love, philosophy, science, theology. Peter was an atheist who became a Christian a few years ago. I grew up in a Christian household and have gone to church my entire life, but lately, I have been questioning my faith, which is very . . . new to me, let's say, and somewhat unsettling.

Jim: I know the feeling. Well, first, let me say how neat that you have a Christian friend who is open to listening, talking, and walking through your questions and doubts. I wish I had had that.

Peter: You didn't?

Jim: *(sighs)* Unfortunately, no, I didn't. My case was a bit more . . . let's say . . . complicated.

Thomas: Complicated in what way?

Jim: Well, let me start from the beginning. I went to college to study theology. I received a master's in divinity, and soon after that, I became the pastor of a small church that ended up becoming a megachurch, with thousands of people coming every week. However, it got to the point where I felt it wasn't for me anymore because, like you, Thomas, I believed some things I couldn't reconcile with my faith.

Thomas: Like what, if you don't mind me asking?

Jim leans forward again, about to share something crucial in his story.

Jim: I am attracted to men.

It seems that Jim expected a stronger reaction from Peter and Thomas after hearing about his same-sex attraction, but Peter and Thomas didn't even flinch. They remained focused and fascinated by Jim's story. The fact that they didn't react in any sense makes Jim feel very pleased and comfortable.

Peter: Was this something you discovered before you became a pastor, or was it during your ministry?

Jim: I was 13 when I realized I wasn't attracted to girls. At that point, I was a Christian and doing well in school. Some said, I was "on fire" for the Lord. Then, I began helping with some teaching and preaching right before my college years. As I was sharing the gospel with other people, I realized there wasn't room for homosexuality in the church, so I did my best to suppress it. After I finished my master's in divinity, I got married to my ex-wife and had a long and happy marriage, at least on the outside. However, I knew something in me wasn't settling well. After we got married, we decided to plant a church, and a few years later, it grew to the point that we could buy our own building with thousands of people coming every week. I spent a few years trying to reconcile my homosexuality with the supposed "truths" of the Scriptures, but at one point, I desisted. I found myself struggling with my identity and what the Scripture considers sin, even though I don't think sin is a thing anymore. As I was struggling with my faith and my same-sex attraction and due to my job as a pastor, I also had the chance to listen and walk through many other people's struggles. However, people were not dealing with "sin" the way I was—some were lenient and indulged in it and then came to church very nonchalantly. This hypocrisy began to disturb me because I was struggling with my sexual identity and my faith while I was pouring myself out to help others who were proclaiming a very superficial, hypocritical faith. I have to say, there were many people in my church who were excellent people and only showed me love when I came out as homosexual. But here is the thing: if someone went on stage on a Sunday and said he or she was dealing with "pride" or "lust," people would pray for them, and it wouldn't be a big deal. However, I knew if I said I was sexually attracted to men, my situation would be perceived differently—with more hate, judgment, and resentfulness. This type of hypocrisy made me begin to question my own beliefs.

I made the horrible mistake of not being sincere with people who would have cared for me as I struggled to find peace through the whole thing. Instead, I got fixated on the hypocrisy of it all. But at one point, I thought finding peace about this wouldn't do anything with the hypocrisy either since the hypocrisy would still be there. So, one day, I told my wife, and it didn't go well. She wasn't disrespecting me but was very disappointed that I never told her. She said many things began making sense about me after I told her. Now, through all this, I started questioning the Bible's morals, teachings, claims, and culture. I wasn't willing enough to see my sexual attraction to men as a bad thing anymore, and a few months later, I quit as a pastor, divorced my wife, and left the faith. I have to say, it feels like one of the best decisions I have ever made. I didn't want to hurt anyone; I just wanted to feel free and be myself. Any pain I might have caused by doing that is a pain I cannot feel responsible for because, ultimately, I know better who I am than anyone else, let alone a God I think is not real anymore. But you know what? I have no hard feelings toward Christianity as a whole. I met wonderful people who showed by their actions that they truly follow Jesus, and many of them were supportive through all of it; not necessarily about my lifestyle decisions, but about me. In summary, I don't think Christianity is true, and I am glad it's over for me.

Peter grew up in a more secular culture where these stories are way more common. However, Thomas is having his first-ever experience with someone who doesn't believe in God and seems perfectly reasonable and happy. Peter wonders what his reaction will be after hearing Jim's story.

Thomas: Did you end up telling the whole congregation about your sexual attraction to men?

Jim: Yes, I had to. It was very uncomfortable, but I did. At first, they thought I was sharing it because I was struggling and needed prayer, but I told them I wasn't struggling anymore but living life as I should have lived it out from the beginning. There wasn't any struggle anymore, but fulfillment.

Thomas: How did the congregation react?

Jim: It broke the church apart. Some wanted me to start an "affirming" church, others wanted me just to leave, and others just left. The church didn't survive the split and closed its doors a few months later.

Thomas: Man . . . I cannot imagine how difficult it must have been for everyone, especially you.

Jim: Yes, it was. After getting divorced, I left my city and moved to Maine to start afresh.

Peter: I hope you don't mind that we are asking you so many questions.

Jim: Not at all. Ask away.

Peter: What about your parents and your sister?

Jim: Well, my father abandoned us when we were little and recently passed away, actually. I was in contact with him during the last few years of his life, which is another long story. My sister and my mother are still Christians, and they have always shown me all the support and love they can as family members, even though they don't agree with my lifestyle.

Peter: And what happened to your ex-wife?

Jim: She had a couple of rough years after it. We tried to be in contact, but I think the connection was hurting us more than helping us. So, at one point, we decided to part ways for good, and I think it was better for both of us. I think she remarried and seems to be happy. We never had any kids together, either.

Peter: I have to say, it's so encouraging to me that you invited yourself to be vulnerable enough to share your story with two strangers like us. Thank you.

Thomas: Yes, thank you.

Jim: Oh, my pleasure.

Suddenly, Lourdes shows up.

Lourdes: Oh, I am glad the three of you are conversing! Here are your coffees. Sir, do you need anything else?

Jim: No, thank you.

Peter: Lourdes, you know Jim is an artist? Would you mind showing her?

Jim: Actually, I can show you one specific drawing I made last week.

Jim opens his notepad and flips through the pages until he finds the one he is looking for.

Jim: *(excited)* Here.

Lourdes looks at Jim's drawing and timidly gasps. It is a drawing of her leaning her head on one of her coffee machines with her eyes closed. One hand is on top of the machine, and the other is holding the handle of the portafilter.

Jim: I apologize if it was an intimate moment I shouldn't have drawn.

Lourdes seems speechless. Her eyes glimmer as tears gradually form. Lourdes wipes the tears off her face and begins talking in a very non-Lourdes way—softly, calmly, and even with a bit of a lower pitch.

Lourdes: I was praying.

Jim, Pete, and Thomas remain quiet.

Lourdes: I think you drew this . . . last Tuesday, right?

Jim: Yes, I think so. How do you know?

Lourdes: That day would have been my Golden Anniversary with Richard. Every coffee I make makes me feel closer to him, but I still don't know how many coffees God wants me to make until I finally see him again. Peace in uncertainty. That was a hard day for me. I miss my "*Richarcito.*" What's your name again?

Jim: Jim.

Lourdes: Jim, I'd like to frame your drawing at my coffee shop. Would that be OK with you?

Jim: Absolutely.

Lourdes: It's a good reminder for me and all my clients. We can still be strong when we recognize that sometimes we aren't.[83]

---

[83] 2 Corinthians 12:9–10: Each time he said, "My grace is all you need. My power works best in weakness." So now I am glad to boast about my weaknesses, so that the power of Christ can work through me. That's why I take pleasure in my weaknesses, and in the insults, hardships, persecutions, and troubles that I suffer for Christ. For when I am weak, then I am strong.

Suddenly, Truman barks a few times, which makes Lourdes jolt and transform back to her usual "Lourdesness." Peter and Thomas wonder if they even know Lourdes anymore. She is crazy and a profoundly deep well of wisdom, both at the same time.

Lourdes: Truman! Don't bark. It's just a cat.

Truman howls while opening and closing his mouth as if he were talking back to Lourdes. Everyone at the coffee shop laughs.

Lourdes: This dog . . . never believe anyone who says that dog cannot speak! Jim, thank you for the drawing.

Jim: You're welcome, Lourdes. By the way, your coffee is fantastic.

Lourdes: Sometimes it's so good to hear others agree with what you know is already true.

Jim, Peter, and Thomas laugh. Yes, Lourdes "is back." She gets distracted and begins talking to a different table.

Peter: Going back to the questions. I am actually very interested in hearing about your life as an atheist, but I'd like to ask you to do us a favor.

Jim: Go ahead.

Peter: Could you tell us about it without referencing Christianity? Some people don't believe in God and live their lives as if God doesn't exist; but when someone asks them to talk about their worldview, they cannot describe it without comparing it to, undermining, or mentioning Christianity in one way or another. Thomas and I are interested in hearing about your life as an atheist in the purest form without making any comments or comparisons to other worldviews, especially Christianity.

Jim: I like that, and I agree. These types of conversations tend to become conversations where the atheist is poking holes in the Christian worldview. In contrast, atheists rarely explore the reason why they think the way they do.

Peter: Also, I am aware atheists might be "united" in their non-belief in God, but each of them has many different beliefs about everything else, so we are not asking you to speak on behalf of all atheists simply because we know it's not possible. We get that.

Jim: Yes. Well, I'll do my best. When I left the Christian faith, it was like starting a painting on a blank canvas. Everything I thought was true didn't have to be so anymore. Therefore, in my case, from Christianity to atheism, I went through a process of rediscovery. I need only to make one assertion about Christianity, but only to contextualize my conversation. Is that OK?

Peter smiles and concedes with a hand gesture.

Peter: Of course. That's OK.

Jim: God doesn't exist, which implies the universe hasn't been created; which implies we haven't been created; which implies our morals and values are based on experience and not on absolutes; which implies my morals and values can be different than anyone else's; which implies that I have the responsibility to find my own purpose and meaning in life. It's a clean slate. That's freedom. Freedom of thought, freedom of purpose, freedom of fulfillment. I try to live my life the way I want while being considerate about the fact that I am not alone, and I need to respect the freedom of others. There are pleasurable and painful things. I do my best not to inflict any pain on anyone around me, and I'd like to expect people to do the same toward me. However, we don't live in a perfect world, and everyone messes up. That's why we have a justice system: to refrain people from doing things we all agree are painful—like killing, stealing, abusing others, etc. Those are universal experiences the majority of the world doesn't want to experience, so we create laws to keep them all at bay in the best way possible.

Thomas: What's your purpose in life?

Jim: To live. I think that's good enough.

Peter: To live doing what, if you don't mind me asking?

Jim: To do things I find pleasurable: drawing, being with people, love, having a nice meal, learning, experiencing my sexuality with other consenting adults, drinking a good glass of wine, etc.

Peter: If you didn't have those things, would you still have a purpose?

Jim: That's a big hypothetical; but if I didn't have those things, I guess I'd find other things to enjoy. I would have to adapt to this new hypothetical situation.

Peter: That's fair.

Thomas: Jim, can I ask you a question about what you find "pleasurable"?

Jim: Yes, go ahead.

Thomas: What if someone's pleasure endangers your personal safety? Let's say, if a person likes hurting others for the pleasure of it; in that case, would you say that person is living out their freedom in a good way?

Jim: As I said before, if a person hurts me, we—as a society—agree that hurt and pain are not good things for us. I would say that a person would not exercise his right to freedom in an ideal way.

Peter: When you say "ideal," where does this concept of an "ideal" come from according to you?

Jim: An "ideal" is a conclusion we arrive at after a long process of trial and error when we realize, for instance, that pain and suffering are bad things. So, we need to do our best not to hurt each other or make anyone suffer for the benefit of all people as a whole. Stopping pain and suffering in the world is an "ideal" we know is beneficial to all of us without invoking any supernatural explanation.

Peter winces as if someone is hurting.

Thomas: Are you OK, Peter?

Peter: Oh, sorry. I shouldn't react that way.

Thomas: React to what?

Peter: To the word "supernatural."

Jim: What's the problem about it?

Peter: I am not saying you are doing this, Jim. Sometimes, the term "supernatural" is used pejoratively, as it pertains to the irrational. It might also imply as if God had created two worlds, one natural and one supernatural. However, God only created one world, not two. The term "supernatural" could very well refer to things that are "natural," yet we still don't understand. For example, abstract yet well-defined truths like sacrificial love, mathematics, or the laws of logic are ultimately non-material, but we don't call them "supernatural."

Jim realizes he might need to be more nuanced than expected, which is an exciting thing.

Jim: That's . . . I never thought about it that way.

Thomas: Me either.

Peter: *(joking)* Same here.

All of them laugh.

Thomas: OK, going back to the conversation about an "ideal." I believe we can say there have been different periods of trial and error that other cultures have undergone, resulting in various "ideals" that highly differ from each other. Once two different groups of people arrive at two different "ideals," what is the course of action then?

Jim: The course of action, according to history, unfortunately, has always been conflict and war. I wish that weren't the case. Ultimately, our "ideal" as a society is to diminish pain and suffering and increase well-being. Therefore, if another society's ideal resulted in them wanting to hurt us, then we would need to defend ourselves.

Peter: Would you say the group that is attacking is doing something "evil" in that case?

Jim: The word "evil" has many theological implications. I would rather say they are doing something they shouldn't do.

Peter: Jim, I was an atheist myself many years ago, and you just mentioned something I found hard to fit in my worldview back then concerning modal verbs like "should." I don't want to bother you with the same question, but when you say "should," would it be fair to ask "should" according to whom?

Jim: Yes, that's fair. There are as many "shoulds" as there are people in the world. We sometimes agree on some things people should or shouldn't do based on experience.

Thomas: Then, are these "shoulds" susceptible to change depending on external pressures like culture, society, environment, etc.?

Jim: Absolutely, I would say so.

Peter: Is it possible, in principle, to imagine a "should" that could work or could have worked out for every person of every time period and culture in history?

Jim: I don't think so; I don't think it's possible. I could perhaps imagine a time in the future when the world will be so communicated and globalized that everyone might think in a similar way, morally and ethically. But even this, I doubt.

Thomas: Why?

Jim: Because we are all trying to survive at the end of the day. Survival is very instinctual, and it makes people do horrible things. I don't think this will ever change.

Peter: Then, in terms of morality, would you say there are good and bad things?

Jim: I would. There are good and bad things people agree on, like the fact that many of us don't want to suffer; but ultimately, even those things we agree on are fundamentally subjective and depend on culture. If you ask me if there is an objective good and an objective evil in the world that transcends our opinion of them, then I would say no.

Peter: Jim, you are doing a fantastic job sharing your worldview as an atheist with us without mentioning or comparing it with Christianity at any point. Trust me; it's challenging to do it!

Jim: Thank you! I get it. I will always have the tendency to compare my views to those I had in the past. But I think you are right. Many times, these conversations end up being very one-sided, and only Christianity is scrutinized. I am glad we are focusing on atheism in this way while taking into consideration that each atheist can significantly differ from others on many topics.

Peter: That's right.

Thomas: I find the idea that "we find morality" interesting, instead of morality "finding us," as it were. I think I am ready to ask you questions about other topics. Is that OK?

Jim: For sure.

Thomas: Do you believe in some type of absolute truth?

Jim: Umm . . . I am open to the idea, but I would expect this absolute truth to be material, one we can understand through our senses.

Peter: Why is that?

Jim: Over the last four hundred-something years, the scientific method has helped us discover and describe things we didn't know about the universe. And any time we find and describe something, there are always causation or correlation connections between one or more things that are fundamentally material. Therefore, I have good reasons to keep expecting more materialistic explanations waiting for us ahead.

Thomas: For matter to be studied, matter first needs to exist. Where does it come from according to your perspective? I am not talking about its properties or potential to change and become other things, but the reason why matter exists.

Jim: That's a great question. My answer to that is: We still don't know.

Peter: Do you expect a materialistic explanation for the existence of matter?

Jim: It is a possibility.

Peter: If matter created matter, this could imply that matter is eternal. Could one of the properties of matter be "being eternal"?

Jim: I don't know. It's an option. Everything could have come out from nothing as well. I don't mean "nothing" in "a quantum vacuum with billions of particles bouncing off each other," but nothing "in the absence of anything."

Thomas: So, matter could have come out of nothing without having a cause?

Jim: I love these questions, but they all inhabit the fringes of physics and metaphysics now. My most comfortable answer is this: I don't know why the universe exists, but I have enough reasons to expect materialistic explanations for how it functions.

Thomas: Why does the universe look the way it does?

Jim: I don't have an answer for that. I don't know.

Peter: Let me ask you that same question in a different way. Do you see any traces of intelligence behind, beyond, or sustaining the universe according to how it seems to obey the laws of physics?

Jim: I think "intelligence" could be one option to explain why the universe looks the way it does . . . perhaps . . . But I don't think intelligence can be beyond the universe because, as far as I know, intelligence is a property of our brains, and brains are material. Beyond space, matter, and energy, intelligence cannot exist on its own because if, at one point, there was nothing, then intelligence would have been "a thing." And nothing is nothing.

Thomas: Could there have been a "material nothing" but "spiritual something" at one point within the framework of existence?

Jim: How do you define spirituality? I ask this because spirituality is a human thing, and if humans didn't exist, then spirituality wouldn't exist either. In a way, spirituality is an idea; only brains can have ideas. Therefore, spirituality, in a sense, is also material.

Thomas: I would say something is spiritual when it is real but cannot be perceived by our senses.

Jim: How do you know something is "real" if you cannot perceive it?

Thomas: It is hard for me to believe at this point that matter caused matter to exist because this could lead us into an infinite regress of causation from matter to matter that also cries out for an explanation of its own existence. I would be more open to believing that whatever "caused" or "prompted" the universe to exist shouldn't have—in principle—the properties the universe has because we know space, time, energy, and matter had a beginning. I would concede that what I call "spiritual" could perfectly be a way to name something that is not material but still real, empirically speaking. And that "thing" doesn't have to be "a god," but something or "someone" completely different.

Jim: I see your point. As I said, these are the most fundamental questions of reality. I don't have an answer for them now, and I believe no one does at this point.

Peter: Is it because you expect the answer to be related in some form to something fundamentally material?

Jim: You could say that.

Thomas sits back, breathes deeply, and exhales with a smile. Peter and Jim also do the same, and the three of them smile together. Jim is being vulnerable with people he doesn't know well, and Peter and Thomas want to care for him through it.

Thomas: OK, Jim! Let's give you a break. Do you want something to eat?

Jim: Haha! Yes and no.

Peter: Isn't that the way we all feel at all times?

The three of them laugh. Peter sits back laughing, but a second later, he jolts in pain, bringing his hand behind his neck.

Jim: Hey, Peter, are you OK?

Peter: Oh yes, yes . . . no worries. It's nothing.

Thomas gives Peter a quick and subtle nod to ensure he is OK. Peter nods back to calm Thomas down. It is unfortunate to be reminded of something difficult while you are having such a good time. Peter keeps massaging the back of his neck to calm himself down. But Thomas knows.

Jim: I mean with "yes and no" that I'd like to get one of those chocolate muffins, but in reality, I shouldn't because of my sugar levels. I've wanted to get one since I saw the girl I drew eating one.

Sofía . . . every time Thomas thinks about her, it feels like time freezes around him, and nothing else matters.

Peter: OK, Jim. It's on me. One muffin is OK. Because of how you are talking about it, I think I have gathered enough evidence to support your wanting one.

All three of them chuckle. Peter raises his voice a little bit so that Lourdes can hear him.

Peter: Lourdes, may we have three chocolate muffins?

Lourdes: Three? Peter! We need to make sure you can still fit in your car whenever you decide to leave this place!

The whole coffee shop laughs. The wit . . .

Jim: I think it's impossible not to have a good time in this place with an owner like Lourdes.

Thomas: 100%.

Lourdes: OK, I'll bring them to you in a second!

Truman doesn't seem to like the fact Lourdes is raising her voice to talk to Peter from the counter, and he barks once at her.

Lourdes: What? Are you trying to train me, Truman?

The laughing continues. Lourdes gets three muffins and brings them to their table. Truman shadows Lourdes everywhere she goes.

Lourdes: Truman, you don't have to follow me everywhere I go. I am just moving ten feet away from the counter. *¡Qué barbaridad!*

Jim: I think he is trying to herd you. These dogs herd humans and animals by instinct.

Lourdes: So, the Lord was right: I am an actual sheep.[84] Thanks for the reminder, Truman.

Truman barks once back at her. This is turning into a show at this point. Lourdes is not trying to be funny; this is who Lourdes is, which makes it even funnier.

Lourdes: OK, Truman, let's go back to the counter and leave them be. The show is over, people.

Peter: OK. Jim, try it. Tell us what you think.

Jim holds the chocolate muffin, looking for all the world like a man in love. Both Peter and Thomas are waiting for his reaction.

Jim: OK, here goes nothing.

Jim bites into the chocolate muffin, remains quiet while chewing, and doesn't stop looking at it.

Peter: And?

Jim: I cannot believe how good this is!

Peter: Have faith, Jim. Believe!

---

[84] John 10:27: My sheep listen to my voice; I know them, and they follow me.

All three of them laugh.

Thomas: Actually, that's a good segway into a different question. When you believe something is true, you never say anything is true in an absolute sense. Am I right?

Jim: That's correct. Even the scientific method, through its inductive method of hypothesis-trial-error-conclusion, cannot give us 100% certainty of anything. I believe something is true in terms of probability. I believe the sun will come out tomorrow with much certainty, not because I know it per se, but because of how many times it has done it.

Thomas: So, in principle, anyone can be wrong about anything at any point.

Jim: Yes, that's a possibility.

Peter: I find this fascinating because there is some soft correlation between your belief and Scripture's words about knowing things. "People cannot see the whole scope of God's work from beginning to end."[85] This helped me better understand the word *faith* on my journey from atheism to Jesus. The example of the sun is brilliant and can be used analogically to understand what Scripture means by *faith*. As the sun comes out every day, your trust increases in that it will do it again tomorrow. It's the same with God: Existence, order, consciousness, beauty, hope, love, Scripture, Jesus, experiences, prayer . . . you trust God exists because of the number of times He shows He is there in your life, and then you have faith. Faith is a consequence of trust.

Jim: The issue is that we see the sun but don't see God.

---

[85] Ecclesiastes 3:11.

Peter: I would say there is a more significant issue at hand, the fact that we have eyes to see the sun and that the sun is there.

Jim: What do you mean?

Peter: Well, for the sun to exist, first reality needs to exist, and the laws of physics have to combine in such a way to permit not only life but life to be conscious of its existence—as it happened with humanity. Only then, things can be "seen." I humbly say that the whole system cries out for an explanation, for which "intelligence" is a great candidate.

Jim: We still need to find an explanation for the whole system, so I would rather say, "I don't know," instead of concluding something without having any evidence.

Peter: What is evidence for you? Or, let me ask you the question in a different way, Jim. Does the universe's existence, specific properties, and functionality suggest some reason for its existence?

Jim: I don't have an answer, but I don't think positing a God is a good answer either.

Peter: I respect that. Now, the universe allows for the existence of intelligence, and you need intelligence to understand it because the universe happens to be intelligible. Could this fact suggest that some intelligence or creative order was a part of its emergence?

Jim: Logically, you could posit such a hypothesis, but there is no way to prove it from within the system.

Peter: When we explore metaphysics, I don't think we are trying to prove anything mathematically anymore but to come up with ideas about how something like mathematics could have emerged. That's what I mean when I say that observing the sun presupposes the existence of intelligence since you need a conscious being—you or me—and a pattern—the sun coming out—to be discerned, to even make sense of it.

Thomas: OK, guys. Phew! That took a bit of work to follow! Let's dial it down a little bit. Jim, what other things can you tell us about your life as an atheist?

Peter: I am loving this, though.

Jim: Haha. OK. A big topic I feel comfortable sharing with you was discovering I was sexually attracted to men and the whole redefinition of sexuality issue. But to talk about this topic, I have to mention a couple of things about Christianity to contextualize it.

Peter: Feel free to say anything you want to challenge us both.

Jim makes a short pause, looking at Peter, and gives him a calm yet puzzled look. Peter is worried he said something he shouldn't have.

Peter: Is everything OK?

Jim: Yes, yes . . . Sorry. I just never met a Christian who was excited for his faith to be challenged this way while asking me with a smile.

Peter: Oh! Jim, but what if I am wrong? I am just like you. I want to know what is true and isn't, and an excellent way to know it is to expose my faith and all my weaknesses, both emotionally and intellectually, so that my worldview can be challenged.

Jim: It's remarkable you think this way. Thomas, as I said before, you are fortunate to have him as a friend.

Thomas: Yes, Peter is a great friend. However, he thinks American football doesn't make sense, so he is not as good as you think he is.

Peter and Jim laugh.

Peter: It doesn't make any sense.

Jim: Why so?

Peter: There is enough evidence to support the claim that it doesn't.

Jim: Show me the evidence!

All three laugh together, raising their voices slightly, and Truman barks at them.

Thomas: Oh! Truman, sorry!

Lourdes chuckles.

Jim: Guys, this chocolate muffin is unbelievable. Thank you.

Peter: You're welcome.

There is silence for a few moments.

Jim: OK, back to the conversation. I think one of the downfalls of the Christian faith is the fact that it doesn't support people like me.

Thomas: What do you mean when you say "support"?

Jim: I mean, I cannot be a part of a Christian church because I am sexually attracted to men, and the same happens with many other people who experience their sexuality in many different ways. I know some people are investing their time into "progressing" theology, trying to accommodate their sexuality into God's vision for the world, but I don't think it works. I believe the Bible is clear about what God feels about people like me.[86] In summary, according to it, I am . . . "unnatural," to put it politely.

Peter: I want to tread this topic carefully because we care for you, so you stop us at any point.

Jim: I appreciate it.

Peter: I would say that since I am the one who believes in God, I am the one who carries the burden of proof here. Therefore, when a person says, for instance, that there are many genders beyond the male and female biological binary system, the burden of proof should fall on them to demonstrate that it is so, not on the one who doesn't believe it is so. So, God says sexuality is something only to be enjoyed within a heterosexual marriage. Then, anyone who hints at a new way to understand marriage and sexuality shouldn't base their entire argument on undermining those who disagree with them but on bringing up reasons to convince them.

Jim: That's fair. But why are you saying this?

Peter: Well, as soon as the topic of sexuality came up, you began talking about it through the perspective of those who disagree with it, in this case, Christianity, instead of talking about it making a positive case despite those who disagree with it. I am just interested in hearing positive cases for your atheism and lifestyle since we already know what Christians think about it or what God's vision is for it. Do you know what I mean, Jim?

Jim: Yes, I do. That's fair.

---

[86] Read, Genesis 2:24; Leviticus 18:22; Leviticus 18:22; Romans 1:26-28.

Peter: You also mentioned that you cannot join the Christian church. What do you mean by that?

Jim: God loves me, yet because of my natural sexual desire, I am an abomination, and I cannot be a part of His family. That's a way to explain it. This way of thinking has made many Christians very hateful toward people like me.

Peter: This topic is profound on an emotional level but outstandingly easy to understand on a theological level.

Jim: *(curious)* I am all ears.

Peter: God loves me but doesn't like my anger, my arrogance, my boasting, my envy, my lust, my greed, my hatred, my lying, etc. Trust me; I have all of those and can still be a part of His family because of Jesus.[87] I know the world struggles deeply with the idea of sacrificial love. You can sacrifice yourself for another person without having to accept everything there is about them. That's precisely what Jesus did for you, me, Thomas, and the world. So, for example, my lust and your attraction to men are exactly at the same level in God's eyes. God doesn't want me to be greedy, hateful, or a liar, and the world agrees that those things are not good. However, within that list of moral truths, God also says His vision for sexuality is for a man and a woman to enjoy it within the confinements of a heterosexual marriage. Still, some people think this is problematic. The question for me is, how much is each individual willing to sacrifice to follow Jesus? The challenge is up to all of us, and it doesn't look the same for any two people. This,

---

[87] Romans 5:8: But God showed his great love for us by sending Christ to die for us while we were still sinners.

however, doesn't make any sense if you first don't believe God exists. These are empty words for a person who doesn't believe.

Jim: Exactly.

Peter: At the same time, Jim, I think you are not quite right about the fact that God doesn't love you. He does so much. Whether you believe it or not doesn't matter to God, because God keeps loving you and eagerly wants you to love him back. His love was sacrificial on the cross,[88] so it's reasonable to think that loving Him back would require some sacrifice from us in return.

Jim: *(somewhat bothered)* And what have you sacrificed, if you don't mind me asking?

Peter: Not at all, Jim. You are being so open and vulnerable to us! I sacrificed the fact that I cannot be with my family back in England, my self-centered pursuit of success, my lust and desire to engage in all my sexual desires, my time, my daily life . . . Following Jesus is not an easy thing to do. If I had focused on how others responded to Jesus' call, I would have plenty of reasons to accommodate His will into how I think I should live my life. But that's the thing, Jim, I believe my life doesn't belong to me. Instead, it is a gift that I have to honor. There are no better or worse people in God's eyes, but *one* broken family—called humanity—in need of redemption because of their actions.

Jim: See? That's very judgmental. How could you know that everyone is broken without knowing who people are? That's very arrogant.

---

[88] Hebrews 9:28: So also Christ was offered once for all time as a sacrifice to take away the sins of many people. He will come again, not to deal with our sins, but to bring salvation all who are eagerly waiting for him.

Peter: Oh, Jim! Not at all! I know this is a fact without having to judge anyone. We are broken because we die! Death is the ultimate enemy to defeat. It is sin that causes death.[89] That's why the resurrection of Jesus is so important.

Jim: *If* it's true.

Peter: Correct. If it weren't, none of my words would make any sense,[90] and I would be the first person to admit it. Plus, there wouldn't be any reason for me not to pursue my own desires and live my life as if I owned it. Also, if I may, I think you mentioned you cannot be a part of the Christian church because of your same-sex attraction. Did I hear that well?

Jim: Yes.

Peter: OK. I just wanted to make sure. Jim, you can be a part of the Christian church while being sexually attracted to men, as long as you do your very best not to indulge in it and you acknowledge that the Bible says that it is sinful. Even if we act on all of our temptations, an authentic Christian would always recognize they are not doing God's will; they would always go back to Jesus in confession and repentance; and they would always ask for forgiveness. This means we will wrestle with the sanctifying process of the Spirit, and embrace the willingness to not engage in those sins anymore. I think there is a passage . . . Is it OK if I read a passage of Scripture to you that I believe communicates this idea very well?

Jim: Yes, go ahead. I don't mind.

---

[89] Romans 6:23: For the wages of sin is death, but the free gift of God is eternal life through Christ Jesus our Lord.

[90] 1 Corinthians 15:14: And if Christ has not been raised, then all our preaching is useless, and your faith is useless.

Peter: I think . . . give me a second . . . Oh, yes, here it is. First John 2:16–17: "For the world offers only a craving for physical pleasure, a craving for everything we see, and pride in our achievements and possessions. These are not from the Father, but are from this world. And this world is fading away, along with everything that people crave. But anyone who does what pleases God will live forever.

Jim: You are asking me to be someone I am not because of your religious beliefs.

Peter: I don't think *I* am—God is. In fact, God is also asking me to be a person I sometimes wouldn't like to be either.

Jim: What do you mean?

Peter: For example, I tended to be prideful, lustful, contentious, etc. Those feelings led to experiencing tons of pleasure, for different reasons, in the past. When I first realized that wasn't God's will for me or anyone else, then it was painful to deliberately put myself aside and die to all of it because of Jesus, and at times I keep struggling with it. Jim, your same-sex attraction and my proclivities toward sinful behavior make us the same in the eyes of God: sinful and desperate. I may not struggle in the same exact categories as you, or as Thomas, or as Lourdes . . . but I do struggle.

Jim: So, how would you feel if I judged your behavior and lifestyle based on my personal beliefs?

Peter: I think you would be contradicting yourself a little bit.

Jim: Oh, really? How so?

Peter: Because, according to what you said before, you cannot judge my set of beliefs as long as my process of trial and error took me to a place where my beliefs don't clash with your well-being in any respect, and they don't.

Jim: Oh, but they do, don't they? I cannot be around you because of who I am.

Peter: You are being yourself, and I am glad you are around me right now. I don't understand. What do you mean?

Jim: Yes, but there is a side of me you don't accept.

Peter: But, Jim, there is a side of me you don't accept either—my beliefs in Jesus. The real issue is where we choose to place our identity and why. For example, Jesus is everything to me, absolutely everything. My identity is in Him. If you said something harsh about Him, should I feel or believe that you don't accept me the same way you think about your same-sex attraction?

Jim: I guess so.

Peter: Then, the question would be, why do you choose to place a big "chunk" of your identity in your same-sex attraction? Do you feel the same when someone doesn't accept or criticize any other aspects of your personality?

Jim: I don't. Because this is not a matter of me nonchalantly liking something or not. This is a matter of who I am, something I didn't choose about myself.

Peter: I respect that. However, I didn't choose to be born prideful or lustful either, but that doesn't entail I have to be those things only because I feel them. My whole point is this: God doesn't see you as a same-sex attracted human being, but a human being who is first created in His image. Your same-sex attraction might be one aspect of yourself, but not who you intrinsically are, at least not to me as a Christian.

Jim: There is so much to say about this. I'll say that your metaphysical assumptions make you see me and the world in a way that deviates from actual reality, which could be dangerous.

Peter: I partially agree. As demonstrated by some people who have claimed to be Christians and whose actions didn't match their supposed beliefs, regrettably, sometimes that is the case.

All of a sudden, Peter leans forward. From Peter's body language, Thomas feels a joke or something similar is coming.

Peter: *(whispering)* Anything can be dangerous in the hands of conscious, free-will agents who cannot be good on their own.

Jim: Wow! What a can of worms you just opened!

Peter: Worms everywhere!

All of them laugh. Some people sitting at the tables next to them are confused, looking to see if it's true. From behind the counter, Lourdes is stunned.

Lourdes: Peter! What are you talking about!?

Peter: Sorry, sorry! We are just joking, everyone.

Thomas: I don't think we are, though.

No one knows what to think anymore.

Thomas: Hey, Jim, how are you feeling? Are you still good?

Jim: Yes, I am.

Thomas: OK. Please tell us a little bit about your lifestyle without getting into too many details.

Jim: Yes. After I divorced my wife, I began exploring my homosexuality with other men, and I felt freedom; I thought I was acting on the person I am. However, I never wanted to live or marry any other person anymore. I began to have casual sex encounters with other consenting adults to satisfy an urge that I believe is natural. There is nothing terrible, evil, or unnatural to it: hunger, thirst, sexual desire . . . all natural components of what it means to be a human.

Thomas: Did your new lifestyle bring you happiness?

Jim: It is hard to be a human being, so my life is as happy or as complex as anyone else's. However, I noticed a change in how I interacted with the world because I wasn't restraining who I had been all along.

Peter: Jim, when you say "natural," what do you mean by it?

Jim: I mean, it's part of nature, and homosexuality is a part of the animal kingdom.

Peter: OK. I think I understand what you are saying, but help me with something. According to evolutionary biologists, one of the leading forces driving the process of evolution is reproduction, but homosexuality doesn't promote the reproduction of our species. At a conceptual biological level, would you still consider homosexuality or the redefinition of sexuality "natural" in that respect?

Jim: It is happening "in nature." Therefore, it is natural. We could reverse this core aspect of evolution because we have developed technology to overcome it.

Peter: Now, in principle, our species wouldn't have existed if it hadn't been for the reproduction that is only possible through heterosexuality. Besides, our technology hasn't overcome the fact that you need a female egg and a male sperm to begin the process of reproduction; so, in that sense, it's still constrained biologically.

Jim: If your problem is the word "nature," then it might be time for you to be open to redefine it, because the world seems to be moving forward and you might be falling behind.

Peter: Yes, but I don't follow the world.

Jim and Peter remain calm; however, the tone of the conversation has become a bit more tense.

Jim: Then I'll follow the world, and you follow whoever you want.

Peter: In that, we agree. We have the freedom to choose who we want to be and become—at least in the West—and I would do everything I could so that you and I don't lose that freedom at any point.

Jim: I agree with that.

Jim's phone rings.

Jim: Do you mind?

Peter and **Thomas:** Not at all.

Jim has a short conversation with someone he seems to know well.

Jim: It's my sister, she needs some help with my mom, so I need to leave in few minutes to help.

Thomas: Oh, OK. Do you have time for one more question?

Jim: Um . . . yes! One more would be fine.

Peter: Jim, do you want another chocolate muffin?

Jim: No! I wish! No! Thank you, though.

Peter: OK, OK.

Thomas: Here is my last question. From Christianity to atheism, as you abandoned your faith gradually, what is the most challenging teaching of Christiani—?

Jim doesn't even need to wait for Thomas to finish his question.

Jim: Hell.

Peter and Thomas remain quiet, waiting to hear Jim say more about it.

Jim: Imagine this . . . I didn't ask to exist; I show up here, I cannot act on my own natural desires; and if I do, I will be tortured forever. That, my friends, is utterly disgusting.

Peter and Thomas don't say anything. Jim is getting more emotional with this question, meaning he cares about it. This is not a time to engage in conversation but to sit, wait, and listen.

Jim: The promise of Heaven fades in comparison with the reality of Hell. I would have rather not existed than have lived and been exposed to the possibility of spending an eternity of torture in Hell. God creates me, knows that I am sinning, does nothing for me while I am having doubts even though I never stopped asking Him for answers . . . And for that, I am destined to suffer in Hell. It is pretty disgusting. I get more emotional because of the idea of it; not because I think it's true, but because I don't think it is.

Peter: You have all the right to get emotional about something you find disgusting. I think this a normal, human reaction.

Jim: What do you feel when you hear me talk like this about Hell, Peter?

Peter: My first reaction is not to say anything but to care for you and give you more time to keep talking about it.

Thomas: I . . . never thought about Hell in that way. And, from that perspective, it makes sense what Jim is saying.

Peter knows he could engage in conversation about Hell, a complex topic for a non-believer but not as difficult for those who peek into the reality of sin face to face—both the one we carry within ourselves and the one that reigns and has enslaved the world from the beginning. Instead, it is better to let some things rest, to struggle with them in solitude for a while.

Jim: There is one thing I'll say about Hell, just as I said it about sexuality. Many people are trying to accommodate their modern views within the moral and sexual framework of the Bible, but I don't think it's possible. The world should accept what Scripture is and isn't and just let it go. I am curious though, Peter, what do you think about Hell?

Peter: Are you sure you are OK with me sharing my thoughts on it?

Jim: Oh, yeah, Peter. Please.

Peter: OK. When you contemplate the possibility of Hell without believing that God exists, the reality and devastation of sin, and what Jesus had to do on the cross to overcome it, Hell doesn't make any sense whatsoever. In my case, I do believe those three things are real. God knows everything that is happening at all times,[91] so imagine having to withstand all the horrible things we do and think about as human beings every single day of our lives: human trafficking, child abuse, torture, sexual immorality, murder, and the incredible myriad of all the horrendous things humanity has done from the very beginning and we keep doing today—me included. We have implemented a justice system to restrain people from doing things like this, and at times, we even condemn specific actions with capital punishment or a lifetime in prison. By the way, if you don't believe there is an afterlife, then in that case, we would be condemning people to spend in prison the only life they have. That's "pretty disgusting" for those who might see justice differently than we do. If you extrapolate this to God's vision of the world for a moment, Hell is a reality that is not as difficult to understand. He created everything, He is holy and wants us all to be holy too,[92], and He set up the parameters of what is just and isn't, just like we do from a secular point of view. Therefore, He has the right to determine what each person deserves according to their actions, and, again, just exactly as a secular judge, He has the right to do within the parameters of justice according to what He believes we should all do.

Jim: That's interesting. What do you think about the nature of Hell though? Is it eternal? Do people burn forever and ever with no possibility of redemption?

Peter: You know, Jim? In Scripture, and primarily because of Jesus, one cannot deny Hell is real. There is no doubt Scripture points to

---

[91] 1 John 3:20: Even if we feel guilty, God is greater than our feelings, and he knows everything.

[92] 1 Peter 1:15–16: But now you must be holy in everything you do, just as God who chose you is holy. For the Scriptures say, "You must be holy because I am holy."

the reality of Hell, a place where people will "live" without God's grace being present anymore. However, concerning the nature of Hell and what Hell looks like, I have suspended judgment.

Thomas: Huh! What do you mean?

Peter: Scripture talks about a dark place,[93] where there is fire.[94] And also that Hell is like a second death,[95] even though there is an eternal component to it.[96] As you can see, it's difficult to pinpoint precisely the nature of Hell. Still, the common denominator is clear: I don't want to be separated from God forever—the same way I don't want to be in prison in this life—and that's why I accommodate my behavior and actions to avoid it. The analogy breaks down at one point, because it is not my behavior or actions that save me. By the way, if you asked me about Heaven, just like Hell, I couldn't tell you what Heaven looks like—at least, not in great detail—although the Scriptures talk about what it will make you feel.

Jim remains quiet. Thomas too.

Peter: The last thing I would say is this: the world should scrutinize Heaven with the same passion they scrutinize Hell. As I said about Hell, I also don't know what the nature of Heaven is like, but it will be the most outstanding, marvelous, fulfilling, and eternally joyful experience ever. It's hard to imagine a place where there won't be

---

[93] Matthew 22:13: Then the king said to his aides, 'Bind his hands and feet and throw him into the outer darkness, where there will be weeping and gnashing of teeth.'

[94] Matthew 5:22: But I say, if you are even angry with someone, you are subject to judgment! If you call someone an idiot, you are in danger of being brought before the court. And if you curse someone, you are in danger of the fires of hell.

[95] Revelation 21:8: "But cowards, unbelievers, the corrupt, murderers, the immoral, those who practice witchcraft, idol worshipers, and all liars—their fate is in the fiery lake of burning sulfur. This is the second death."

[96] Revelation 14:11: The smoke of their torment will rise forever and ever, and they will have no relief day or night, for they have worshiped the beast and his statue and have accepted the mark of his name.

any suffering or pain because we are in pain and we suffer every day. But I want to be there.

Peter gently touches the back of his neck.

Peter: And the *only* thing you need to be there, even if it's a huge thing to do, is to surrender your life to Jesus Christ and obey Him out of love, and not out of legalism.[97] It's challenging and revolutionary thinking to believe "your life" is not "yours" after all, but a gift you are called to honor, and you can honor it by loving others.

Jim seems unsure and after a sigh, he really must go.

Jim: Well, gentlemen, I must take care of my mom. I wish I had more time to talk to you and delve into more big questions with you.

Peter: Jim, what an absolute pleasure it has been to spend time with you.

Thomas: Same here, Jim. It's sad you don't live around here.

Jim: Well, you know? It all depends on my mom. Maybe I'll have to spend more time in town moving forward.

Peter: Jim, I know we don't know each other well, but I could share my phone number with you, and you can let me know if your mom ever needs anything. It would be my pleasure to help her and your sister.

Jim: That's very kind of you. Here, please take one of my cards. My phone number is there.

---

[97] Matthew 16:25: If you try to hang on to your life, you will lose it. But if you give up your life for my sake, you will save it.

Thomas: Before you leave, I have two more things for you. First, I will buy three chocolate muffins for you, your mom, and your sister.

Jim: Oh, no! You know what? I surrender my life to the chocolate muffin!

The three of them laugh.

Jim: Thank you.

Thomas: And lastly, I want to ask you a question Peter asked me the first time we met. Ultimately, when you think about your journey from Christianity to atheism, did it happen because of Jesus?

Jim sits back in his chair, giving the impression that no one has asked him this question before. After taking a few seconds to reflect on it . . . he seems puzzled . . . and gets ready to give them an answer.

Jim: No, ultimately, it was not only because of Jesus.

Thomas: OK, Jim, thank you again for spending time with us. Let us know if you are ever around again.

Jim: I need to leave on Sunday. But I'll let you know whenever I return. I enjoyed the conversation too. Before I go, this is for you.

Jim leaves an envelope on the table.

Jim: But, please, open it later.

Peter: I am so curious now. Thank you, Jim! Take care, my friend.

Thomas: Lourdes, would you give Jim three muffins to go?

Lourdes: Sure!

Jim: I was hoping you forgot about it.

All three of them laugh. Lourdes gently places three chocolate muffins inside a paper bag. Jim holds the bag, waves back to Peter and Thomas, bends down to pet Truman, and leaves the coffee shop. Peter and Thomas are very curious about the envelope Jim left on the table. What's in it? *They wonder.*

Peter: Thomas, do you want to open it?

Thomas: OK.

Thomas opens the envelope. It's a drawing of Peter and Thomas sitting at "their" table with two steaming coffees, having a conversation. A note at the bottom right corner says: "Bad things happen when we stop talking. May the conversation never stop!" Jim. They both get emotional.

Thomas: Whenever we look back at this drawing in the future, it will bring back so many memories.

Peter: Jim is great. You should keep the drawing. Would you like to meet next week to discuss everything Jim said?

Thomas: Yes, I need some time to process everything.

Thomas and Peter pay for all the coffees and muffins, say bye to Lourdes, bend down to pet Truman, and leave the coffee shop, heading toward their cars.

Thomas: Peter, let me know if you get a call from the hospital with a date for your surgery.

Peter: I will, thank you. See you next Thursday at the same time?

Thomas: Sounds good.

Thomas' car is parked closer to the coffee shop. He gets into his car, thinking about everything Jim said, and looks at Peter as he walks toward his car. Peter doesn't move as quickly as he used to anymore. He feels bad for him and, begrudgingly, finds himself saying a small prayer in his head: Please, help him . . .

Thursday, October 26

It's a cloudy, rainy day. Peter arrives at The Shire *and moves slowly toward the entrance, not caring about the rain falling on him. It is raining like it does many times in England—in a sprinkling kind of way. According to his friends in his hometown, "Only cowards carry an umbrella." In his bedroom back at home, he could see the rain falling on his window, seeing how each drop followed a different path from the top of the window to the bottom. He would spend hours imagining and describing the life of each drop of water falling down his window according to the path it would take and how quickly it would do it. Each drop, a person. Each person, a life. Now here, then not anymore. Lourdes, Sofía, Landon, Jim . . . and Thomas . . . just like the water drops finding their life path on his bedroom's window years ago.*

Lourdes: Hey, Peter! You are getting wet!

Peter responds to Lourdes without opening his eyes as he keeps enjoying the sprinkling rain falling on him.

Peter: It's raining, Lourdes!

Lourdes: Oh, really? I didn't notice!

Lourdes smirks and rolls her eyes. Peter is floating.

Lourdes: Are all of you the same back in England?

Peter cannot contain the laugh and gets back to reality. He starts heading to the entrance of the coffee shop while Lourdes is holding the door for him.

Peter: *(exaggerating his British accent)* No, Lourdes, no. I am weirder than the usual English chap.

Lourdes: Then, we are so lucky we got you, *verdad*?

Peter: No, I am lucky we have you.

Lourdes: Aww, Peter, you'll need to try harder to get free coffee today.

Peter laughs.

Peter: Hi, Truman!

Truman jumps out of his bed and runs toward Peter, leaning all his weight on him and expecting all the attention he can give him.

Peter: Oh, Truman! You are a good boy!

Truman shares a soft howl and gets back to his bed. Peter looks around the coffee shop.

Peter: Oh, wow! There is no one here. This place is empty, Lourdes!

Lourdes: Thanks for the encouragement and the reminder, Peter . . .

Peter: Haha! I am sorry. I didn't mean it like that.

Lourdes: I'll stop giving you a hard time now. Yes, evenings get lonelier at *The Shire* as we approach winter. Are you meeting with Thomas?

Peter: Yes.

Peter looks behind the counter to the wall and sees Jim's drawing of Lourdes leaning gently on the coffee machine while praying with her eyes closed. Jim has a talent to draw people in their most vulnerable moments, whether he realizes it or not. Lourdes notices Peter is looking at the drawing.

Lourdes: Oh, you are looking at the drawing.

Peter: Yes.

Lourdes: If I only could make one coffee for Richard and bring it to his table . . .

Peter smiles.

Lourdes: One day.

Peter: One day.

Lourdes: Will there be coffee in Heaven?

Peter: How dangerous would it be for me to answer that question with a "no"?

Lourdes laughs, and Peter is proud he could make the queen of wit laugh like that.

Lourdes: Actually, Peter, it was a serious question.

Peter: Imagine the best things in the world, enhanced to infinity, with no trace of evil and suffering ever again. That's how much I can say about Heaven.

Lourdes: Best things of the world, according to whom?

Peter: According to whom? Lourdes . . . Of course! According to you!

Lourdes laughs again. Peter is on a roll.

Lourdes: Then there will be coffee there and Richard.

Peter: And Jesus.

The door to the coffee shops opens; it is Thomas. Truman jumps again out of his bed to say hi to him.

Thomas: Truman!

Thomas looks around for a second.

Thomas: There is no one here, Lourdes!

Peter: Oh boy . . .

Lourdes: You both are so encouraging to me!

As Thomas is about to apologize, Lourdes interrupts him and begins to mimic Peter's British accent.

Lourdes: *(with an exaggerated British accent)* I didn't mean it like that, Lourdes!

Thomas realizes Peter had said the same thing to Lourdes before he arrived, and they all laugh at Lourdes' imitation of Peter's accent.

Peter: I don't sound like that!

Lourdes exaggerates his accent even more.

Lourdes: *(imitating a British accent)* I don't sound like that!

It's a lost battle at this point. Between laughs, Peter and Thomas go to their table, and Lourdes begins preparing their coffee.

Peter: Thomas, how are you?

Thomas: I am doing well.

Peter: Thomas, how are you?

Thomas smiles.

Thomas: I am fine, truly. I'm just a bit confused about everything that is going on. Have they scheduled your surgery yet?

Peter: Yes.

Thomas: What? I told you to let me know!

Peter: They told me yesterday, so I thought I would rather tell you in person.

Thomas: When is it?

Peter: Thursday, December the 14, early in the morning.

Thomas: How do you feel about it?

Peter: I get excited when I think about not having to go through all the pain I went through in the past. This time, we caught it before it got worse. But, on the other hand . . .

Peter's body seems to sink slowly into the floor.

Thomas: You are going to make it out of this, Peter.

Peter: I think so too, but how do you know?

Thomas: I don't *know* it, but it's what I want.

Peter: I wish I could ask you to pray for me.

Thomas doesn't know what to say and feels somewhat uncomfortable.

Peter: No worries, mate. You are with me. Your presence and your friendship are very valuable to me.

Thomas: You know? Before we debrief about our conversation with Jim, can I ask you a question about prayer?

Peter: Yes. I think we haven't talked about that yet. What do you have in mind?

Thomas: Do you think prayer works?

Peter: You know? I wouldn't like to put my philosopher hat on again and ask you about definitions, mostly because I am no philosopher. But allow me to do it once. What do you mean by "works"?

Thomas: Umm . . . if it works . . . you know? If prayer changes things, if you get what you ask for from God.

Peter: This reminds me of a friend in England who once quoted a Bible verse to me to prove that "the whole prayer thing is a hoax."

Thomas: Which one?

Peter: I think it was . . . give me a second.

Peter checks his phone.

Peter: Yes, Matthew 18:19: "I also tell you this: If two of you agree here on earth concerning anything you ask, my Father in heaven will do it for you." He told me many people gather in the name of Jesus to pray about things, but those things don't happen at all. This, for him, was proof that prayer was a hoax and that Jesus was lying.

Thomas: OK . . . That sounds to me pretty convincing. But . . .

Peter nods at Thomas in a joking way.

Peter: You say it . . .

Thomas: Of course! Context!

Peter: Exactly! The word "context" often sounds like a cop-out in these conversations. But you can still disagree with me after I share the context with you; there is no problem with that. See? I just gave you context about the context.

Thomas laughs.

Thomas: Fair. What's the context?

Peter: Do you remember about Jesus' prayer in the garden of Gethsemane?

Thomas: Yes. What about it?

Peter: That prayer models the life of prayer of every Christian. In it, Jesus says this: "He went on a little farther and bowed with his face to the ground, praying, "My Father! If it is possible, let this cup of suffering be taken away from me. Yet I want your will to be done, not mine."[98] Do you see how Jesus is praying to get something, but then He brings more attention to the Father's will than His own? That's precisely what happens when we pray. God has already given us everything we could have asked for in Jesus and the promise of eternal life. Prayer is not something that "works," or doesn't work. Prayer manifests the Father's love for His people, who He allows to call Him "*Abba*,"[99]—*Dad*—and have conversations with Him whenever we want to. Our prayers cannot change the will of the Creator of the universe. If our prayers align with His *will* for us, then one could say prayer "works," using that terminology.

Thomas: So, when you pray, you don't ask Him to heal you?

Peter: I do, but that's not my ultimate desire. I ask Him for His will to be done in my life first, and then I ask Him to heal me if that's His will for me. When He doesn't "answer my prayer," He is, in the meantime, blessing me in a million different ways, in ways I cannot comprehend. I don't need God to answer my prayer to know He loves me. I know He loves me because He wants me to pray and because of Jesus.

Thomas: So, you pray without expectations.

---

[98] Matthew 26:39.

[99] Romans 8:15–16: . . . Now we call him, "Abba, Father." For his Spirit joins with our spirit to affirm that we are God's children.

Peter: Exactly. I pray because I love Him, not because I want things from Him. I pray with full expectation that He will answer my prayer in the way that best fulfills His will for me. At this point, Jesus has already given me everything. However, He does answer many prayers, and when He does, it's a very humbling experience.

Thomas: One thing I would say, though, is if you prayed for God to heal you, but then it is the surgeon who removes the tumor, is it the surgeon who heals you or is it God?

Peter: Both. God often works through people. God even worked through people to write the Scriptures! He has been working with and through people from the beginning. Besides, God created a world where there is order, nature can be studied, and we can understand it so that we can be stewards of creation in His name.[100] Jesus commissioned us to make disciples of all nations to reach the world with the news of the kingdom of Heaven.[101] God's will for His people is that they participate in accomplishing His will. So, my surgeon will be doing just that, whether he realizes it or not, whether he is successful or not.

Thomas: So, wouldn't you instead want him to be successful?

Peter: Yes, Thomas, I would. But I would rather want God's will to be done because if the surgeon cannot help me and I pass, then I'll immediately be with Jesus, and eternal life will begin for me[102], and that's not a bad thing for me at all.

---

[100] Genesis 2:15: The LORD God placed the man in the Garden of Eden to tend and watch over it.

[101] Matthew 28:19–20: Therefore, go and make disciples of all the nations, baptizing them in the name of the Father and the Son and the Holy Spirit. Teach these new disciples to obey all the commands I have given you. And be sure of this: I am with you always, even to the end of the age.

[102] Philippians 1:21: For to me, living means living for Christ, and dying is even better.

Thomas: How can you be so sure this is what happens when you die?

Peter: Remember when we talked about faith and trust last time? I have enough reasons to trust Him at this point in my life. He has shown me so much love and care for a few years now.

Thomas: But then, you are afraid of the process of dying . . . How can I make sense of that?

Peter: Aren't we all afraid of things we have never experienced?

Thomas: I guess so.

Peter: You are making a good point, though. If I truly believed with all of my heart that as soon as I die, I'll be with the Creator of the universe, then one would expect me not to have any fear at all. I respect that. However, Scripture is full of examples of people who experienced the presence of God firsthand, and afterward, they were still scared of things. The apostle Paul is one example.[103] Dealing with fear in a broken world is unavoidable. This world is painful, and there are many things I still don't understand. In summary, I don't pray to see if it works or doesn't work, but I pray because I love Him and *want* to talk to Him. At the same time, I am beyond thankful that He allows me to pray to Him and even answers my prayers when they align with His will.

Thomas: Can I tell you something?

Peter: Yes.

---

[103] 2 Corinthians 1:8: We think you ought to know, dear brothers and sisters, about the trouble we went through in the province of Asia. We were crushed and overwhelmed beyond our ability to endure, and we thought we would never live through it.

Thomas: Last Thursday, when I got into my car, I did pray for you even though I felt I didn't want to do it.

Peter: Really?

Thomas: Yes. I mean, it wasn't a long, heartfelt prayer. I just found myself instinctively saying, "Please, help him." But then I wondered, "Who am I talking to?"

Peter seems lost in his thoughts all of a sudden.

Peter: *(whispering)* "Please, help him."

Peter gets emotional, showing sadness with his eyes but joy through a smile.

Peter: To be honest with you, that's one of the most heartfelt prayers there is, the one that comes out of absolute uncertainty, fear, confusion, and doubts.

Lourdes: Enough with both of you!

Peter and Thomas get scared out of their chairs.

Thomas: What?! What?!

Peter: What's going on!?

Lourdes walks firmly and confidently to their table, grabs a chair, and sits next to them.

Thomas: Where's our coffee?

Lourdes: No more coffee for you!

Lourdes's volume stirs Truman, who begins barking at her.

Lourdes: Enough with you too!

Truman lowers his ears and lies down in his bed again. Peter and Thomas don't know what to say. Lourdes is mad!

Peter: Lourdes, what's happening? Have we done anything wrong?

Lourdes: Absolutely!

Thomas: What did we do!?

Lourdes breathes in deeply and exhales while sitting back in her chair.

Lourdes: The whole town is worried about you two!

Peter and **Thomas:** Us!?

Lourdes rolls her eyes and throws her hands in the air.

Lourdes: Please, no more games! What's going on with all of you?

Peter and Thomas look at each other, wondering what she knows about them.

Lourdes: Thomas, we don't see you at church anymore. You, Peter, are crying half of the time I look at you from behind the counter, plus you seem to be moving . . . like . . . slower. What a pair, you two! You no longer drink my coffee or eat my muffins until you tell me what's happening!

The more she talks, the softer her tone gets. Her voice breaks a little bit. She really cares for them.

Lourdes: I am worried about you two.

Lourdes tears up. Peter looks at Thomas, and Thomas realizes Peter is about to give up and share the news about his tumor.

Thomas: It's all because of me, Lourdes. Everything is OK with Peter.

Peter: Thomas, it's fine. I think Lourdes should know about my surgery.

Lourdes: What surgery?!

Peter: Lourdes, remember I had a tumor back in England? It's back, and I am starting to have trouble moving. The surgery is scheduled for December 14.

Lourdes doesn't even know what to say.

Lourdes: But . . .

Peter: It's OK. I didn't tell anyone because I didn't want anyone to worry about me. Last time, my family was devastated by the whole thing, and I don't want any of you to worry about me the way they did.

Lourdes releases a big sigh.

Lourdes: So, no one knows about this? Not even your family back in England?

Peter: No one. They would be worried sick, and they wouldn't be able to do anything for me. My father's health is declining too.

Suddenly, Lourdes turns to Thomas . . .

Lourdes: Thomas, what about you?

Peter nods to Thomas, inviting him to tell her too.

Thomas: *(sigh)* I don't know if I believe Christianity is true anymore.

Lourdes remains quiet.

Lourdes: You two are out of your mind.

Peter and Thomas seem confused.

Peter: Lourdes, have you heard what we just said?

Lourdes: Yes, I did.

Peter: Then, why are we "out of our minds"?

Lourdes tears up. The sight of it breaks both apart. There is room for tears even within the stronger people in the world.

Lourdes: *(her voice breaking up)* Because you are not supposed to go through this alone.

Thomas and Peter didn't expect Lourdes to say that. They look at each other, and both of them get very emotional. They know it; Lourdes is right.

Lourdes: Why didn't you tell me?

Peter: I don't know what to say.

Thomas: Me neither.

Lourdes: I understand this is not the type of thing you tell everyone you know, but what about the ones who love you?

Peter and Thomas never heard Lourdes say that to them.

Lourdes: Come here, you two.

Lourdes puts her arms around them and hugs them both at the same time. Peter feels as if his mom was hugging him. Thomas, however, is worried because he knows Lourdes doesn't know how to keep secrets well.

Thomas: Thank you, Lourdes. Now, I am serious, though. You cannot tell anyone about me, please.

Peter: I will tell everyone at church about my surgery on Sunday.

Thomas: What?!

Peter: It's true. I was being so selfish and silly. It is counterintuitive, but sometimes we can even be selfish about our suffering. We are not supposed to carry it alone. How could I not want more people to pray for me? I don't know what I was thinking. I guess it's the fear of hurting people with the news. I don't want people to be sad for me. I won't like the attention, but there is no reason to be alone.

Lourdes: Thomas, you can count on me. I won't tell anyone. People miss you at church; people miss your insights and questions. Even if you have doubts, why would you not let people walk through them with you?

Thomas: I don't know. I guess I don't want to become a burden to others, and I am afraid of how people will react.

Lourdes: Thomas, everyone will react and say things about anything and everything we do, whether we are Christians or not. People's opinions, fears, insecurities, doubts . . . there is nothing we can do about them. But you can choose to be vulnerable with people that you trust. And there are many people who you can trust: me, Peter, Sofía.

Thomas: Well . . .

Lourdes: Well, what? Sofía? I know you are not engaged anymore.

Thomas: How is it that I am not surprised? You know? At this point, it doesn't matter anymore. Sofía is not doing well. She wishes she could go through this with me, but she physically can't.

Lourdes: Probably because of her experience with Landon.

Thomas is shocked.

Thomas: I guess you know it all.

Lourdes: When Sofía's father died, and his brother Landon became bitter toward Christianity, she developed a fear of abandonment. She shared this in a women's group a few months after everything happened. I guess she is afraid that you, too, will abandon her.

Thomas: Abandon her? Never.

Lourdes: How deep are your doubts? You don't believe at all anymore?

Thomas: I am between two worlds now, not knowing where to go.

Lourdes: Pssh . . . as if that was surprising.

Thomas gets offended.

Thomas: What in the world, Lourdes?

Lourdes: *Relájate hombre*! You don't know what I mean yet. Thomas, the apostle Peter doubted;[104] when Jesus resurrected, some doubted;[105] Adam and Eve,[106] Abraham,[107] Sarah,[108] Moses,[109] David,[110] Elijah,[111] John the Baptist,[112] and the list goes on. They all were doubters. Even Jesus' family thought He was crazy.[113] All the disciples ran away in doubt,[114] not just Thomas, but God never gave up on them. So, don't give up on yourself just yet, Thomas.

Thomas: I see . . . Sorry I reacted that way, Lourdes.

Lourdes: You take it easy, Thomas. You are not the first doubter and won't be the last one. And you, Peter . . .

Peter gets nervous because her attention shifts quickly from Thomas to him.

Lourdes: Do you have any symptoms now?

---

104 Matthew 14:30–31: But when he saw the strong wind and the waves, he was terrified and began to sink. "Save me, Lord!" he shouted. Jesus immediately reached out and grabbed him. "You have so little faith," Jesus said. "Why did you doubt me?"

105 Matthew 28:17: When they saw him, they worshiped him—but some of them doubted!

106 Genesis 3:11 . . . the Lord God asked. "Have you eaten from the tree whose fruit I commanded you not to eat?"

107 Genesis 15:8: But Abram replied, "O Sovereign Lord, how can I be sure that I will actually possess it?"

108 Genesis 18:12: So she laughed silently to herself and said, "How could a worn-out woman like me enjoy such pleasure, especially when my master—my husband—is also so old?

109 Read Exodus 3.

110 1 Samuel 27:1: But David kept thinking to himself, "Someday Saul is going to get me. The best thing I can do is escape to the Philistines. Then Saul will stop hunting for me in Israelite territory, and I will finally be safe."

111 1 Kings 19:4 Then he went on alone into the wilderness, traveling all day. He sat down under a solitary broom tree and prayed that he might die. "I have had enough, Lord," he said. "Take my life, for I am no better than my ancestors who have already died."

112 Luke 7:19: And he sent them to the Lord to ask him, "Are you the Messiah we've been expecting, or should we keep looking for someone else?"

113 Mark 3:21: When his family heard what was happening, they tried to take him away. "He's out of his mind," they said.

114 Matthew 26:56: . . . At that point, all the disciples deserted him and fled.

Peter: Yes. I need to move slowly because sudden moves can make the tumor press the nerves in the back of my neck, and it hurts.

Suddenly, the coffee shop's door opens, and a few clients get in line to get their coffee.

Lourdes: *(whispering)* You two, keep me posted and tell me if you need me. I'll bring your coffee and two chocolate muffins on the house.

Thomas: Thank you, Lourdes.

Peter nods and smiles at Lourdes in gratitude. Lourdes returns the chair to the table next to theirs and heads toward the counter.

Lourdes: Welcome! Are you here to try the best coffee in town? If not, this is not where you should be!

Peter and Thomas smile at each other and get back to their conversation.

Thomas: I guess we are more obvious than we thought.

Peter: I guess we are.

Thomas: Are you sure you want to tell everyone?

Peter: Lourdes is right. Why should I not want people to pray for me? It doesn't make sense as a follower of Jesus. My emotions and my empathy for others were getting in the way. What about you? How do you feel after hearing what Lourdes said?

Thomas: I wouldn't say I like that she knows that much about me and Sofía, I'll be honest with you. The thing about people doubting in the Bible took me by surprise. It helps me not to feel as isolated.

Peter: Good! You shouldn't!

Lourdes approaches their table with their chocolate muffins and coffees. She grabs them both again to hug them, but she does it with such passion that Peter jolts in pain because of his neck.

Lourdes: Oh, no! I am sorry!

Peter: Ouch . . . It's OK. I stopped you before you pulled me in. The way you hugged us earlier was perfect.

Lourdes: I hurt you while trying to love you, which hurts me! Sometimes, I can be a little bit overwhelming, I have been told.

Thomas cannot contain his laugh.

Lourdes: What's so funny?

Thomas: Just a little bit, you said?

Lourdes gasps.

Lourdes: *(with irony)* Thomas Leonard Lennox, I didn't know about your sassy side . . . and I love it!

Peter and Thomas laugh.

Lourdes: I am overwhelming. Overwhelming is me. We are both the same person. My Richard is probably decompressing in Heaven right now after being married to me on Earth.

Lourdes leaves while the three of them are laughing.

Peter: Man, Lourdes is a force to be reckoned with.

Thomas: Then, may her force be with you, but not me!

Peter almost spills his coffee after hearing Thomas' joke.

Thomas: *(still smiling)* I admire Lourdes in so many ways. She is thoughtful, attentive, empathetic, and sometimes unexpectedly profound.

Peter: Indeed.

They both take a bite of their muffins, listening to the rain gently tapping on the roof of the coffee shop and "their" window.

Peter: Hey, Thomas, why don't you tell me your thoughts about our conversation with Jim? What do you think about atheism from his point of view?

Thomas releases a big sigh in preparation to explore the big questions.

Thomas: You know? I have been thinking about it. I like the consistency of it from the point of science concerning what we can and can't know. Also, I appreciated his willingness to avoid making assumptions about things we don't have answers for. He was very candid and sincere. Then, at the same time, it caught me off guard when he began making assumptions about how he thinks we should all behave to maintain our sense of individualism and freedom. I appreciate his explanation about how a trial-and-error process led us to distinguish what things are good for us and what things are not. However, I didn't find it convincing.

Peter: Why? You said something similar to me a few weeks ago.

Thomas: Well, I have been thinking about it. When it comes to discerning our morality, this process of trial and error runs the danger of assuming that all human beings experience the same type of process. But we know this is not so since we have many ways of understanding concepts like morality, freedom, etc. When two distant cultures meet, presupposing the way the other is supposed to behave, there is no foundation to expect anyone's behavior to be like yours. From this perspective, I think Jim believes morality to be objective in a pragmatic sense, meaning, it is conducive to thinking morality is objective because it helps us set clear boundaries. However, in essence, Jim's view of morality is relative to time, space, and cultural conditioning and is susceptible to change at any point if necessary. So, when Jim believed something was good, he believed it in the sense of "it is good for now," not "it is good no matter the circumstances."

Peter: Why do you think that is problematic?

Thomas: Understand me. It makes sense to think that way; the problem is that this way of seeing morality, again, expects people to make certain moral decisions while internally knowing that they are neither good nor bad in an absolute sense. That's a very volatile way to think about morality. If you apply any external pressure to a society that views morality like this, let's say with a war, a famine, or the spread of disease, probably most people wouldn't be challenged enough to keep doing as many good things under those circumstances as they should, or could, simply because they believe that—under certain circumstances—the "good" stops making sense. Do you know what I mean?

Peter: Yes, I think so.

Thomas: I don't know. Maybe this is silly. But I don't think we should call it "good" if we consider morality that way. We should say, "What works for us now and what doesn't." The good seems to me to transcend our opinions, and we can arrive at that conclusion without having to believe God exists and is the source of our sense of morality. I do think morality is objective, with or without God.

Peter: I see what you mean. What else did you find interesting?

Thomas: Another thing I found lacking about his worldview was that for everything he believes and doesn't believe about himself, others, and the world around him, he needs a system within which all those things exist, including himself. He didn't seem to show as much wonder or curiosity about why things are the way they are. He said, "I don't know" when it comes to metaphysics or the reason for it all, but I think he assumed that the answer to those questions, if there is any, must also be material. I also thought this was a good argument at one point, but I don't anymore. I don't know . . . when it comes to morality and metaphysics, I found his worldview somewhat empty, and I think that's why he tries to be as pragmatic as he can regarding these types of questions.

Peter: What do you think about his sexual attraction to men and what happened to him at his church?

Thomas: It's a challenging situation. Probably, it was horrible for him to go through all that. From a Christian point of view, it is frustrating that pride, jealousy, lying, etc., are not as visible and apparent as a same-sex attraction can be. I wonder if that's why people are more judgmental toward that type of sin than the ones that reside deep in our hearts and are harder to see.

Peter: I agree with you. What do you think about the redefinition of sexuality and everything we said about that?

Thomas: I liked what you said about the fact that Christians are not the ones redefining sexuality, so they don't have to carry the burden of proof to demonstrate it. At this point, I can only say two things: people are people, and I still believe they are intrinsically valuable just for being people. That's one thing. The other thing is this: I agree that anyone can do whatever they want with their body. The problem is not the freedom we all have or should have but what we do with that freedom.

Peter: What do you mean?

Thomas: Well, I didn't know any of this before, but after hearing what Jim said, I got curious and read more about it. There seem to be some adverse effects on people who engage in same-sex relationships; for example, a higher rate of HIV infection among gay men and higher rates of psychological distress among lesbians. It seems there is also some risk of developing certain chronic diseases, cancer, and mental health problems. However, heterosexual people who are promiscuous may also be at a higher risk of developing prostate cancer, cervical cancer, and oral cancer as a result of having multiple sexual partners. So, science might be pointing to the fact that the safest way to engage in sexual relationships, oddly enough, seems to match what God expects from it.

Peter: Huh . . .

Thomas: But wait a second. I am not saying it is "good" or "bad." I am just talking about the negative effects of it beyond our opinion of it or how much we need it or find pleasure in it; that's a different conversation.

Peter: OK . . .

Thomas: So, I have thought, if we were consistent with the science, which seems to be one of the core foundations of atheism, then we wouldn't be promiscuous, have same-sex relationships, drink alcohol, smoke, or take drugs or a vast myriad of behaviors that have a factual negative impact on us. However, many keep participating in them. This demonstrates that, for some, science and critical thinking might go hand in hand at a conceptual level, but not regarding how they choose to live their lives. That seems to be somewhat inconsistent within their worldview. Unless one deliberately distinguished between scientific truth and pleasure . . .

Peter: Interesting . . .

Thomas: In the end, I am not convinced atheism leads to more certainty than Christianity. This is a good way to put it: Christianity makes way more sense in a practical sense, in how we should live our lives, but then makes enormous assumptions about a spiritual world it cannot demonstrate is there. Atheism seems to be more cautious when it comes to answering big questions for which they have no answers. Still, on a practical level, I don't think that many people realistically follow the science, because many keep making decisions that are inconsistent with what the science says about human behavior.

Peter: You sound to me like a classic agnostic at this point.

Thomas: Maybe. Ultimately, I don't think we should tell people how they should live. The question is, can people coexist having radically different ways of seeing the world?

Peter: We all would like that. However, at some point, some decisions we make will always affect people around us, so conflict of some sort seems unavoidable.

Peter seems frustrated all of a sudden.

Peter: If we just obeyed Jesus . . .

Thomas: What?

Peter: If most Christians obeyed Jesus and loved their enemies, Christians would be the easiest people to live around, even if others disagreed with them. The problem is that following Jesus requires us to make a big sacrifice—to let the self go—and even many of us who consider ourselves Christians struggle to make that sacrifice. We still focus much of our energy on just being right about things instead of loving people sacrificially the way Jesus loved us. Thankfully, there are many Christians who do obey Jesus and are a light for the world. So, instead of bringing our attention to how others should follow Jesus, Jesus is yearning for us to become the followers we'd like to see in others. I am not a Christian because of Christians; I am a Christian because of Jesus. So, no one should ever become a Christian because I am a Christian. That's not a good reason to follow Jesus. Sorry, I digress a little bit, but do you know what I mean?

Thomas: Even if those things make sense, there is no way to know if Christianity's claims are true.

Peter: Is there anything you know for certain?

Thomas: No, there isn't. But God? Should we expect to be uncertain about whether something or someone as immense as God exists, who is allegedly omnipresent, omnibenevolent, omniscient—as we are uncertain about the rest of things in this world?

Peter is startled.

Peter: That's . . . wow . . . very insightful.

Thomas: Come on, Peter, do you think it makes sense to ask each other the question, "Does God exist?" if He really does? I would understand it if we said something like: "You know? God exists, and there is no doubt of it. Now, about His attributes or character, I am not sure . . . " OK. But what does it say about God, the fact that we question His existence, which probably should be His most tangible attribute?

Peter: You are making me think so hard on this! You are so good at asking questions, mate. Let me see . . . I struggled with this idea myself on my journey from atheism to Jesus. Let's play with this idea a little bit. In a world where everyone seems to be free—at least in principle—to make their own decisions to do good and bad things . . . how would people behave if they, let's say, always saw God's presence right there in the sky, while having the freedom to keep doing whatever they want to?

Thomas: Huh, I guess people would feel forced to comply with God's will instead of having the freedom to choose to follow Him. It would be too intense, I presume.

Peter: That's a way to put it. Sinners cannot be in the presence of God. That's why we are not with Him or see Him the way we would love to, and that's why it makes sense to keep asking the question, "Does God exist?" even if He does. At the same time, God came to earth in Jesus, and we saw Him.[115] And you know what people did?

Thomas: What?

[115] 1 John 1:1: We proclaim to you the one who existed from the beginning, whom we have heard and seen. We saw him with our own eyes and touched him with our own hands. He is the Word of life.

Peter: We killed him. Think about it this way: God creates the universe,[116] lives among his people in the Tabernacle,[117] becomes a human in Jesus, chooses to give up His divine privileges to become a slave to the world,[118] and ends up dying for it to save it.[119] That same Creator of the universe, because of Jesus, allows us to call Him "*Abba*,"[120] and he sees us as His "friends."[121] From holiness and supremacy, to call us friends. How much do we want God to do for us, so we know that He "exists" at this point? He died for us, yet we keep doubting He exists. At one point, we need to realize that there is no "evidence" to convince a person that God exists if he or she is determined not to believe it. First, you need to be at least open to it, which is an option God seems willing to give everyone, a freedom He couldn't give us if we always saw him in a "tangible" way. As I said before, even if He were present in an "obvious" way, people would still not choose to repent from their sins. You cannot ask anyone to love you against their will.

Thomas: Well, wait a second. In a way, God is forcing me to believe Him. If I don't believe in Him and follow Jesus, then I'll experience some horrible torment due to my nonbelief. So, at the end of the day He is forcing me to believe in Him no matter what. I cannot freely choose to love Him or not.

---

[116] Genesis 1:1: In the beginning God created the heavens and the earth.

[117] Exodus 40:34: Then the cloud covered the Tabernacle, and the glory of the LORD filled the Tabernacle.

[118] Philippians 2:6: Though he was God, he did not think of equality with God as something to cling to.

[119] John 3:16: For this is how God loved the world: He gave his one and only Son, so that everyone who believes in him will not perish but have eternal life.

[120] Romans 8:15–16: . . . Now we call him, "Abba, Father." For his Spirit joins with our spirit to affirm that we are God's children.

[121] John 15:14: You are my friends if you do what I command.

Peter: If, and only if, He is the creator of the universe and the creator of reality itself, freedom is a concept that would ultimately be framed according to His will, not ours. You still have the option to evaluate the consequences of believing in Him with the same passion you assess the consequences of a potential non-belief. And if you believe God loves you to the point of sacrificing Himself for you in Jesus, and you obey Him, living right by God and other people, then you'll have eternal life in a glorious, joyful, indescribable way, with no pain or suffering whatsoever.

Thomas: But . . .

Peter interrupts him.

Peter: Give me one second, Thomas. Sorry that I am interrupting you. You see what happened when I said "eternal life" to you? You didn't bring any attention to it. I think you should be fair and consider eternal life for what it is. Have you considered what the promise of eternal life truly entails in this conversation?

Thomas seems confused.

Thomas: I don't know if I understand what you mean.

Peter: When we doubt and have questions about God, we focus on building cumulative cases with reasons not to believe in Him, but what about the reasons why we should? Eternal life is a good reason to believe in God, and to get there, He wants you to love Him and then love others the way you love yourself. Why don't we just do that while being excited about eternal life? Why isn't sacrificial love a good reason to believe in God?

Thomas: I don't know.

Peter: I believe it is because it is the most challenging thing to do. *Knowing* many things is easy, but the real challenge lies in loving people *sacrificially*. Not many people seem to want to face that challenge when following Jesus and believing in God. And do you know why I think this is the case?

Thomas: Why?

Peter: Love hurts in many ways: It makes us feel vulnerable, points out our weaknesses, and shows the world our imperfections. But intellectual knowledge doesn't. Sacrificial love leads to eternal life. Why? Because of Jesus. I believe all questions, doubts, challenges, successes, hopes, fears, and life itself will eventually make sense depending on the answer we give to Jesus whenever we face His ultimate question.

Thomas: Which is?

Peter: "Thomas, do you love Me and others the way I love you?"

Thomas remains quiet for a second.

Thomas: I felt goosebumps for a moment. But it sounds too simple to be true.

Peter smiles and takes a sip of his coffee.

Thomas: Peter, what if all of this is false, man?

Peter: Thomas, but what if it isn't?

They smile at each other, feeling this is a good time to end the conversation until next time. It keeps raining outside. Could a few answers lead me back to God? *Thomas wonders.* Could a few questions lead someone back to God? *Peter wonders.*

The conversation continues in their minds as silence is present momentarily. It is time to get some rest from it.

Peter: Thomas, are you attending the pumpkin carving party Lourdes is hosting here this Saturday?

Thomas: Oh, it is October 28th already?

Peter: It's hard to believe.

Thomas: I don't know if I will.

Peter: Why?

Thomas: I don't know. There might be many people from church, and I don't feel like having to go into details about everything happening.

Peter: Well, if you want to come, let me know. I'll try to be here to help Lourdes as much as my body allows.

Thomas: Are you going to tell everyone at church about your surgery?

Peter: Yes, this Sunday.

Thomas: Well, if you need anything in the meantime, you know that I am here.

Peter: Thank you so much, Thomas.

Thomas and Peter leave The Shire, *but not without chit-chatting a little bit with Lourdes and petting Truman. As soon as they open the door to their cars, they both realize how much the temperature has decreased over the last few weeks. Fall is here. Thomas and Peter hug each other. Thomas notices Peter's moves are slow and carefully premeditated. His tumor must be hurting more than he shows. Their conversation echoes in the solitude of his thoughts.* Why, all of a sudden, do I think some of Peter's answers are not as convincing as I would've thought just a few months ago? Is there something else going on, something more personal, causing me to doubt? Even if my questions are sincere, and I believe they are, am I trying to hide something from people, or myself, that I am not aware of? *Thomas keeps mulling over everything as he drives back home. Questions hiding behind questions. Questions yearning to be asked. People afraid to find answers. Answers that do their best never to be found.*

Thursday, November 2

Thomas arrives at The Shire *and notices all the fall decorations are gone. He wonders what the pumpkin carving party was like and, most of all, who went to it? Thick, gray clouds cover the sky, and the wind blows stronger than usual. All the trees in the trail have almost dropped all their leaves, forming a yellow, red, and brown carpet that extends way into the forest. At a distance, the gray color of the sky seems to merge with the color of the lake's water, making it hard to distinguish one from the other. Thomas gets to the entrance of* The Shire *and opens the door. Before saying hi to Lourdes, he looks around the coffee shop to see if he sees anyone he knows, and he does.*

Oh no . . . *He says to himself. He is not ready to open up to anyone, let alone his pastor.*

Pastor John: Hi, Thomas! It's been a few weeks since I last saw you at church. Is everything all right?

Thomas: Hi! You know? I have been busy and unable to take a moment for myself and God for a while.

Great thing to say if you are trying not to talk about it, Thomas, *he says to himself, frustrated. He smiles and approaches Pastor John. They both shake hands.*

Pastor John: By the way, Thomas, thank you so much for caring for Peter like you do. You are very thoughtful.

Thomas: Oh, yeah, it's my pleasure.

Thomas remembers Peter told him he was going to share at church the news about his tumor and the soon-to-come surgery.

Pastor John: Would you like to sit with me for a second?

A "yes but no" answer never made more sense to Thomas than at this moment. It's not because of Pastor John, but because he doesn't want to be vulnerable with anyone else.

Thomas: Sure. I am meeting Peter here in a few minutes.

Pastor John: Oh, that's great. Can I buy you both a coffee? By the time Peter arrives here, the coffee will still be burning hot, so that won't be a problem.

Thomas: Haha! That's true. Sure. Thank you.

Pastor John: Give me a second.

Pastor John goes to the counter to talk to Lourdes and orders two more coffees. Thomas and Lourdes wave at each other from a distance. Thomas pulls out his phone and texts Peter.

Text conversation:

Thomas: Peter, Pastor John is here and invited me to sit with him.

Peter: Are you OK?

Thomas: Yes, I just wanted to let you know. Maybe we should let the big questions rest for today. I don't know if I feel like explaining myself to anyone else.

Peter: Oh, I see. No worries. Whatever you feel like, Thomas. I'll be there in five minutes.

Thomas: OK.

End of the text conversation.

Pastor John gets back to the table.

Pastor John: Lourdes will bring your coffee and Peter's. I have tried to hold them myself in the past, but I still remember the pain.

Both laugh.

Thomas feels very uncomfortable and doesn't know what to say.

Pastor John: Thomas, is everything OK?

Thomas: *(nervous)* Yes, it is. Why do you ask?

Pastor John: It's because you said you were "busy." Years in ministry have taught me that "busy" sometimes means "something is going on, but I don't want to talk about it."

Thomas smiles nervously. Pastor John remains quiet.

Pastor John: Thomas, why don't you do what you do best?

Thomas: What is that?

Pastor John: To ask the best questions I have ever heard. You don't have to answer my questions. Instead, I could try to answer yours if you have some.

Thomas wonders if Pastor John knows he is doubting and questioning his beliefs.

Thomas: How do you know I'd like to ask you questions?

Pastor John: Because it is who you are, and I pray that most of us would be as inquisitive as you are, Thomas.

Thomas: Has anyone told you anything?

Pastor John: I pray for everyone constantly, including you. Over the past few months, I have seen you struggling at church and asking more and more questions about the core doctrines of our faith. Then I heard you and Sofía are not engaged anymore, and I prayed for an opportunity to talk with you because I don't want you to feel alone throughout anything you might be going through.

Thomas: I guess it doesn't make sense to hide it anymore.

Pastor John: To hide what?

Thomas: Pastor John . . . I don't know if Christianity is true anymore.

Pastor John: I see . . .

Pastor John doesn't seem surprised by what he just heard. In fact, as Thomas is breaking the news to him, he can even see a hint of . . . nostalgia.

Pastor John: You remind me so much of a friend I met in seminary.

Thomas: How so?

Pastor John: He was a pure intellectual, always learning and having an insatiable thirst for knowledge, who also tended to be alone and keep things to himself.

Thomas does see how Pastor John made that connection after hearing what his friend was like.

Thomas: What happened to him?

Pastor John: He was prone to feel lonely even when around people, and all his knowledge didn't allow him to enjoy the simplest things in life. He was in his head all the time. Understand me, he was a genius. He taught himself how to read in Greek and Hebrew before college. I remember one time he corrected our professor in Hebrew class on the first day of school.

Thomas: Oh man, really? How did that go?

Pastor John: I mean, I didn't know him then. It was the first day of class. Our professor didn't know what to say, and I felt pretty uncomfortable. I would see him eating lunch alone, reading books alone . . .

Thomas: How did you both become friends?

Pastor John: Haha!

Thomas feels there is a long story behind that laugh.

Thomas: What's so funny?

Pastor John: The way it happened. One day, in pastoral care class, our professor asked the class this question: "How would you explain *agape* love, sacrificial love, to someone who doesn't understand it?" He raised his hand and gave the most brilliant explanation about the word's etymology and how it was understood within its first-century Middle Eastern context. A few jaws dropped in class, including our professor's. However, I knew he was wrong.

Thomas: Huh? Wrong?

Pastor John: Yes, it's insufficient; because sacrificial love is not something you can adequately explain but *do*.

Thomas smiles but wouldn't have expected that answer in a million years, either.

Pastor John: Well, I raised my hand after he finished talking and said: "I don't think that's right." Imagine his face when I said that. "The best way to explain *agape* love to someone who doesn't understand is to love that person in a way no one has loved them before, to be like Jesus in the way you speak to them, treat them, and think about them even when you are not with them . . . loving them even if they despise you."

Thomas: Oh man, what happened when you said that?

Pastor John: My friend stood up and stormed out of the class. No one knew what to say. However, I knew I had to go after him to see if he was OK. He was almost out of the building when I stopped him. By the way, his name was Edward. I said: "Edward! Are you alright?" He said: "No, I am not!" Then I said: "Why?" and he said: "Because you were right!" And that's how our friendship began.

Thomas: Haha!

Pastor John: Edward was always asking questions and couldn't stop learning. That's the way you remind me of him. Now, he was different from you in that he unfortunately became a slave to knowledge, and his relationship to knowledge made his life very hard. After we became friends, he taught me so much about . . . everything. Again, he was a genius. But I taught him to see people not as mere recipients of knowledge but as human beings who cannot know everything there is to know, who sometimes don't feel well, who sometimes are afraid, and who need to be loved and to know Jesus. I prayed for him for months, asking God to use me to help him be free from his obsession with knowledge and to value it as much as anything else. Paul is right when he says: "You say, 'I am allowed to do anything'—but not everything is good for you. And even though 'I am allowed to do anything,' I must not become a slave to anything."[122] I remember in our preaching class, we were asked to preach in front of the class for the first time. I wanted to do it well to impress my professor, but I cared much for Edward. So, knowing Edward would listen to me, I prepared a sermon specifically for him based on a few passages from the Bible.

Thomas: Which ones?

Pastor John: Ecclesiastes 1:17–18: "So I set out to learn everything from wisdom to madness and folly. But I learned firsthand that pursuing all this is like chasing the wind. The greater my wisdom, the greater my grief. To increase knowledge only increases sorrow."

Thomas remains quiet.

---

[122] 1 Corinthians 6:12

Pastor John: The other was a message about how God "chose things the world considers foolish in order to shame those who think they are wise. And he chose things that are powerless to shame those who are powerful."[123] How Jesus prayed to the Father, saying: "O Father, Lord of heaven and earth, thank you for hiding these things from those who think themselves wise and clever, and for revealing them to the childlike."[124] And what Paul said in 2 Corinthians 12:9: "Each time he said, 'My grace is all you need. My power works best in weakness.'" Edward thought knowledge was who he was, not a talent he had. He became a slave to it. When I finished preaching, I remember him looking at me, feeling very emotional. The Holy Spirit moved in his heart so deeply that day. God answered my prayer.

Thomas: What happened after that?

Pastor John: He kept going to classes but stopped studying for weeks—not that he needed to study much, to be honest with you. He just went to the chapel, knelt, and prayed for hours daily. I remember sometimes joining him to pray, and we wouldn't say anything to each other. One day, he showed up to class, and Thomas, you should have seen his face. I promise you . . . that smile, the relief I felt from him. He wasn't battling himself anymore; he wasn't being hard on himself anymore or finding his identity in knowledge and how much he knew about different subjects. It's almost like seeing a person breathe for the first time. The Holy Spirit took hold of Edward and freed him from himself.

Thomas: That's a remarkable story. What is he doing today?

---

[123] 1 Corinthians 1:27

[124] Matthew 11:25

Pastor John: He became a missionary and spent years and years feeding people and talking about Jesus in the poorest neighborhoods of New Delhi, India. Due to the poor air quality in the city, he developed both respiratory and cardiac issues, and two years ago, I learned he passed away. He began a ministry called *khao aur seekho*, which in Hindi means "eat and learn." He would feed the poor and talk to them for hours about the love of Jesus. As he was teaching them about it, he also demonstrated it by his actions. He began a church-planting movement in India, which continues to multiply today. I remember the last time we had a phone conversation. I'll never forget what he said: "John, how easy it is to obtain a doctorate in any field of knowledge, but how strenuously difficult it is just to get a minor in love!"

Thomas is lost in the story he just heard, finding similarities and differences between Edward and himself. Suddenly, Lourdes says something from behind the counter.

Lourdes: OK. Here are your coffees. I think I just saw Peter pulling up just now.

Pastor John: Oh, great! Thank you, Lourdes.

Thomas looks out the window to find Peter . . . and there he is. His left shoulder is slightly elevated, probably to overcompensate for the pain he is feeling. He moves even slower than last week. It breaks his heart to see Peter this way. Thomas heads quickly outside to help Peter get to the coffee shop. In the meantime, Pastor John and Lourdes are looking at them in the coffee shop.

Lourdes: These two . . .

Pastor John: Their friendship is something else.

Lourdes: Do you know if Peter told his parents?

Pastor John: Not yet. Maybe we can ask him.

Thomas holds Peter's hand to help him get to their table. Every few steps, he winces in pain.

Lourdes: I am worried about Peter.

Pastor John: At this point, the only thing we can do is help him, love him, and pray constantly for God's will to be done in his life.

Thomas opens the door for Peter and helps him sit in his chair.

Peter: Hey, Lourdes, Pastor John!

Lourdes: Hi, Peter!

Pastor John: Here is your coffee.

Peter: Thank you! Steaming hot . . . When did you prepare it, Lourdes?

Lourdes: This morning.

Everyone laughs.

Thomas: Have a seat, Peter.

Peter sits down slowly, sighing as soon as he does it.

Pastor John: Peter, how are you feeling?

Peter: I . . . I don't know if I am going to make it to December 14 in this pain.

Thomas: What did you do in England while waiting for your surgery?

Peter: Well, at this point, I think I was already hospitalized around one month before the surgery.

Lourdes: Does your doctor know you are feeling this way?

Peter: No, it has gotten worse the last few days. When the tumor presses the nerves in my neck, it shoots very sharp pains all over my shoulder and arm, and my muscles become very stiff. I remember they gave me tons of muscle relaxers to keep me going 'til they were ready for my surgery.

Pastor John: Peter, I have set a meal train for you until December 14. People from church will bring you food and give you company as much as needed.

Peter: Thank you.

Lourdes: Peter, I think it's time to take some of those muscle relaxers. You don't seem to be doing well.

Thomas: You know what? I can take you to the emergency room right now.

Peter feels discouraged but knows it's time to do something about it.

Peter: Thomas, why don't we have a conversation here? If I don't feel better by the end of it, you take me to the hospital. Deal?

Thomas: Peter, no more of this, "mate." I am going to take you now. You can hardly move! By the way, how did you drive here by yourself?

Peter: I don't know. Pretty slowly, I guess, avoiding quick turns and taking it easy.

Lourdes: Thomas, please take two chocolate muffins for you and Thomas in case you are hungry in the waiting room.

Peter gets a bit emotional.

Peter: Thank you, Lourdes.

Pastor John: If you need any help, please call me. Let's gather and pray over Peter.

Everyone gathers around Peter, including Thomas, although he is unsure and feels out of place. Thomas places his hand on one of Peter's shoulders to make sure Peter knows he is there for him.

Pastor John: Lord Jesus, we love you with everything we have. You allow us to come to you as children of God, our *Abba*, to ask you for things; this is precisely what we are doing right now. Lord, Peter's in pain, cannot move well, and he needs you. Please, help him find rest through the storm. We ask you that, if it's Your will, You heal Peter from this tumor, and if not, then that You find a way to glorify Your name through all this uncertainty. Thank You for the promise of eternal life and for always being here 'til the end of the age.[125] Lord, thank You for the joy we experience through sufferings of all kinds as we hope for what will come. We love Peter so much. We pray all these things in the name of Jesus, Amen.

Everyone says amen, even Thomas, although his was more of a doubtful whisper.

Lourdes: OK, take your muffins; they are on the counter.

Pastor John: Thomas, if you both need anything . . .

---

125 Matthew 28:20: . . . And be sure of this: I am with you always, even to the end of the age.

Thomas: I know. Thank you, Lourdes and Pastor John. OK, Peter, let's go to my car. Depending on how you feel after seeing the doctor, we'll see if you can drive your car back home. Lourdes, could Peter's car stay in the parking lot for the night in case he cannot drive?

Lourdes: Yes.

Peter: OK. Thank you, everyone.

As they leave the coffee shop, Lourdes holds the door for them, and Pastor John accompanies them to help open Thomas' car. Peter leans on Thomas and Pastor John while trying to sit in the car. Suddenly, Peter winces in pain.

Peter: Ah! Sorry, it's no one's fault. I just cannot extend my right arm anymore.

Thomas: The fact you wanted to have a conversation with me while feeling like this . . . Peter, you are crazy.

Peter: *(trying to smile)* The big questions don't care much about my health, they are just there waiting for us to explore them.

Thomas rolls his eyes and sighs in frustration.

Thomas: Peter, Peter, Peter . . . let's go to the hospital to get you some help.

Peter manages to sit in Thomas' car and lets out a big sigh. Pastor John taps the top of the vehicle twice while waving at Peter and closing the door. As Thomas goes around his car to sit in the driver's seat, Pastor John shakes hands with Thomas.

Pastor John: Thomas?

Thomas: Yeah?

Pastor John: Don't be afraid of your journey; don't be afraid of your questions. Keep asking them. But remember, it's all about sacrificial love and Jesus, not the number of questions you know the answer to. The best evidence for God's existence is to love people the way Jesus loved us all and see what happens.

Thomas nods and smiles at him while getting in his car, although a feeling of uncertainty overwhelms him any time God is brought into the picture. As soon as he sits in the driver's seat, he too lets out a big sigh. For a moment, there is just silence. Peter is holding his head with his right hand, so it doesn't move with all the turns and bumps on the road.

Peter: Thomas, could you please drive slowly?

Thomas realizes Peter's eyes are trying to communicate a level of fear his mouth is doing its best to hide.

Thomas: Peter, I have an idea. Let's stop at a pharmacy. I'll buy you a neck brace, so you don't have to worry as much about your neck.

Peter cannot hold it back any longer and begins crying.

Thomas: What's going on, Peter?

Peter: *(crying)* I cannot believe I must go through this again, Thomas. I am scared.

Thomas: Peter, it's not the same this time. I am here, Lourdes and Pastor John and the whole church are here. You are not alone, and we won't leave you alone.

Peter: *(Peter keeps crying)* I had to tell them. I had to tell them.

Thomas is confused.

Thomas: Tell what to whom?

Peter: *(voice cracking)* My parents . . . They know I'll have another surgery, and the tumor is back. I worry for them. I could hear their worry over the phone. I think I heard my mom crying in the background. I don't want them to suffer anymore because of me.

Thomas: Peter, I think it's normal to worry for them. But now it's time for you to focus on yourself for once. You cannot carry the burdens and worries of others all the time. Your parents know how to take care of themselves.

Peter: But why?

Thomas remains silent.

Peter: Why again? Why do I have to go through this again? I don't want to do this again. I am scared.

Thomas quickly considers God's love and why He would allow someone like Peter to go through this again, but it's not the time for theology; it's a time to listen and mourn with his friend.

Thomas: Peter, here is the pharmacy. Give me a second while I get your neck brace. Would you be OK being alone for a few minutes?

Peter: Yes.

Thomas is about to close the door, but . . .

Peter: Thomas?

Thomas: Yes?

Peter: Thank you.

Thomas smiles back at Peter.

Thomas: I'll be right back.

As Peter sees Thomas leaving, he turns to God in prayer. He tries to control his breathing. Peter, *he says to himself.* You feel like this because you are trying to control what's happening to you. You can't. You need to let go. It is moments like this when Scripture comes alive and makes sense. *It's the last thing anyone would do, but as a follower of Jesus, the first thing that comes out of Peter's mouth is a "thank you." He is not thankful for the pain and the fear, but because both point to something beyond themselves, to the One who suffered for Peter so that Peter's suffering could make sense at all. Peter breathes deeply and exhales slowly, saying: "Thank You, Jesus." Peter can see Thomas inside the pharmacy paying for the neck brace. He couldn't have asked for a better friend. "Lord . . . call him back to Yourself," he whispers. Thomas gets back to the car and sits in the driver's seat.*

Thomas: Here, Peter. Let me help you with it.

Peter: Thank you.

Thomas puts the neck brace around Peter's neck and adjusts it tightly enough to support his head well but soft enough that it isn't uncomfortable.

Peter: Oh, man . . . this is way better.

Thomas feels some relief.

Thomas: I am so glad. Let's go to the hospital.

They drive for a few seconds without saying anything to each other. Thomas' mission is to take Peter's mind off his pain as they drive to the hospital.

Thomas: I meant to ask you how the pumpkin carving party was.

Peter is no longer holding his head and seems more relaxed.

Peter: Oh! It was fun. I couldn't help Lourdes as much as I wanted to. Also, Sofía's mom and Lourdes argued about how to carve a pumpkin "corrcctly."

Thomas: Again?

Peter: Haha! Yes, every year is the same.

Thomas: Who won the contest for best design?

Peter doesn't say anything because Thomas already knows the answer to that question.

Thomas: Sofía.

Peter: Her designs are so good they don't even make sense anymore.

Thomas: What was her design this year?

Peter: She made a portrait of Lourdes and her husband, Richard. When Lourdes saw it, she got very emotional and began saying inappropriate things, "Lourdes style."

Thomas: Haha! Like what?

Peter: Things like, "I like it, Sofía, but unfortunately, the pumpkin will end up being like Richard, underground!"

Thomas: Oh, man! Haha! Do you think she sometimes uses that type of humor to hide how she feels about something?

Peter: . . . Maybe? I don't know.

Peter feels a question about Sofía is coming. Thomas is driving slowly. He is looking at the road but isn't at the same time. Thomas "is not" in the car but lost in his thoughts, reliving all the moments he shared with Sofía in their town. Every building—a memory; every street—a path he wished could take him back to her. Towns have feelings.

Thomas: Did you talk to Sofía?

Peter: Yes.

They don't say anything for a few seconds. Peter is cautious in choosing his next words as he wonders how to care for his friend.

Peter: She asked me how you were.

Thomas: What did you say?

Peter: I said you are asking all the right questions and missing her deeply.

Thomas: Did you say that?!

Peter: Isn't it true?

Thomas: . . . yes but . . .

Peter: Do you know that after our incident with her brother Landon, he told her to forget about you a few times? She told him: "You don't know Thomas, Landon. But I do."

Thomas feels some relief.

Thomas: Did she know about our conversations?

Peter: To answer that question, I must tell you what happened at church on Sunday.

Thomas: Oh, yeah! Did you tell everyone about the surgery?

Peter: Pastor John wanted me to sit before the congregation to tell everyone about it. But . . .

Peter's naughtiness is back, and Thomas doesn't know why.

Thomas: Oh, no . . . what did you do?

Thomas knows Peter. He can be both the most serious and silliest person simultaneously. He notices Peter trying to hold back a smile, which Thomas thinks is another horrible joke "made up in Peter's mind."

Peter: I sat down in front of everyone. The whole church was looking at me, and I was even making it seem as if I was in more pain than I was feeling. "I have something to tell you." For a moment, I felt no one was breathing because of how quiet it was, and then I said, "Thomas threw a stone in the lake, which reached the island in the middle."

Thomas: You are absolutely out of your crazy mind. You cannot be serious!

Peter starts laughing.

Peter: At first, no one believed me, but then I gave them more details, and some of them did. You are everyone's hero now.

Thomas: Oh . . . my . . .

Peter: I mean, this has been a few generations of people trying it, and, as far as I know, no one made it. Some were skeptical because we didn't film it, but then I said: "Well, you believe Jesus resurrected, and no one filmed it either."

Thomas: Peter! You didn't say that! Hahaha! Are you serious?!

Peter: I did. I know what I saw, and the apostles, too.

Thomas: Hahaha!

Peter: At that point, half the church laughed, and half the church was challenged by what I said. Pastor John covered his face and shook his head, laughing, not knowing what to do. But then I told them everything about my tumor. Everyone gathered around me and prayed the most beautiful prayer. Lourdes offered to pray for me.

Thomas: . . . everything went well?

Peter: Yes, except the way she began praying. She mimicked my British accent and said: "Lord, Peter is the English chap we didn't know we needed in our life and without whom now we cannot live." What a church we have.

Thomas: I somehow miss it.

Peter: Oh, we miss you too. But don't be hard on yourself. Your questions are important. After that, and a few laughs here and there, Lourdes said the most beautiful things about Jesus: fear, hope, and the importance of being thankful. "Lord, thank you for the blessings we have eyes to see and the millions of blessings we can't see."

Thomas keeps listening.

Peter: After the prayer, Sofía approached me and asked me how I was. She and her mom offered to help me in any way possible, and then she said to me, "Thank you for helping Thomas in a way I cannot help him right now, Peter."

Thomas tears up.

Peter: She told me she is listening to "atheist thinkers" to empathize more with you, even though she is not "particularly enjoying it." The more she listens to them, the more she thinks . . .

Thomas interrupts him.

Thomas: "Jesus is not as complicated."

Peter is pleasantly shocked.

Peter: That's exactly what she said! How did you know?!

Thomas: Just like she said about me, I also know her.

Peter cannot shake the thought of how sad he would be if Sofía and Thomas didn't end up sharing their life together.

Peter: After that, she and her mom hugged me and told me again to call them if I needed anything.

Thomas: Oh, look! Here we are.

The hospital is less crowded than expected. Fall is here, and dusk seems eager to set faster than the day before. The light from the streetlights makes it easier to see the gentle mist falling and dancing to the comings and goings of the breeze. Thomas pulls up, helps Peter get out of his car, and helps him check in at the front desk. After waiting a few minutes, a nurse calls Peter's name, and Thomas helps him get to the doctor's office. As soon as the doctor sees Peter, she recognizes him and begins asking him questions.

Doctor: Hi, Peter, is the pain getting worse?

Peter: Yes.

Doctor: I can see your surgery is scheduled for December 14. We might need to do it sooner, after all. I think the tumor is growing faster than expected.

Peter begins feeling very nervous.

Thomas: Doctor, Peter said that back in England, when this happened to him, they gave him muscle relaxers to help him live a semi-normal life until the day of the surgery. Is this something you could do for him?

Doctor: Well, I think he was accepted as a patient a few weeks before the surgery. We might need to do that for him again.

Peter jumps into the conversation, doing his best to find an alternative.

Peter: Can I try some muscle relaxers first, and if they don't help, then come to the hospital?

The doctor pulls up Peter's patient history and makes a few observations about the potential effects of some of the muscle relaxers he took the first time.

Doctor: The issue here is that your tumor seems to be growing at a faster pace this time. We could try it for a week. However, I wouldn't recommend doing much or moving much, even if you are taking these and they are working. The tumor has some calcification in it, which can cause extra damage to the nerves. If your symptoms worsen after a week, you must be admitted to the hospital immediately.

Peter: *(sighing with relief and uncertainty)* I can do that. Thank you, Doctor.

Doctor: I'll prescribe you a very potent muscle relaxer that might make you feel very drowsy, but I think that's better than feeling the pain you are feeling. It'll be ready for you in 20–30 minutes at the pharmacy we have on file for you.

Thomas: Thank you for your help.

Doctor: Peter, if you feel worse, you must come to the hospital immediately. Do you hear me?

Peter: I do.

Doctor: OK, take care of yourself.

Peter and Thomas return to their car to drive together to the pharmacy. On their way out, Thomas glances around the waiting room. Some elderly people have difficulty breathing, a middle-aged woman is sleeping on a stretcher, and several parents are waiting for the nurse to say their names while their kids are playing, oblivious to what is going on around them. Do you truly love the world, God? Because it doesn't seem so. *Near the exit, Thomas notices a crucifix hanging on one of the walls inside the receptionist's office. "What a way to answer my question . . . " he whispers in frustration.*

Peter: Did you say something?

Thomas: No, No. Peter, how are you feeling?

Peter: I am fine. There is nothing I can do about it right now. I need to let it go. The neck brace is helping me keep my neck straight and avoid some pain, so that's good.

Thomas: I am glad.

Thomas seems puzzled, lost in his thoughts.

Peter: *(joking, making his tone sound as if he was annoyed)* Ask me the question.

Thomas: What in the world? How do you know I want to ask you a question?

Peter: Thomas, what if I told you I know what you are thinking?

Thomas: You scare me sometimes.

Peter: You too.

Both laughs.

Thomas: OK, what do you think I want to ask you?

Peter: I think . . . hmm . . . I think you are confused.

Thomas: OK . . .

Thomas could not be more curious.

Peter: I think you are confused because you know I am scared, but I have hope in Jesus. So, "What do I need my faith for then?"

Thomas cannot believe what he is hearing. He stares at Peter for a few seconds with his eyes wide open.

Peter: Thomas! Eyes on the road!

Thomas: Man, how did you even know?

Peter: Because this is the mystery of all mysteries. Jesus weeping, "sweating blood," and asking the Father to see if it's possible for this "cup" to pass, probably referring to the crucifixion and the separation from the Father and the Spirit as sin was judged in Him once and for all.[126]

Thomas: And how would you be able to explain that?

Peter: Thomas, there is no way to explain or rationalize this. We can only contemplate it, observe it in awe, and wonder about it.

Thomas: Jesus knew he was going to be with the Father soon after His death, yet He seemed to have suffered tremendously before it, even though He was the one who planned all of this from the very beginning.

Peter: Again, you can ask questions and wonder, but the only answer you'll get will be contemplation. This is the will of God we are talking about. Why did it have to happen this way? Why did God choose to suffer if He could have forgiven us in any other way?

Thomas: And what about the fear of Jesus? He was God!

Peter: He was also human, and humans suffer and feel fear. I have no easy explanation for this mystery; I can only stand in awe of it with you. For all of eternity, the Son had never known displeasure or separation from the Father. Yet, to pay for our sin, He had to experience both—bearing God's full wrath upon sin. Believing this is not the same as understanding it. It's a truth beyond my

---

[126] Matthew 26:38: He told them, "My soul is crushed with grief to the point of death. Stay here and keep watch with me."

imagination. But Scripture is meditative literature. It invites us into a state of wonder, and that wonder is its own kind of answer. Let's see. For example, have you ever dealt with resentment? Have you ever felt the heavy burden of wanting to forgive a person while your whole being is telling you not to?

Thomas: Yes.

Peter: How did that make you feel?

Thomas: It debilitates you physically and emotionally.

Peter: That's a good word. It does debilitate you. Now, imagine bearing all the resentment that has ever existed on Earth . . . See? I cannot explain it; the only thing I can do is wonder, contemplate, meditate on it, etc.

Thomas: So, are you saying there are no answers to some questions?

Peter: Oh, that's exactly right, both theologically and physically. Theologically, only God knows everything He has done from beginning to end,[127] and physically, we can only describe the appearance of things and their behavior, but not what those things intrinsically are. We are made to wonder.

Thomas: So, how can I make sense of your fear of death and your belief in eternal life?

Peter: You won't be able to "make sense" of it; you can only rest in the paradox it presents.

Thomas: What do you mean?

---

[127] Ecclesiastes 3:11.

Peter: God can do anything He wants, but He chose to sacrifice Himself for His creation; Jesus is both God and man; you can be joyful through suffering; you can be afraid yet full of hope, etc. These paradoxes are true not because they make sense in a "logical" way, but they are true in the sense that you can find rest in them if you solely focus on experiencing them. Thomas, when we say that something makes sense what do you think we mean?

Thomas: We see correlation, dependency, or a cause-and-effect principle that helps us understand the process a being or a thing undergoes. Also, if that process can be replicated and we get the same outcome each time, that's even better. We can make sense of something if we follow this principle.

Peter: I love that. Now, you know me so well; what would I say to that?

Thomas: That correlation, dependency, cause-and-effect are relationships of physical things for which we have no explanation for their existence. So, beyond their functionality, we cannot make sense of anything we think we claim to understand. Science describes things that exist but doesn't explain why things exist at all.

Peter: You know me too well. Now, if this is the case for the physical and tangible world, how could I expect, as a follower of Jesus, to "make sense" in a mathematical way of the most profound truths of existence? I cannot. The only thing I can do is to be in awe and contemplate God's will as it unfolds . . . and worship.

Thomas: OK, so your fear of death and your hope for eternal life don't make sense. Is that what you are saying?

Peter: Exactly. From the world's perspective, it doesn't make sense at all. As a follower of Jesus, I live in a world that hurts while I hope for the promised world that won't. I aim to find rest in the paradox, a peace where logic cannot take me.

Thomas: Would it be fair for me to assume that your faith is not as strong as you think it is because you still are afraid of death?

Peter: That's fair. It is possible that my faith is not mature enough at this point. However, I do know I have reached maturity in Jesus because even though I am afraid of the process of dying, and I don't want to go through it, I am not going to fight it if it's God's will for me. See? Another paradox: I don't want to die, but then I don't mind it if it could bring some good and glorify God in ways I cannot understand. That's Jesus' prayer in the garden of Gethsemane all over again. Thomas, once I know what being alive *feels* like, the thought of ceasing to exist on this earth terrifies me. If Jesus is telling the truth, then there is no reason for me to fear death anymore, but only the process of dying.

Thomas: Thank you for being sincere about that.

Peter: If I follow Jesus, which means I obey him, and He bled Himself out on the cross because of His love for us, I cannot expect my life to be perfect even if I am doing the right thing.

Thomas: Let me ask you about something. Are you suggesting we suspend our rational judgment and logical thinking to reach truth?

Peter: No, no. Our rational judgment and logical thinking, as extraordinary as they are, can only take us so far. Because of our rational judgment and logical thinking, we can reach places like trust or faith because they point to something beyond themselves.

Making analogies is difficult sometimes, but, let me try one . . . Do you love Sofía?

Thomas: Yes, I do.

Peter: You can come to know that you love her; that's rational. However, everything that involves loving her doesn't "make sense" as something that you *know*, but only as you experience it and risk your love for her by the things you *do*. "How should I love her? How much should I love her? Can I love her more?" These questions cannot be rationalized; they can only be put into practice through experience. So, rationally, I know I am afraid of death, but my hope for life brings me a peace that, from a rational point of view, will never make sense. Followers of Jesus live in a continuous paradox, and the sooner we stop trying to understand it but *rest* in it, the faster we experience things the world deems as "irrational," such as joy through suffering; peace through uncertainty; pride in our weaknesses; loving our enemies; etc. And all of it is possible because of Jesus.

Thomas: Man, I'm not sure I understand what you mean.

Peter: Thomas, I might be afraid of the process of dying, but I am not afraid of showing to the world my weaknesses, my lack of knowledge, even my sins, if all of it helps me point them to Jesus. Remember what Paul said: "Jewish people are always asking for proofs from God. Non-Jewish people are always looking for so-called 'wisdom.' But we always proclaim Christ, the one who was nailed to the cross! This is embarrassing to Jews and nonsense to people who are not Jews."[128]

---

[128] 1 Corinthians 1:22-24.

Thomas: So, if the world thinks you are foolish, that doesn't bother you?

Peter: Even if someone thinks I am speaking foolishly, my desire is to show how sacrificial love can reveal Jesus without using words.

They both remain quiet for a while. After a few turns, they find themselves at the pharmacy. Thomas pulls up in the parking lot. Peter tries to reach for his wallet, but Thomas stops it.

Thomas: I got it. I'll get your medicine and bottled water. Wait for me in the car.

Peter: Thank you, Thomas. Thank you for wanting to help me the way you do, even though it cannot be "rationalized."

Thomas laughs and rolls his eyes while heading to the pharmacy. Peter stays in the car laughing with himself too. His laughs bring him many memories, especially one he cannot wait to share with Thomas. Thomas returns to the car and gives Peter his medicine and bottled water. Thomas sees Peter is still laughing, which makes him laugh too.

Thomas: What's so funny?

When Thomas asks him, his question makes Peter laugh even more.

Thomas: Peter, what is it?

Thomas cannot stop laughing, even though he doesn't know what he is laughing about. In reality, it doesn't matter. Thomas loves seeing Peter having such a good time, even if it comes and goes quickly, as it usually happens with good moments in life.

Peter: After talking about things that make sense or don't, rationality and whatnot, it came to me what Lourdes' mom told her when she was a child.

Thomas: Lourdes' mom? She was from Spain, wasn't she? I cannot wait to hear this . . .

Peter: Yes. Do you know the verse, "Fear of the Lord is the beginning of wisdom"?

Thomas: Yes, another conversation right there.

Peter: Yes, and I'd love to have it. Anyway. Lourdes told me that when her mom used to get frustrated with anyone, she would quote the verse with a twist: "A slap in your face is the beginning of wisdom."

Peter tries to mimic Lourdes' mannerisms.

Peter: "One slap in your face, and you are set."

Peter and Thomas cannot stop laughing, and it goes on for minutes. There are no questions, pain, surgery, or fear for a moment—just a simple and silly laugh between two friends. After a few minutes, they both try to breathe and relax from all the laughing.

Thomas: *(in a somber tone)* Peter, so why don't you take off your neck brace so I can slap you in the face, and we take care of the tumor right now?

At this point, both are laughing out of control. Peter feels well enough to be dropped off at The Shire *and drives his car back home. What a great way to finish a day driven primarily by pain, suffering, and uncertainty.*

Thursday, November 9

Thomas is sitting at their favorite table, waiting for Peter to arrive. Lourdes seems uneasily calm today. Truman is "chinning" on his bed. There are a couple of customers inside the coffee shop. It is cold, very cold. However, the sun has been out all day today, making the cold feel crisp and not as bad. Perhaps it is a good day to go on the trail again? Thomas sees Peter pulling up in the parking lot. He seems to be moving better. The muscle relaxers may be helping after all. Peter exits his car and walks slowly but steadily toward the coffee shop. OK, he is feeling better. *Thomas says in relief. Peter opens the door and looks excited to get something out of his pocket.*

Peter: Hey, Truman!

Truman jumps out of bed and runs toward Peter as if he hasn't seen him in years.

Lourdes: So, this is what it is, uh? Truman goes first now?

Peter: Yes! Look, Truman, I brought you a pack of treats from the store!

Truman begins running in circles, barking in excitement.

Lourdes: And not only that, but you bring stuff for him too?!

Thomas joins "the party."

Thomas: That's true, Lourdes! Peter never brings anything to you.

Peter: Guys! Come on!

Thomas: And he told me that he doesn't like your coffee anymore.

Lourdes: You really know how to hit where it hurts.

Peter keeps petting Truman.

Peter: Come on, Lourdes, you know Thomas is just joking.

Lourdes goes around the counter and hugs Peter.

Lourdes: How are you feeling?

It takes Peter a few seconds to answer her.

Peter: *(doubtful but hopeful)* I am feeling . . . better. The muscle relaxers are helping for now.

Lourdes leans over to Peter's ear.

Lourdes: *(changing her tone to make it sound like a joke)* I might need to get some of those myself . . .

Both Peter and Lourdes laugh.

Peter: Can I open the treats for Truman?

Lourdes: Go ahead, but make him work for them.

Peter makes Truman sit, lay down, go through his legs, etc. He quickly runs out of treats.

Peter: That's it, Truman!

Truman barks at Peter once and goes back to his bed.

Thomas: Lourdes, how's the training going?

Lourdes: Was I supposed to be training him?

Thomas: No, I meant Truman's training of you.

Lourdes lifts one of her feet and slowly removes one of her shoes.

Peter: No, no, Lourdes! Don't throw him your shoe!

Lourdes points at Thomas with her shoe, waving it back and forth to let him know what'll happen if he says something like that again. Lourdes is just having fun though.

Peter: Guys, sometimes I think you wouldn't survive each other for that long if I weren't here.

Peter meant it as a joke, but Lourdes and Thomas looked at each other with a hint of sadness because it reminded them of Peter's surgery. Lourdes shakes the feeling off and gets back to her coffee-making.

Lourdes: I'll bring you both your coffees in a second.

Peter: Thank you, Lourdes.

Thomas gets up and hugs Peter, being conscious of his pain. Thomas doesn't say anything.

Peter: It's good to see you too, Thomas.

They both sit down.

Thomas: So, you are feeling better?

Peter: Yes. It's night and day. I still need to be conscious of how I move my neck and shoulders, but I am not in as much pain as last week.

Thomas: Are you having symptoms from the muscle relaxers?

Peter: Uh . . . the first few days, I did feel very drowsy. But trust me; I would rather feel drowsy than the sharp and paralyzing pain I feel when the tumor presses my nerves.

Thomas: I understand.

Peter: What about you?

Thomas: I am fine. I have been listening to this podcast about world religions and arguments for the existence of God.

Peter: Oh, interesting. What are you learning?

Thomas: Ummm . . .

Thomas suddenly looks out the window. He seems distracted, even a bit disappointed...

Peter: Thomas, what's going on?

Peter leans forward to look out the window. Someone is about to enter the coffee shop. It's Karl, a Christian friend from church. Thomas doesn't have a good relationship with him for two reasons. One, he also liked Sofía—or maybe he still does—but Sofía never liked him in a dating kind of way; and two, he doesn't have the best skills to engage in conversation, let alone with anything concerning the big questions in life.

Thomas: *(whispering nervously)* Oh man, did you invite him to come?

Peter: No, I didn't. He might be here to grab some coffee and will be on his way.

Thomas: Sorry that I am reacting this way. It's just hard to be around him sometimes.

Peter: Tell me! I feel the same when I am with you.

Thomas smirks and leans over to hit Peter playfully but soon realizes Peter is in pain.

Peter: Eh! Eh! Are you mental?

Peter points at his neck without believing what Thomas is about to do.

Thomas: Oh yeah! Yeah! I'm sorry, man. After the surgery is over and you feel better, though, get ready . . .

Peter laughs, and Thomas sits back in his chair, waiting for the door to open.

Thomas: Here we go . . .

Karl: Hi, Lourdes, may I have a coffee to go?

Karl looks around, sees Thomas and Peter, waves at them, and they wave back at him.

Karl: Hey, Thomas, it's good to see you. It's been a while since I last saw you at church. Is everything all right?

Thomas: Yeah, I have been busy, so that's it.

Hopefully, busy just means 'busy' for Karl, *Thomas says to himself.*

Karl: I heard Sofía broke the engagement with you. I am sorry to hear that.

Thomas' demeanor changes and gets more defensive.

Thomas: Are you?

You can feel the tension already. Peter doesn't know what to say.

Karl: Thomas, relax, man, the past is the past. I thought we had moved on from that.

Thomas: I don't know, Karl. You have been trying hard to make my relationship with Sofía harder than it should have been.

Karl: How, exactly?

Thomas: The last thing I heard you say to someone at church was that Sofía should be careful with me because the many questions I ask about God might be a sign of not being a true believer or something like that. Is that true?

Peter feels he has to intervene.

Peter: Hey guys, hey . . . Let's start over. Karl, what are you doing here?

Karl still feels annoyed by Thomas' comments and tries his best to answer Peter's question.

Karl: Well, I was trying to say hi and be polite, but now I wonder if all this anger is why Thomas is not at church anymore.

Thomas sighs in frustration.

Thomas: You know what, man? Why don't you grab a chair and sit with us, and we say everything we have to say to each other once and for all?

Peter: Thomas, I don't think this is a good idea, mate.

Karl: I don't know if I want to do this.

Thomas: But you do because of everything you say about me behind my back. Why don't we talk as civilized people and see if the rumors are true or not? We have been playing this game for too long.

Karl: *(defensive)* I wouldn't mind, but what about Peter? Does he need to hear all of this?

Thomas: Oh yeah, no worries about him. In fact, remember what Jesus said about having problems with a "brother"? It is good that Peter is here.[129]

---

[129] Matthew 18:15–16: If another believer sins against you, go privately and point out the offense. If the other person listens and confesses it, you have won that person back. But if you are unsuccessful, take one or two others with you and go back again, so that everything you say may be confirmed by two or three witnesses.

Peter: I wonder if one day we'll have just a pleasant and relaxing conversation about "the big questions" in one of our meetings, Thomas.

Karl: Oh . . . is that why you meet?

Peter realizes that by mentioning "the big questions," he indirectly implies that Thomas keeps asking questions and doubting his faith.

Peter: Yep.

Karl: Well, then, I was right. You keep asking questions that are moving you away from the truth of God, and that's why you are not at church.

Thomas tries to contain himself.

Thomas: Karl, I ask questions because I want to find answers, answers I am humble enough to recognize I don't have.

Karl: See? That's your problem.

Thomas: Enlighten me.

Karl: You are not asking questions because you are curious; you are asking questions because you are suppressing the truth of God.[130]

Peter: Wait, wait, wait . . . wait a second, Karl. If someone is suppressing the truth of God, would that person keep asking honest questions with an inner desire to really know if God exists? Because that's Thomas's case.

---

[130] Romans 1:18: God's punishment is being revealed from heaven against all sin and ungodliness of people who use sin to hide the truth.

Karl: When you question God's authority and deviate from a plain reading of Scripture, you risk falling into idolatry and believing man's knowledge and questions can pose real challenges to the truth of Scripture.

Thomas: So, my questions are the result of sin?

Karl: I believe so.

Thomas covers his face with his hands and sighs deeply in frustration.

Peter: I need to understand what you mean, Karl. A follower of Jesus cannot ask questions?

Karl is feeling uptight and insecure, which makes him feel everyone is his enemy when that is not the case. This is not Karl's first time giving this vibe to people around him.

Karl: God's authority should never be questioned; that's a sign of the rebellion of our hearts. Do you think we should question God's authority, Peter?

Peter: Listen to the way you asked me that question, Karl. "Do you think we should question God's authority, Peter?" You are cornering me into giving you the "right" answer according to your bias. That's not the way to ask a question.

Karl: OK . . . *(Karl smirks and rolls his eyes)* How should I ask you a question, then?

Peter: At least in a way that you are not assuming anything about me, and you give me some time to think about my answer. Then, you can say anything about it.

Karl: See? See? This has always bothered me about you two. You always talk about "the big questions," "the big questions" . . .

Karl says in a mocking tone, making quotation signs with his hand.

Karl: But all the big questions have already been answered in Scripture. When you must ask "big questions," your faith is not strong enough. But answer my question about God's authority, Peter. I am not letting you off the hook with it.

Peter: God's authority cannot be understood without considering how much He loves us. Jesus told us to refer to God as Father.[131] God's authority is not the authority of a dictator obsessed with right belief, but the authority of a father whose son died for me and who is willing to guide me through my errors to know the right way of living and loving others because of Jesus. It's an entirely different way to see it. I am not questioning His authority if I ask questions to try to understand it.

Karl: It sounds to me like you are just watering down the truths of Scripture because you are afraid of how they will sound to those who don't believe.

Peter: It sounds to me like you are worshipping your own understanding of theology, which has become your idol. Your beliefs about Scripture, not Scripture itself, have become the filter through which you judge people around you and their intrinsic value as people.

At this point, Thomas feels like he is watching a football match, and his favorite team is scoring a goal.

---

[131] Matthew 6:9: Pray like this: "Our Father in heaven, may your name be kep holy."

Thomas: Ouch!

Peter: I don't want to play games like this with you, Karl. But if you come to this conversation the way you are coming at us right now, I also need to be sincere and honest about why I think you tend to assume things about other people and are usually wrong about them. Am I wrong about that?

Karl: Yes, you are.

Peter: Of course, I am.

Karl: This is not about me but about the truth of Scripture. My opinion doesn't matter; I'm just trying to speak truth into people's lives.

Thomas: You speak it, but do you obey it?[132]

Karl: *(scoffing)* Well, I am the one who is at church, Thomas, am I not?

Thomas: Karl, people supposedly saw Jesus resurrected right before them, and some doubted.[133]So, don't tell me that attending church fully demonstrates that someone obeys Jesus. For example, you go to church, but apparently, you speak poorly of me behind my back. So, does "going to church" mean anything to you? Because, as far as I know, "you can identify people by their actions."[134]

Karl: I regretted the times I said stuff about you behind your back, but now, at least, I realize I wasn't wrong about it.

Peter: Karl, seriously?

---

[132] John 15:14: You are my friends if you do what I command.

[133] Matthew 28:17.

[134] Matthew 7:20.

Karl: I am just saying . . . You both meet here trying to look sophisticated with your arguments and questions, but the truth of Scripture is clear. I am worried about you too, Peter.

Peter: Oh, Karl, you are not alone, trust me. I worry about myself all the time; that's why I follow and obey Jesus instead of worshipping a god called "theology."

Karl: You seriously are not saying that theology is wrong, right?

Peter: No. You are *assuming* that I am. What I *am* saying is that we need to be careful to worship the God of theology, not the theology of God. Theology is not God, but it is our attempts to better understand Him. God desires that theology leads us to repentance, a change of heart, and to love others the way Jesus loved us.

Thomas: This is another way to put it: sometimes you come across as worshiping your own understanding of theology in a similar way the Pharisees worshipped the law.

Peter: Oh, man . . .

Peter and Thomas are obliterating Karl.

Karl: Well, you shouldn't have any opinion about "my theology" being the unbeliever you demonstrate you are by your questions.

Thomas: Could you, for once, ask me a question without assuming something about me?

Karl: Some things are evident because "you can recognize them by what they produce." Isn't that true, Thomas? Look, guys. You are the ones who are coming at me relentlessly, so don't look at me like that. I have the right to defend myself too. I would be disappointed in any Christian friend who wouldn't talk to me about the truth the way Thomas needs to hear it. I care for you, Thomas, and I don't want your soul to be tormented in Hell for the rest of eternity. I have heard you talk about Christianity before, Peter. You make Christianity sound palatable because you are afraid of people's reactions to the truths of God in Scripture.

Thomas: Man, you and I have way different opinions about what the word "care" actually means.

Peter: OK. What if I told you I have evidence to suggest that you are not a Christian at all?

Thomas notices Karl has tapped into Peter's rebellious side—the same side Landon stirred a few weeks earlier.

Karl: OK, let me hear your "evidence."

Karl makes the quotation gesture once more.

Peter: In Galatians 5:22–23, Paul said: "…the Spirit produces: love; joy; peace; patience; kindness; goodness; faithfulness; gentleness; and self-control." When I arrived at our church, you had been a Christian for a while. Therefore, the Spirit of the living God has supposedly been in your heart for a few years. Why, then, is it so hard to see "the fruit of the Spirit" in your life?

Thomas: Ouch!

Karl: I think you are just a young Christian who doesn't understand the urgency of Scripture and the seriousness of God's wrath yet.

Thomas: *(out of patience)* Man, again, instead of just assuming things about us, why don't you ask us a question and give us a chance to answer it ourselves?

Karl: Look, I am not here to give you my opinion, but God's opinion. You can take it or leave it; that's not my responsibility.

Thomas: You know what? I don't think this conversation is going to go anywhere.

Peter: Agreed. Karl, if the truth you believe in is not communicated as you think it should, then it is not "the truth." It gives me the impression that you are just slightly arrogant about it. I'm sorry that I have to say it this way. Thomas might be doubting his faith, but even the apostles begged Jesus: "Show us how to increase our faith."[135] We cannot become judges of anyone's relationship with God, let alone of people who, like Thomas, are not denying that God exists, but are just asking questions about Him.

Thomas: In fact, what is worse? To doubt about God and sin—that's me according to you—or to claim to believe in God and keep sinning—that's you according to me?

Peter: Hat-trick.

Karl: *(furious)* You know what? I am going to tell Pastor John about you, Peter. I am sorry that you are going through all of this with your tumor. But all this nonsense makes me doubt whether you should even be serving in our church anymore.

Peter: Karl, since I have been part of our church, you have had problems with three staff members and several people in our congregation. You are an engineer, aren't you? Why is it so hard to apply the simple mathematical rule of the "common denominator" to all those situations to see who the real problem is?

---

[135] Luke 17:5.

Thomas: Man!

Karl: I have had enough of this crap. By the way, I am glad Sofía broke the engagement with you. You don't deserve her; I have been right about it all along.

Thomas: There it is! Now it's time for you to go, Karl.

Thomas makes a fist and clenches his teeth, avoiding looking at him.

Karl: I wish I didn't have to see you anymore.

Karl gets up and leaves the coffee shop, forgetting the coffee Lourdes was preparing for him. Peter and Thomas don't say anything to each other for a while as they see Karl getting into his car and leaving the parking lot. At this point, there wasn't anyone else in the coffee shop. Lourdes could hear everything they said when they all began raising their voices. As soon as Karl leaves, Lourdes goes around the counter, grabs a chair, and sits at Peter's and Thomas' table.

Lourdes: That wasn't OK . . .

Peter: *(confused)* What wasn't, OK?

Lourdes: The way you both treated Karl.

Thomas: Seriously, Lourdes? The way we treat him? He came at us the way he always does with everyone—with arrogance, assuming untrue things about us, and acting like the world revolves around him. At what point should a person like that be put in his place?

Lourdes: *Pero qué dices*! You have no idea what you are talking about. Everyone knows Karl is a difficult person; there is no denying that. But where would someone like him go if it weren't for our church? Or who would have the patience to love him? He has a lot of turmoil; as a church, we are supposed to be a family. God wants our church family to love on Karl in a way that perhaps no one would out there. Who are we to deny God's love to a person? Isn't God patient with all our shortcomings every day? That wasn't ok!

The Holy Spirit is profoundly convicting Peter through Lourdes' words. He and Thomas messed up. Thomas, on the other hand, vehemently disagrees with her.

Lourdes: *(with a mom tone)* Look, boys, even if everything you said to him was "true" or "right," you are the ones who are aware of what's going on with him, and he isn't. So, shouldn't you be the ones that behave according to that knowledge instead of becoming what you criticize about him and know is not right?

Thomas: Yeah, but what about what he has been saying about me and Sofía for years?

Lourdes: Thomas, who is the judge? You or God?[136]

Thomas gets furious suddenly at hearing about God again. He begins yelling.

Thomas: And who cares about God if God is not defending the people I love?! Should I let Karl ruin my reputation and Sofía's and do nothing about it?! Should we let him go on his way whenever he hurts people around him? This is ridiculous!

Lourdes raises her tone as well. Truman begins barking.

Lourdes: Thomas, you don't stop hate with more hate; you stop it by doing exactly the opposite of what hate wants—you love! There

---

[136] James 4:12: God alone, who gave the law, is the Judge. He alone has the power to save or to destroy. So what right do you have to judge your neighbor?

is no other way to stop it! That's what Jesus came to tell us, and that's why it's so difficult to follow Him! We are supposed to do something the world would never do—love our enemies![137]

As Thomas listens to Lourdes, he begins tearing up and getting all emotional and frustrated.

Thomas: *(embittered)* I am sick of all of this! I lost Sofía, I might lose Peter, and then I need to let someone like Karl, who isn't aware of how much pain he causes everywhere he goes, get away with this, thinking he was right all along when he isn't? SOMEONE LIKE KARL WHO DOESN'T CARE ABOUT ANYONE'S FEELINGS?! FORGET YOU!

Truman keeps barking.

Lourdes: Truman! Go to your bed!

Truman lowers his ears and returns to bed, sharing a timid bark as if complaining.

Peter: Hey, hey, hey . . . Thomas, don't let the moment's anger make you believe or say untrue things about yourself and others. Calm down. Lourdes is right. Karl has some work to do, but that shouldn't change how we behave around him.

Lourdes: Thomas, Sofía knows you and won't believe anything Karl says because she knows of all the turmoil and issues in his life. Besides, Pastor John is aware of it. This is one of the subtlest ways the devil tempts us: you build so much resentment toward a person that you slowly end up becoming the person you hate.

Thomas cannot take it.

---

[137] Matthew 5:43–45.

Thomas: Lourdes, stop with the God stuff once and for all! I need a break from this! I cannot take this right now. I need to leave this place. What a bunch of . . . ugh!

Thomas storms out of the coffee shop, gets in his car, and leaves. Lourdes and Peter stay inside the coffee shop, not knowing what to say to each other. Peter is leaning on this table, covering his face, hopeless.

Peter: Lourdes, come on. You are right about how we handled it with Karl. However, it would help if you recognized that he is prompt to cause situations like this everywhere he goes. At what point should we set some boundaries for him?

Lourdes is still agitated because of what just happened.

Lourdes: Karl is a difficult person, but I believe the Spirit and the church are keeping him from being even worse. A person experiencing the turmoil he experiences inside, without having somewhere or someone to go to, could even become a dangerous person to himself and others. The church is a place for people like Karl. It doesn't surprise me that the church is a mess sometimes because *we are* the church, and we are a mess, even though we have been forgiven.

Peter: What type of turmoil are you talking about?

Lourdes: I don't know if I should tell you this.

Peter: No worries, you don't have to.

Lourdes leans over to Peter to whisper to him even though no one is at the coffee shop.

Lourdes: Karl doesn't know how to love people because he never experienced love himself.

Peter: Really? What do you mean?

Lourdes: His mother abandoned him and his father when he was a toddler, and his father has always been very distant toward him. In one of our retreats, he told Pastor John, me, and other adults that he was afraid other people would abandon him too. All the "theology talk" is just like a ribcage protecting a terrified heart. When Sofía said no to him years ago, he didn't hear, "I don't like you that way, sorry." He thought he was being abandoned once more, but this time, Sofía kept being part of his daily life, so he irrationally held onto the hope of being with her the same way he had hoped to be with his mom again all his life. He just cannot let it go. Theology and "right belief," as you said to him, are good things, but for him, they have become the ultimate thing because they are the only things he feels would never abandon him: his knowledge about God. He doesn't understand what having a "relationship" with God means, how to put into practice all the theology that is stuck in his brain, and the reason is simple: he doesn't know how to love because he has never been loved the way we all are supposed to be loved.

Peter: That's why you and Pastor John always seem so patient and understanding with him even though he causes so many struggles at church.

Lourdes: If not us, Peter . . . if not us, who will love him? Peter . . . "but God showed his great love for us by sending Christ to die for us while we were still sinners."[138] Who are we to restrain the love God showed us first?

Peter: *(sigh)* I have nothing else to say. I am sorry.

Lourdes: But please understand the word *love* here. Loving Karl doesn't mean we always need to tolerate everything he does in light of how much trouble he causes. Love entails discipline and truth, and both those things hurt when applied. He needs to be challenged as well, and he needs to know that people have the right to move away from him if they lack the patience he requires sometimes, but without wishing anything bad happens to him because of it.

Some people pull up in the parking lot, and Lourdes returns to the counter to start the coffee machine again.

Lourdes: Peter, is Thomas going to be OK?

Peter: I hope so. He is going through a lot. It's just too much to take in such a short time. I'll check on him in a few days. He needs his time away from me too.

Lourdes: Well, you let me know if you both need anything.

Peter looks outside the window as he gets ready to leave. An old couple strolls toward the coffee shop. The old man is trying to be goofy and make his wife laugh. Peter wonders about the number of times this man might have told the same joke to his wife and the number of times his wife might have heard the same joke over the years. That wife's love is sacrificial love. *Peter's joke makes him chuckle.* Man, would I ever marry? *The thought and uncertainty of his situation make his heart sink to the floor. Peter says "goodbye" to Lourdes and*

---

[138] Romans 5:8

pets Truman once more, then rushes to the door to hold it so the old couple can enter. The old woman is actually laughing.

Old woman: Oh, thank you, young man.

Peter: You're welcome.

He might be funny after all. *Peter lets the door go and walks toward his car, wondering if it's a good idea to call Thomas. He remembers his journey from atheism to Christianity as if it had happened yesterday. Sometimes, you must let people, especially those you love the most, struggle and mourn alone for a while. Those are the moments God uses to grow people the most if they see those same moments as an opportunity to do so. Lourdes was right, "For the Lord disciplines those he loves, and he punishes each one he accepts as his child."*[139] *Perhaps it's best to leave him alone for a few days and let him reach out if he wants to. Concerning Karl, Peter decides to text him and tell him how sorry he feels and how much he would like to meet with him to discuss what happened. Karl answers back, saying he is "very disappointed," but, weirdly enough, Karl's attitude doesn't irritate Peter anymore. Peter knows he desperately needs love, and all his frustrations and attitudes are just a terrified heart crying out for someone to care for him. Perhaps this is what Lourdes meant, if the world knew this about him, what would it do with that information, would they use it to take advantage of him? Peter, however, knows what he will do with him from now on, to love him more.*

---

[139] Hebrews 12:6: For the Lord disciplines those he loves, and he punishes each one he accepts as his child.

Thursday, November 16

It's been a week since Peter last saw Thomas at The Shire. *He didn't leave in a good way, and Peter decided to give him space to wrestle with his questions and feelings on his own. In fact, he showed some frustration toward God when answering Lourdes concerning Karl. However, it's hard not to check on a person you love. But we often unconsciously hurt others while trying to help them. One word, one gesture, an attitude, a specific tone in a specific context, unsaid expectations . . . Hurt is a potential reality in any relationship. Peter always looks forward to spending time with Thomas at* The Shire, *so he decides to go there and sit at their usual table alone for a while, hoping he will show up to talk. It's starting to get cold outside, even for "an English chap." Peter is wearing a winter hat, a scarf, and a coat his mom bought him the last time he visited with them. Peter's mom, Mary, wasn't very expressive with her words, but she clearly showed how much she adored him by taking care of him in all the practical and tangible ways mothers take care of their children. Peter's coat reminds him that, for his mom, he will always be "little Peter." "It doesn't matter if it's cold or not; you get your coat no matter what!" It wasn't enjoyable for Peter to carry all the coats his mom had bought him everywhere throughout the years! Today, however, his coat has become a simple and profound reminder of the most essential thing in this life: love. Peter arrives at* The Shire *and is welcomed by Truman, but not in the usual Truman way.*

Peter: Truman! Oh, no! What happened? Why are you limping?

Lourdes is attending to other clients, so she hasn't even seen Peter get there yet. Truman leans on Peter, trying to lick his face as if he isn't in pain at all. Peter wonders if there is anything a dog cannot teach humans about "the big questions" in life. After all, they at least get what faithful, forgiving, and constant love really is, no matter the circumstances. The Shire *is full of people, and no tables are open at the moment. Peter gets in line to order some coffee and sends Truman back to bed, but not before cuddling with him again.* I wonder why he is limping? *He says to himself. It takes some time for Lourdes to be freed up, but just as he is going to say hi . . .*

Jim: Peter!

Peter turns around and doesn't realize Jim is sitting at one of the tables.

Peter: Hi, Jim! What are you doing here?

Jim: I came to visit with my mom for a couple of days. Would you like to join me?

Peter: Sure! Could you give me a second while I order?

As soon as he turns around, Lourdes looks at him with her arms crossed.

Lourdes: *(imitating Peter's accent) I hope you order today and not tomorrow, mate.*

Peter laughs.

Peter: *(imitating Lourdes' American/Spanish accent)* Your British accent is sounding better and better!

Lourdes laughs. Peter leans over to whisper something to her.

Peter: Actually, Lourdes, I'll get two chocolate muffins too. I know Jim loves them but does everything he can to avoid them. Haha! By the way, what's wrong with Truman? Why is he limping?

Lourdes: He is limping because he wishes to be young but is not; he still acts as if he is young. This dog's energy is crazy; you should see him jumping to get his frisbee. I think he landed weird and got hurt.

Peter: Oh, poor boy. Did you take him to the vet?

Lourdes: I am waiting to see if it goes away on its own. If not, I'll take him in a few days. I'll bring you your coffee and the muffins in a few minutes.

Peter walks over to Jim's table and sits across from him.

Jim: Hey, where is your friend Thomas? Didn't you guys meet every Thursday to talk about the big questions? I came to see if I could join you!

Peter: Well, I think Thomas needs a break from this right now.

Jim: Huh . . . Is he OK?

Peter: Well, it's a long story. He is going through a lot. I haven't seen him for a week, but it's good for him to be away from people for a few days, even from me.

Jim: If you don't mind me asking, does it have anything to do with his questions about Christianity?

Peter: Unfortunately, it has a lot to do with it. But I prefer to let the topic rest since Thomas is not here. Is that OK?

Jim: For sure. The journey from one worldview to another can be a painful one. What about you, Peter? What's your story? I shared mine with you guys, but I never heard either of yours. Would you mind if I asked you a few questions?

Peter: No, not at all. Ask away.

Jim: How did you become a Christian from atheism?

Peter: You are quite right. It was intense for me too. Many things changed. My family and friends struggled because following Jesus made me behave in ways that didn't match their expectations of me. The hardest part was what happened with some of my friends, who, unfortunately, moved away from me because of my beliefs.

Jim: What about your family?

Peter: Some members of my extended family were more in the, "I don't understand what's going on, so let's not talk about it, camp." Others didn't want to be around me anymore. However, my parents have been supportive in their way my whole life. They are not Christians, either.

Jim: Do you have any siblings?

Peter: No, unfortunately. My mom had one miscarriage before having me, and it was devastating for her. So, I guess I do have a brother or a sister, but I don't know them yet.

Jim: Yet?

Peter: I hope I can meet them in Heaven.

Jim: Here we go!

Both laugh.

Jim: I think it's precious to believe you would meet a sibling one day in the afterlife. But that's just a thought, not a thing you know.

Peter: That's why I said, "I hope" instead of "I know."

Jim: I get that. But sometimes Christians use "hoping" and "knowing" as synonyms when they shouldn't.

Peter: Jim, please, don't tell me you believe "hope" is a matter of blind faith. Do you think that?

Jim: I am sorry to disappoint you. But yes, I do.

Peter: Well, I don't hope in a vacuum, but I hope because I have reasons to hope.

Jim: What reasons are those?

Peter: Well, existence, matter, beauty, consciousness, love, life, Jesus, God, Scripture, relationships . . .

Jim: Still, you don't "know" you'll meet your sibling one day in Heaven.

Peter: I don't "know" it; I hope because I have reasons to hope. Isn't it true that you behave according to some prior knowledge and make predictions about what the outcome will be? Isn't that hope?

Jim: Yes, but I make predictions of things that exist and are real, not imaginary things.

Peter: Oh, Jim! But a human being is not imaginary, they exist, siblings exist, hope exists, life exists, those things are real too.

Jim: But you assume there is an afterlife without knowing it.

Peter: I assume there is an afterlife because I have reasons to believe so, mainly because of Jesus and His resurrection. Would it be fair to say that you assume God doesn't exist without having actual evidence to support your conclusion?

Jim: Peter, I don't believe unicorns exist for obvious reasons. For example, we have never seen one. The same is true with gnomes or bigfoot. Why would God be different?

Peter: Well, for starters, Christianity is rooted in history: Jesus, His death on the cross, His empty tomb, His resurrection, His appearances, the way the church began against all odds, billions of people on earth who profess the faith, lives are changed for good every day, our moral basis is founded on Judeo-Christian values, etc. I don't think comparing God with unicorns or Bigfoot is fair, do you?

Jim: I see what you mean. Then, we could say God is the "most important unicorn" ever.

Peter: Haha! Then, how do you feel about a unicorn being the basis for all your moral, societal, and value assumptions? I am sure it must be weird!

Jim laughs.

Jim: Whew! We went from zero to one hundred in less than a minute!

Peter: I know! Haha! Sorry about that!

Jim: No, please, don't be. I wish I had someone like you to talk about these things without having to pretend anything but just saying what I think about everything. Let's go back to your story.

Peter: Haha! OK.

Jim: At one point did you feel ready to make the leap of faith?

Peter: With faith you mean the things we don't see but "hope" they are there because of the things we do see?

Jim: Not at all! But go ahead.

Both laugh.

Peter: The question that began everything for me was, why is there something rather than nothing?

Jim: Oh, yeah, that's a biggie. Now, we do know the answer to that question.

Peter: Really?

Jim: Absolutely. The answer is, "we don't know."

Peter: Oh! Haha! I agree with you, in a sense.

Jim: Then, if you agree, how do you go from, "I don't know" to "God did it"?

Lourdes approaches their table with Peter's coffee and two chocolate muffins. As soon as Jim sees them, he looks at Peter in shock.

Jim: No! No! You tricked me! Now I have to eat it!

Lourdes and Peter laugh.

Peter: See, Lourdes? I told you!

Jim: You both planned this!

Lourdes: No, sir! This is just Peter's idea. The good thing is that he is paying for both. At least you can find some relief in that.

Jim smiles while looking at the muffin. There is pure love between them.

Jim: Thank you, Peter.

Peter: You are welcome.

Jim: So, going back to the question: how do you go from, "I don't know" to "God did it"?

Peter: If I were to answer the question from your worldview, scientific materialism, I would say: I don't know, but!

Jim: But what?

Peter: "I don't know, but" why *is* there something rather than nothing? Why *is* the universe the way it is? Why *is* the universe ordered or behaves so that only conscious beings can decipher it? Why *is* conscious life a potentiality in the universe? And if I combine all these things, do they suggest or point to something beyond themselves? My answer to that would be yes, to some intelligence. I could easily arrive at that conclusion from your worldview, except I am a follower of Jesus, not a scientific materialist. Therefore, the question "Why *is* there something rather than nothing?" does have an answer in Scripture, which I believe is the message of God to humanity. That answer is: "He created out of His own will to have an eternal relationship with His creation, which includes us." Or, as Paul puts it: "God planned long ago that we become His own children through Jesus Christ. This would please God; it is what He wanted."[140] So, either from your worldview or from mine, I have good reasons to believe there is some intelligence beyond the created order or the "universe," as you might put it.

Jim: OK. So, when you accepted the possibility of some type of intelligence beyond or even sustaining the universe, how did that take you specifically to Jesus? As far as I know, there are thousands of religions out there.

Peter: You know? That was a struggle for me. On one hand, if God exists, the fact that there are so many religions makes it harder to believe that one of them is "truer" than the rest of them. It felt as if

---

[140] Ephesians 1:5

"religion" is just something humans do, that's it. However, I looked at it from a different perspective and wondered: why is 85% of the population—as far as I remember—religious? Does that evidence point to there being something divine, or rather, that all of them are wrong? If 85% of the population is religious, I would carefully consider *why* that is the case before dismissing the whole thing.

Jim: That sounds to me like a textbook case of the majority fallacy.

Peter: You are correct that it "sounds" like it, but it isn't because I am talking in terms of probability. If 85% of the worldwide population believes in some type of divinity, does that say something to you?

Jim: Yes, 85% of the worldwide population assumes something they have no idea about. The 15% who say, "I don't know," are closer to reality than the 85%.

Peter: Why is there something called "reality" at all, Jim?

Jim: I don't know.

Peter: OK, but does reality suggest something about its own existence?

Jim: It exists?

Peter: Why?

Jim: I don't know.

Peter: There it is! That's your scientific materialism right there.

Jim: Wait a second, Peter. I am saying: "I don't know." Is there a problem with that answer?

Peter: No. But when I ask you to suggest, hypothesize, predict, or even imagine a possible answer, you don't want to do it. Why?

Jim: Because I don't know.

Peter: I don't believe that. You'll like to do it, but your worldview restricts the way you think about it. Within your worldview, there isn't room for intelligence, except for the one you use to claim, "you don't know." I believe reality reeks of intelligence everywhere.

Jim: You said it well, "you believe."

Peter: I believe after I know first.

Jim: What do you know?

Peter: I know something exists and that what exists can be studied. Everything that can be studied exhibits patterns and some behavior, and the only thing that can decipher those patterns and behaviors are intelligent beings like you and me. I repeat myself a lot on this point, haha. Is it insanity to suggest that intelligence explains reality when the only way to understand reality within the system is through intelligence?

Jim: When you put it like that, I think it's OK to wonder; there is no problem. But wonder shouldn't become an actual assertion of the world, and that's where you and I part ways.

Peter: I get that. But my wonder doesn't become an assertion because of metaphysics, but because of Jesus.

Jim: How is that?

Peter: Jesus makes sense of metaphysics—He is God, and physics since He is the sustainer of everything He created.[141] He also makes sense of all my feelings and emotions as a human being. All three levels find rest in Jesus.

Jim: But see? That's a matter of belief, not a matter of knowledge. You are saying things because I am hearing you talking, but at the same time, in a way, you are not saying anything tangible.

Peter: Of course! I understand because your worldview doesn't allow for the existence of something beyond or even sustaining the created order. That's a conscious choice you make without having evidence to support it. That's belief, not assertion.

Jim: We have absolutely no reason to suggest something like that.

Peter: Well, we do—the universe reeks of intelligence everywhere we look.

Both laugh and sit back in their chairs.

Peter: OK, I think we have reached a wall here. Let's let it rest for a second.

Jim: I think this "wall" you mention is my "I don't know." You are the one who is claiming to know what is over the "wall" without being able to see it.

Peter: I am the one looking at "the wall," wondering why it is there and what type of essence could cause a wall called "I don't know" even to exist.

---

[141] Colossians 1:17: He existed before anything else, and he holds all creation together.

Jim: You know what? I am going to eat a bit of my chocolate muffin right now.

Peter: Haha! Go ahead.

Jim and Peter both bite into their chocolate muffins.

Jim: Do you think this chocolate muffin is real? It doesn't feel real to me.

Peter: And it reeks of intelligence because it was made by an intelligent agency who was manipulating the created order around her.

Jim laughs. Suddenly, Peter's phone rings. Normally, he wouldn't look at it while having a conversation with another person. However, he is worried about Thomas and hopes he is the one texting him.

Peter: Do you mind if I look at my phone for a second?

Jim: No. Please, Peter. Go ahead.

Peter: Thank you.

It's Thomas. Peter gets nervous and curious about his text when he sees his name. Things are happening too fast. No one knows what to expect anymore. Peter begins reading his text:

"Peter, I wanted you to be the first one to know this: I don't believe anymore. Thank you for all the conversations and time spent exploring the big questions together. I now need to mourn my old life, and I am still not ready to engage in conversation about anything related to it for a while. Peter, I hope this doesn't change our friendship. I'll let you know if I feel like hanging out next Thursday. In the meantime,

if you need anything, ANYTHING, let me know. I am here to support you through it all."

Peter's heart sinks to the bottom of his body and beyond. His face blushes and his hands begin shaking a little bit. His breathing becomes short and anxious. How is this all happening so quickly? *Peter wonders.*

Jim: Peter, is everything OK?

Peter doesn't answer for a few seconds, not because he doesn't want to, but because he can't.

Peter: Jim, I need a second. I'll be right back.

Peter gets up and leaves the coffee shop, trying to figure out what to do or think. He gets closer to the trail and looks up to the sky. Being in nature makes Peter feel closer to God. His thoughts are chaotic, questions coming, questions going, talking to himself and God, all at the same time . . . "Why?" *He whispers. Peter begins to tear up and get anxious.* "Why did You bring me here, to leave my family behind, to suffer again because of my tumor, and to be a witness of my best friend leaving You? This doesn't make sense at all, Lord. How can I be thankful in a moment like this?" *Peter tries to calm down and thinks:* Peter, you need to trust that He sees something through all of this that goes beyond your own understanding . . . Oh . . . I see . . . I can trust You simply because I know You love us so much, and You made sure we knew this because You died for all of us on the cross. You don't play with our future; You lovingly walk toward it next to us. Lord, use me as a living sacrifice to be anything You want me to be for others because I already have everything in You. Thank You for allowing me to mourn with You, for teaching me to see everything and everyone through the love you showed us when You were with us, when You died for us, and when You gave us hope for eternal life. *In the stillness, he hears the Lord impressing upon him, "Are you loving others the way I loved you?" Peter answers,* "Yes, Lord, teach me how to do this more and more without having expectations of what the result might be. I cannot wait to be with You . . . but not yet . . . thank You for giving me peace in a moment when peace is the last thing the world could give me. I love You, Lord. Be with Thomas."

Peter wipes off his tears, turns around, and returns to the coffee shop. With every step, a word resonates in his heart: "Thank you, thank you, thank you . . . " *Peter gets back to Jim's table to continue with their conversation.*

Jim: Peter, are you OK?

Peter: Yes, I am.

Jim: I'll be honest with you; sometimes, I miss prayer.

Peter is confused.

Peter: Why do you say that?

Jim: Oh, sorry, Peter. I don't want to pry at all. I was just looking at you outside the window, and I think you went outside to pray.

Peter: . . . I did . . .

Jim: That's what I mean. That text message you got made you stop for a second, be introspective, and look up. Even though I don't believe God is there anymore, I remember one of the most impactful lessons I taught as a pastor. According to what people told me, it was one about prayer.

Peter: What was it?

Jim: We live our lives looking on a horizontal plane of existence. However, prayer makes us look down within ourselves to connect to something transcendent, which is up there. Therefore, the more we connect vertically, our inner selves and God, up and down, the more we can walk joyfully, despite all the pain and suffering, on the horizontal plane of existence, forward and backward.

Peter: I never heard anyone talking about prayer that way. Why do you miss it?

Jim: I "miss it" in the sense of reassurance that someone always cares for you. However, I don't think there is someone out there anymore.

Peter: I understand. Oh! I see you ate the whole muffin! Do you want another one?

Jim: Peter! Stop! No! I cannot keep eating these things!

Jim interrupts himself.

Jim: Wait, actually, I can . . .

Peter: Haha! OK, OK.

Jim: Let's keep talking about your story. How did you go from "some type of intelligence beyond the universe" to Jesus?

Peter: OK.

Peter tries to shake off his emotions and thoughts about Thomas momentarily.

Peter: There is something about Jesus . . . I mean, whether you believe in Him or not. Even if you think the Bible is just a story, a novel, wishful thinking, there is a story there. The story's climax is the main protagonist, the One who made reality itself, sacrificing Himself for His own creation, which in turn despised Him. That story is so unique, so special, so transformative. I don't think it is a story, though—I think it is *history*. I remember reading the Sermon on the Mount[142] for the first time and thinking: what in the world is this? Jesus said the things we think about impact the real world because everything comes from the heart.[143] I realized then that there was a disconnection between my inner world and my external actions. My inner world was and keeps being wild, full of terrible thoughts directed toward me and others, but then, with my actions, I was trying to act differently. It was very hypocritical of me. I don't want to criticize, insult, desire that other people hurt, have lustful thoughts toward women whom God has created in His own image, etc., and then act in front of people as if I weren't those things. I was living two lives, and I couldn't take it anymore. Jesus was the one who helped me bring attention to it. I wanted to be the same person inside and outside. That's when I realized something was wrong, and Jesus came to save me from it.[144]

Jim: Um . . . so you assume there is a disconnection in every person you meet?

Peter: I cannot know it, but if I look around and see people's struggles, the state of the world, the decisions we all make, and most of all, the fact that God says this disconnection is totally real, then I have reasons to believe there is a disconnection in every person I

---

[142] Matthew 5–7.

[143] Matthew 15:18: But the words you speak come from the heart—that's what defiles you.

[144] Romans 3:23: For everyone has sinned; we all fall short of God's glorious standard.

meet. However, I don't know what you think about when you are alone, and no one is looking. The only way I can "know" this is by paying attention to your actions. Many people have this . . . let's call it "capacity," to be OK with having two lives: one that is internally wild, raw, and dark; and the other is that they act and behave as if their inner world didn't even matter to the external world. But it does.

Jim: Is it "life" when an external being continually monitors your thoughts? Do you call that freedom?

Peter: It depends on the character of this external being. In the case of the Christian faith, God loves us so much. Therefore, His "monitoring of my thoughts" is better than my thoughts running wild because I cannot love myself the way He loves me.

Jim: You cannot love yourself the way God loves you?

Peter: No, I can't. The things I say to myself, the things I think about myself . . . God doesn't think those things about me, and I know this because of Jesus. It's in Jesus that I find my identity. Where do you find your identity, Jim?

Jim: Identity is a very vague term. We are socially conditioned by culture, our upbringing, the language we speak, the morals we hold, our personality traits, the things we do . . . I find my identity as I make decisions in life and the world I live in.

Peter: So, how would you answer the question: "Who are you?"

Jim: My name is Jim?

Peter: No, that answers the question, "What's your name?"

Jim: How would *you* answer the question: "Who are you?"

Peter: I would say, "I am a child of God,"[145] which doesn't make me better than anyone else, but it does make me part of a family where all are equal because of Jesus.

Jim: If I told you that I was the child of the Spaghetti Monster, would you believe me?

Peter: Well, you don't look like a spaghetti.

Jim: That's the point. Why wouldn't you be as thorough and logical when it comes to God?

Peter: The comparison between God and a "spaghetti monster" fails at the most basic level. One is a physical caricature, whereas God is understood to be spirit. Therefore, when we say we "bear the image of God," it has nothing to do with physical appearance. It means we have the unique potential to reflect God's nature—who He is and what He does—in our own lives and actions. Through Jesus's sacrifice, we are invited to become His children and live out this high calling.

The comparison is intellectually weak. Has the Spaghetti Monster introduced world-changing ideas about love and divinity? Has it inspired the creation of countless hospitals, universities, and orphanages? Is there a complex library of interconnected and hyperlinked books, written over thousands of years that tells a unified story that leads to Himself, like the Bible? The historical and cultural impact of one is undeniable, while the other is a modern caricature. It's simply not a serious comparison.

[145] John 1:12: But he gave the right to become God's children to those who did accept him, to those who believe in his name.

Jim: However, the Spaghetti Monster hasn't killed thousands of people throughout history, but God did. Let alone the people who profess to follow Him. So, in that respect, Spaghetti Monster 1, God 0.

Peter: It seems you're reading God's actions in the story as arbitrary, but they are consistently framed as a response to human evil—a divine justice that mirrors our own innate desire for wrongs to be righted. Evil, in the scriptural worldview, is a corruption of God's good creation, introduced by our choices. The truly mysterious part is how God intends to restore creation by working through our very flaws and failures. I also think it's important to remember that violence, corruption, and tribalism are not Christian inventions; they are part of the human story long before Jesus. Why, then, is it so surprising when Christians act just as broken as anyone else? The gospel itself is built on the premise that something is deeply wrong with all of us. So, if the actions of broken people are enough to discredit a system of belief, shouldn't we also abandon all trust in humanity itself, which has an even longer and more consistent record of failure?

Jim: Um . . . It's a struggle, and it's true, but at least humanity struggles with something that is real and tangible. God isn't.

Peter: So, let me ask you a question: Are you completely closed off to the idea of God?

Jim: Do you want me to be completely honest with you?

Peter: Are you seriously telling me you haven't been honest with me all this time?

They both laugh.

Jim: *(while smiling)* I would like for something like a loving God to exist. I would like to, but there is no reason to believe He does.

Peter: Why would you *want* God to exist?

Jim: I am not talking necessarily of the God of Christianity, but He is certainly the one who gets the closest to this idea of a "loving God," although He falls short of it in the end. The idea of having been created, having a purpose, and being loved is a nice idea; but we don't have evidence it's real. I think we make it feel real because it brings value to people's lives, and value is something tangible.

Peter: So, Jim, besides all the evidence, philosophy, science, this, that, and the other thing . . . what happens when you see a person like me telling you that my life has radically changed because of Jesus? Does that mean anything to you?

Jim: It means the same as if someone said the same happened to them because of Allah, Buddha, Krishna, etc.

Peter: OK, OK. So, many people radically change their behavior when they focus on something transcendent and they put the self aside, all because they found something non-tangible they consider better than themselves. Doesn't that at least suggest that, in many cases, it is positive to search for truths that our physical realm of existence cannot account for?

Jim: Not at all. An idea is part of the physical world and cannot exist without a brain. So, we could say that some ideas are better than others.

Peter: What do you mean by "better"?

Jim: An idea is better than another if one promotes the well-being of people and the other doesn't.

Peter: Oh . . . but the idea of well-being is not one, but many.

Jim: What do you mean?

Peter: Could your idea of well-being have been applied in any situation, circumstance, society, and period of history from the beginning of civilization?

Jim: I guess it could, but we have been learning about well-being after thousands of years of being here.

Peter: So, do you think there is an ideal or universal way to understand well-being that transcends culture?

Jim: I think so.

Peter: OK. Fair. Are you suggesting there is something good we are all aiming for and getting to learn from as we experience life, as in, we are discovering it?

Jim: Not in a transcendent way, but in a trial-and-error way.

Peter: So, the physical realm has ingrained in it a certain way to go about morality?

Jim: Yes, that could be an option. There is always a better way to do anything. That could be the case of morality.

Peter: Anytime you say "better," Jim, I feel your "better" is directionless. Would your concept of well-being change within the context of a war, where your survival is at risk?

Jim: Yes.

Peter: Exactly. Your ideal of well-being is susceptible to change according to the circumstances around you. I don't want to be dramatic, but I'll use an example to make my case here. If you tell me, "Peter, I care for you." Should I hear, "I care for you always, or "I care for you, depending on the situation?"

Jim: You should hear, "I care for you as much as I can, to the best of my capacities."

Peter: That's why Jesus is a revolution! Jesus cares for you no matter what. Period. Therefore, those who follow Jesus should care for everyone, no matter the circumstances. That's way better than well-being.

Jim: Conceptually, yes. But do they do it?

Peter: I know. But that's not the issue here. The issue here is this: If you can recognize it conceptually, then why don't you become the Christian you'd like to see in others?

Jim: Because Christianity is not true.

Peter: Neither is, in principle, any value or moral judgment you make about the world because everything comes from a purely subjective perspective.

Jim: Wall!

Peter laughs.

Peter: Yes, I think so. I think we have reached an impasse here. I am loving this, by the way.

Jim: Me too. Let me go to the bathroom; I'll return in a second.

Peter: Of course.

Peter knows exactly what he is supposed to do. He gets up and goes to talk to Lourdes.

Peter: *(whispering)* Hey Lourdes . . .

Lourdes: *(Lourdes whispers back)* Hey Peter . . .

Peter laughs.

Peter: May I have another chocolate muffin? I'd like to place one on the table for Jim before he comes out of the bathroom. I'll pay for it later, is that OK?

Lourdes: I don't even know if this is a good or bad thing anymore.

Peter: No worries. For him, morality is intrinsically subjective. He will be fine.

Peter made this joke thinking it was hilarious, but Lourdes didn't find it funny.

Lourdes: Your humor is so weird.

Peter: OK! OK! May I have the chocolate muffin?

Lourdes: Yes! Yes! Here you go!

Peter gets it, rushes back to his table, and places it on Jim's side of the table. Jim gets out of the bathroom and sees Peter acting "all normal" and a flagrant chocolate muffin waiting for him.

Jim: Peter! What in the world? Where did this come from? I shouldn't eat these anymore!

Peter: This muffin came out of nothing. Do you believe in miracles now?

Peter laughs at himself.

Jim: You, my friend, are one of a kind.

Peter: You don't have to eat it, man. Maybe you can eat it later or give it to your sister or your mom. By the way, how is she?

Jim: She is fine. She just needs someone to be with her most of the time.

Peter: Have you been drawing more?

Jim: Of course. Look at this one.

Jim takes his notepad from the bag next to his chair and flips through the pages until he finds what he wants.

Jim: Here.

Peter is in awe.

Peter: It's *The Shire*! Have you shown it to Lourdes?

Jim: Shh! Shh! *(whispering)* I haven't because if I do, she'll ask me to give it to her, and I want it.

Peter laughs.

Peter: Your drawing is brilliant.

Jim: Thank you.

Peter: Jim, it's getting late, but I have another topic on which I'd love to hear your thoughts.

Jim: What is it?

Peter: Social issues: politics, abortion, sexuality . . .

Jim: Wow. Are you the only Christian who is excited to talk about anything?

Peter: I hope not!

Jim: What would you like to talk about?

Peter: Well, these topics are so emotionally charged that I find it difficult to talk about them with others.

Jim: Me too.

Peter: Let's jump right in. What do you think about everything happening with sexuality?

Jim: Um . . . people who have been persecuted throughout history in many ways, having a voice in today's world to say and express what they want, as everyone else should? I think it's a good thing. But I part ways with a certain sector of it when they become radical with it.

Peter: What sector is this?

Jim: Well, I don't think the whole issue of gender should be a topic taught in schools, for instance. I also think parents should have the right to teach their kids whatever they want until they reach adulthood at their homes. But just as the Bible shouldn't be taught in public schools, I don't think gender and sexuality should be taught either, especially because these days, it is almost impossible to separate it from a particular political way of looking at the world. There is a good reason for this: This whole issue of gender and sexuality is somewhat of a "new field" of study in the sense of gender being a spectrum beyond our biological constraints. Nothing should be taught in public schools until it becomes part of the scientific consensus. Right now, I wouldn't trust anyone who says it has because people are very emotional, tribal, and belligerent about this topic. Scientific progress is seen more as a cultural battle than a neutral knowledge acquisition.

Peter: Wow . . . that is very refreshing to hear.

Jim: You said something I really liked last time we talked, and Thomas was here.

For a moment, Peter thinks about Thomas and feels emotional, but the conversation continues.

Peter: What was it?

Jim: Since you say that God exists, the burden of proof should fall on you to demonstrate it. So, since Christianity is not proposing a redefinition of sexuality, the burden of proof shouldn't fall on them. I think that is 100% true.

Peter: Do you think there is evidence for a gender spectrum?

Jim: It's happening, so there is something real about it. But I think there is a problem with it, and it has to do with social media. I think the percentage of people who think they are non-binary is rapidly increasing because they are exposed to the idea of it continually. There is no other way to explain why this wasn't such a huge issue at all only a few years ago, and all of a sudden, many people seem to be struggling with it. This, in turn, makes it harder to believe there is a biological component behind most cases, but just an ideological one. Would "gender dysphoria" be such a prevalent issue if people stopped talking about it? I don't think so. Gender dysphoria would still exist because it's real. However, I don't think it would be so prevalent. This reminds me of Christianity in a sense. People tend to believe things about themselves and the world only because they are told to, not because they really believe them. For instance, many people become Christians because of all their suffering, and you see something similar with young people who end up struggling with gender issues or think they are struggling. In reality, many of them feel alone, anxious, depressed, and dying to be a part of a world in which it is increasingly getting more and more difficult to find your own place. As you know, I am sexually attracted to men, and men exist, so I am attracted to something that does exist. However, being attracted to someone who claims to be neither a man nor a woman is something difficult to grasp because I don't know if a person can be attracted to something that first needs to be explained. It's almost as if attraction were to transcend the physical aspect of people in a sense. It becomes too metaphysical for my liking. However, I want everyone to be free to express who they are, just like I do.

Peter: So, as a gay man, does this new way of understanding sexuality represent you?

Jim: It does, and it doesn't. But enough from me, what do you think about all of this?

Peter: I mean . . . I am shocked to realize that you and I think very similar about this. Something I find interesting at a biological, conceptual level is thinking about the redefinition of sexuality under the umbrella of biological evolution. It takes so long for biological changes to happen according to evolution, but we do not see any biological change per se; it is just a rapid ideological one. Another thing I find interesting is how the word gender was redefined. I do believe gender is a social construct in the sense that men and women can behave in so many ways, and culture has something to do with it; but they never stop being men and women, no matter what their behavior is. I also think there is a huge crisis of identity in the world, and many people are struggling to find meaning in a world that is intrinsically meaningless for many of those same people. I wish . . . I wish!

Peter sighs.

Peter: I wish people from any side of the conversation would sit down with each other instead of constantly fighting a physical, emotional, and digital battle.

Jim: I think that would be helpful, but let me press you a little on it.

Peter: Please do.

Jim: Imagine that we all discuss this to understand each other. Now, what happens after the conversation? Would those people change the way they feel about themselves and the whole issue of sexuality?

Peter: I see. I believe it would decrease the hate, but ultimately, as we keep living out our lives, sooner or later, worldviews end up clashing in so many ways. But beyond all this complicated and unresolvable situation, there is Jesus saying: Love your enemies. Could you imagine if we did just that?

Jim: The problem is that your enemies wouldn't love you back, and then you would die.

Peter: That's exactly what Jesus did. If it weren't for the promise of eternal life, it really wouldn't make any sense because this life would be everything we'd get.

Jim: What do you think about homosexuality?

Peter: I think of it as I think about my lust and promiscuity of the past, it's a deviation of God's sacred plan for sexuality.

Jim: *(frustrated)* Every time I hear the phrase "God's plan . . ." Imagine if I asked you to live your life according to someone else's plan whom you cannot see, touch, hear, or talk to. Would you do it?

Peter: Well, that case doesn't apply to me because people could see, touch, hear, and talk to Jesus.[146] But I know what you mean. It would be very strange to live according to someone I cannot see, touch, hear, or talk to. I am glad that's not my case.

Jim: It totally is, Peter . . . come on . . .

Peter: OK, I accept the challenge, Jim. I'll try to be as pragmatic as possible here. Who should I follow, a person who lived and died two thousand years ago and who started a movement that radicalized the way we see human beings, the way we understand our intrinsic value, how we understand morality, and so much more? More than two billion people all around the world from almost every nation, culture, and tribe, subject themselves to the ways of Jesus. Should I follow the One who said things like: "love your enemies," or "I came to serve, not to be served," who claimed to be God and gave His life for me so that I could have eternal life . . . Or should I follow a human being like you or me with a finite life and an intrinsically subjective way to see everything around him?

Jim: You don't have to follow anyone. Why do you have to follow anyone?

Peter: Oh, come on, Jim. We all follow something or someone.

---

[146] 1 John 1:1: About the Word of Life: What has existed since the beginning, we heard, we saw with our own eyes, we watched, and we touched with our hands.

Jim: I don't follow anyone.

Peter: You are influenced by many people and things around you, Jim. The way you speak, your accent, the work that you do, the technique you use to draw, the things you eat, the way you think, everything about you; everything has been influenced by someone or something. It is inevitable. You are, consciously or subconsciously, always following or being influenced by something or someone. Whether you choose to be aware of it or not is a different thing, but we all "follow" something.

Jim: Well, there is no denying that, but I am being influenced by things that exist, at least.

Peter: There it is!

They both laugh.

Jim: Let's keep going with this rapid set of questions. What do you think about politics? How do you interact with it as a follower of Jesus?

Peter: Well, politics attempt to moderate our behavior; Jesus wants to save us from it. Politics is both necessary and challenging, simultaneously, because all the policies and political decisions we make originate from someone's worldview. That's where the problem begins. Whose worldview should dictate the way everyone should behave and why? I don't think Christians should use political power to spread the gospel, but they should still spread the gospel through sacrificial love, prayer, and relationships—just as Jesus did. In fact, that's the way it happened originally. Jesus wants to change people's lives through relationships, not policies.

Jim: So, you think Christians shouldn't participate in the political discourse?

Peter: Oh, no, no. I think they should participate, knowing where the focus is—to point people to Jesus—not primarily to just "be right" or "win an election."

Jim: What a dangerous thing to do . . . mixing politics and religion . . . have you read a little bit of history?

Peter: Oh, I know. But don't we all mix politics with our own ways of understanding our world? In the same way, it should be concerning to mix politics with a subjective way of seeing morality, for instance. But, ultimately, it's not about politics and religion, but about the world and Jesus. The world is not how it is supposed to be, so nothing that happens within it will be ideal at the end of the day. For example, I remember you said the "ideal" way to live is by bringing more pleasure to most people, less harm to most people, and the most prosperity to all. Am I right?

Jim: Yes, that's a way to say it.

Peter: OK. I don't want to assume your view on this, but what do you think about the topic of abortion? When we terminate the life of a human being, do we bring more pleasure to most people, less harm to most people, and the most prosperity to all? The reason I am asking about this now is because the issue of abortion has been redefined from being a life-and-death situation to now being just another political matter to discuss.

Jim: See? You are assuming that we are terminating the life of a human being.

Peter: How am I assuming that?

Jim: I don't believe a fetus is a human being.

Peter: Really? OK. Jim, are you sure you are a scientific materialist?

Jim: Yes. What does that have to do with anything?

Peter: Jim, a fetus is one of the stages of human life. We all go through it at one point.

Jim: Yeah, but a fetus cannot make decisions on its own, it's not a human being in the sense that is aware of its own existence.

Peter: You are not aware of your own existence while you sleep, yet you are still considered a living human. I think your point is not valid. Is there anything other than a fetus in the known universe with the intrinsic potential to become a human being?

Jim: No.

Peter: This is something I find very unsettling. I think there is no denying a fetus is a human being. The problem is why we are questioning it at all.

Jim: Why do you think we do it?

Peter: I would be more interested in hearing your response to this, Jim, because I am not questioning it.

Jim: Fair. Sex's primary goal is reproduction, but reproduction entails a huge amount of responsibility and a radical change in a person's life, and people have the freedom to choose otherwise. Actually, no one has restrictions on people who want to have kids.

Peter: Yes. As much as we'd like to talk about all the ethical, biological, and societal aspects of this conversation—things like freedom of choice, pleasure, independence, etc.—none of that changes the undeniable fact that a fetus is a human being. There is no other way to look at it. I am surprised you would believe this as a scientific materialist. So, if you believe it isn't, the reason cannot be biological but ideological. Science does answer this question.

Jim: What would you do if your wife was raped and became pregnant? Would you have the child?

Peter: Wait, so now you are calling the fetus a child?

Jim: Huh . . . you got me there.

Peter: Well, Jim. I don't have conversations to "get you." I want to explore these topics with any person who is open to talking about them. If we kept talking for a while, you would "get me" as well. But I don't care about that; I care about exploring potential truths together.

Jim: Would you have your wife's child if it belonged to a person who raped her?

Peter: Arguing from a minority case is always very difficult; but one thing I'll say, beyond the moral implications of a decision like that, abortion in any case is undeniably equal to terminating someone else's human life, whether the child is the result of love or the result of an aggression. No moral implication would change the fact a human being would have lost their life.

Jim: Would you force a woman to have a child if she doesn't want it?

Peter: I know this is a hypothetical, but it is hard to imagine a case where I would be the judge and enforcer of a decision like this. According to God, and how He loves us, He can bring so much good out of any situation. So, to answer your question, and because of how precious life is in God's eyes, I would do everything I could to save the child's life. But, Jim, even though these questions are important, they don't address the core issue here. The real question is this: How did we get to the point where terminating the life of a child became a matter of freedom of choice, another subject of our political discourse, and not plain murder? Doesn't it worry you? What is the goal of redefining life, marriage, goodness, evil, love, freedom, tolerance, truth . . . ?

Jim: I think part of the purpose of it is to free us from a close-minded and morally restrictive system of thought that has caused the world to be stuck in an old way of seeing and understanding the world.

Peter: I think your feelings got the best out of you in that answer, but appreciate the honesty, even though you didn't answer my question. Think about this. In a world where a fetus is not a human being; marriage can be anything you want it to be; goodness and evil are relative and susceptible to change according to the circumstances; love is not sacrificial but capricious and a slave to our thirst for pleasure; freedom becomes a hyper-individualistic and self-centered lifestyle; tolerance doesn't mean knowing how to coexist with people who don't think like you, but to shame those who don't think like you, and truth is a matter of opinion. This is a way to describe some of the current sentiments of our Western civilization. Do you think people are safer, healthier, and more fulfilled? From my perspective, this is a big, firm, and confident step toward absolute chaos.

Jim: I guess we'll see . . .

Peter: *(sigh)* I guess we'll see . . .

Jim: Peter, I have one more question for you before I leave. I need to go to take care of my mom and give her medicine before going to bed.

Peter: Yes. What is it?

Jim: Why is it bad for Thomas to lose his faith? What's the purpose behind your conversations?

Peter didn't expect this question and needs time to think about the answer.

Peter: I want him to live forever. I want everyone to live forever. I don't want anyone to die.

Jim didn't expect this answer either.

Jim: I have mixed feelings about your answer. I think it is the most beautiful yet insane answer.

Peter: Haha. I understand. There is nothing I can do about that. Jim, before you leave, again, it's so intellectually and emotionally stimulating to find someone like you; someone willing to both be vulnerable and recognize things we still don't know. Yet, brilliant all at the same time. I don't take for granted one second of the time we have spent together today, even though you are clearly wrong about so many things.

Peter and Jim laugh.

Jim: Yeah! It's so weird to look forward to hanging out with someone who is wrong about so many things too. The feeling is mutual.

Peter and Jim laugh even harder.

Peter: Thank you, Jim. Remember, let me know if your mom needs anything while you are not here.

Jim: Thank you. I appreciate that.

Peter and Jim shake hands and say goodbye to each other. Peter talks to Lourdes, pays for everything, pets Truman, and finds his way out of the coffee shop. Once in his car, Peter releases a huge sigh and winces. The tumor is starting to hurt a little bit more despite the muscle relaxer he is taking. That's not a good sign . . . not a good sign at all. In the quietness of his car, he reads Thomas' text again and begins writing an answer:

Peter: *(through text)* Is it because . . .

"No, not yet," *he says to himself. He deletes his message and tries again.*

Peter: *(through text)* Even if I need to mourn you as a brother in Christ, I'll still adore you as a friend. I am your biggest fan, Thomas. If you ever want to keep exploring the big questions with me, I'll always be there for you. If not, I'll be there regardless. I hope you can find rest through this difficult season. I won't stop being myself, though, and I'll never stop praying for you. Never. Thank you for being my best friend, Thomas.

Chapter 11: No More

Monday, November 27

Text conversation.

Peter: Thomas?

Thomas: Yes?

Peter: Sorry to bother you, but I cannot move. I need someone to take me to the hospital.

Thomas: Oh no . . . I am sorry, Peter. The muscle relaxers are not working anymore?

Peter: No. I think it's time to be admitted to the hospital.

Thomas: I'll be at your place ASAP.

Peter: Thank you, Thomas. It's going to be great to see you again.

Thomas: You too.

20 minutes later, at Peter's apartment, Thomas knocks on his door.

Thomas: *(from outside the door)* I am here, Peter!

Thomas' phone rings. It's Peter.

Thomas: Hey, Peter, are you OK? I am outside.

Peter: I cannot move well enough to walk anymore. I just felt a massive pain behind my neck that made my whole body shake uncontrollably, which meant the tumor is exerting more pressure on my nerves. I won't be able to sleep or swallow anymore without stronger muscle relaxers. I need to be monitored from now on. Do you still have the key to my apartment?

Thomas: Yes, I do.

Thomas unlocks the door and enters Peter's apartment. Peter is sitting on his bed, holding his head with one hand and squeezing the side of the bed with the other. There is a continuous expression of pain in Peter's face. Thomas looks at Peter without knowing what to say for three reasons. It has been a while since they saw each other. It's the first time they have been together since Thomas finally abandoned his faith, and he has never seen Peter in such dire conditions.

Peter: Thomas, don't look at me like you see a monster!

Thomas smiles nervously.

Thomas: Oh . . . haha . . . I just, I don't . . .

Peter: Do I look that bad?

Thomas: You look horrible.

Peter tries to laugh, but even that hurts him. Peter winces in pain.

Thomas: Hey, hey, hey . . . are you OK?

Peter tears up. Thomas gently hugs him, but Peter doesn't move or stop holding his head with one hand. At this point, any motion makes him hurt.

Peter: This is when my body gives up. I remember all of this from last time. Now, the only thing that needs to be strong is my heart. All these years, I have been trying to forget about the pain, but here it is again. Could you take me to the hospital?

Thomas: Peter, I think you need an ambulance.

Peter: . . . but please . . .

Thomas: What?

Peter: Don't be the driver . . .

Thomas laughs. Peter wishes he could laugh.

Peter: You might be right. I need an injection of stronger muscle relaxers before I can lay flat on a bed. At least that's what they did last time to take me to the hospital.

Thomas: Let me call them.

While Thomas is calling the ambulance, Peter is looking at him intently. It's the same Thomas, but not the same Thomas at the same time. He never had a conversation with "atheist Thomas" before. Is he an atheist, though? His beliefs cannot be assumed anymore. Their spiritual journey has parted ways. However, there he is, helping Peter in his most vulnerable moment.

Thomas: *(on the phone with 911)* Yes, apartment 204 . . . No, I won't leave him alone . . . No, he cannot lie in bed anymore, it hurts too much. Yeah, his neck looks very stiff. He is holding his head with one hand to help with sudden motions . . . Yes . . . OK, I'll ask him. Peter, do you still have the neck brace I got you at the pharmacy?

Peter: Yes, it's on the side of my bed. But I don't know if I can put it on.

Thomas: I'll help you. *(on the phone)* Excuse me, sir? Yes, I'll help him put it on, and we'll wait for the ambulance to arrive. OK. Thank you. Bye.

Thomas finishes his phone conversation with the hospital and heads to Peter's room to grab the neck brace.

Thomas: Here it is.

Thomas gently places the neck brace around Peter's neck.

Thomas: OK . . . does that help?

Peter: I think so. At least I don't have to hold my head myself. How long will it take for the ambulance to arrive?

Thomas: I don't know. They'll be here in just a few minutes.

Peter and Thomas have so many things to say to each other, but they remain silent for a while, not knowing how to start.

Peter: Thomas, I am afraid to ask you how you are.

Thomas: Why?

Peter: Because if you say "good," I know that's not true, and then I'll ask you again, "How are you?" expecting an honest answer. And then, that real answer might entail talking about a topic you might not be open to revisiting for now.

Thomas smiles.

Thomas: It's almost like you have this creepy superpower to talk directly to the version of me I do my best to hide from everyone.

Peter: Hey, real Thomas, what's up?

Thomas and Peter laugh, but Peter is still in pain.

Thomas: I am mourning.

Peter keeps listening.

Thomas: I am mourning my faith, life, and relationship with Sofía. It's time to let go of everything.

Peter: What do you mean "let go"?

Thomas: I am moving, Peter. I cannot be around anymore.

Peter: Moving? Where?

Thomas: I am not sure yet, but I need to breathe and find myself away from Christianity and Christians.

Peter: Are you moving away or escaping?

Thomas rolls his eyes and smiles.

Thomas: Who taught you to ask questions like this?

Peter: You.

Thomas: Well, I wish I hadn't taught you.

Both laugh again.

Peter: So, moving away or escaping?

Thomas: A little bit of both.

Peter: What about Sofía?

Thomas' demeanor changes when hearing her name. There is love but more frustration in his tone.

Thomas: Sofía left me when I most needed her. Through all the pain, I have taught myself not to need her anymore.

Peter is trying his best not to break apart in front of his friend, but each word that comes out of Thomas makes him feel like he is talking to someone he doesn't know anymore.

Peter: Have you told her?

Thomas: Tell her what?

Peter: That you are moving away, that you are moving on, that you don't believe Christianity is true anymore.

Thomas: No, I haven't. I think she'll know once I am gone.

Peter: What have you been doing all this time alone?

Thomas: Thinking.

Peter: And, according to your answers, building resentment toward people who actually love you?

Thomas sighs in frustration.

Thomas: Peter, do you think it's a good idea to talk about this right now?

Peter gets a bit nervous and emotional.

Peter: Don't pity me because I am feeling like this. Should this stupid tumor refrain me from caring for you?

Thomas keeps quiet.

Peter: Your worldview might have changed, but if you let resentment grow within you and go unchecked, it will destroy you and make you become someone you don't want to be.

Thomas raises his voice.

Thomas: I am sick of people telling me what to do or not to do because of their beliefs, according to an ancient book that has little to nothing to say about who I am or what I should do with a life that belongs to me.

Peter: Thomas . . .

Thomas tears up.

Thomas: Do you also want me to leave?

Peter: Also? Who else told you to leave?

Thomas: Everyone around me.

Peter: See, Thomas? No one is asking you to leave. Please, don't leave me.

Thomas sits down next to Peter in his bed and lets out a big sigh.

Thomas: I am sorry, Peter. This is being so weird and hard. It's just . . . everywhere I go, everything I do in this town revolves around Christianity. I don't know who I am without it. I think I deserve to explore the world away from it.

Peter: Yes. You do. That's the biggest question you might ever ask, Thomas.

Thomas: What is it?

Peter: Who can I become *away* from Jesus?

Thomas keeps quiet.

Peter: I lived my life for so many years, thinking my life belonged to me, and God was patient enough to give me time to experience the person I would become without Him being in my life. I didn't like what I saw. You never know how deep a hole goes until you jump in it, but we risk falling so deep in it that we'll never be able to come out.

Thomas: It might be that I'll look at the person I can become away from Jesus, and I like it.

Peter: By all means. At the same time, it's not intellectually or emotionally consistent to conclude that everything you learned and did until today was a waste of time. Don't let resentment dictate your life. Whether you believe Christianity is true or not, there are things about Christianity that are true: love, compassion, community, forgiveness, etc.

Thomas: I might get to the point where I'll be able to distinguish between my beliefs and what is good in a practical way. But right now, I need space and time away from everything.

Peter: I know. You do.

Peter and Thomas keep silent for a while.

Peter: But are you also going to move away from me?

Someone knocks on the door. The ambulance is here. Thomas opens the door for them, and the EMTs rush immediately to check on Peter. After a few explanations of his medical history, they decide to inject a potent muscle relaxer and wait until Peter can stretch, move, and lay down on his own. As they take him to the ambulance, Thomas ensures everything is in order before leaving his apartment. Right above the entrance is a sign with one of Peter's favorite verses written on it: "Tears came to His eyes."[147] *Everyone used to poke at Peter because of it.* "That's *your favorite verse? Seriously?" But seeing Peter lying on a bed and on his way into an ambulance turns this verse into something other than "the shortest verse in the Bible." Thomas notices a small phrase written on the corner of the frame. It's Peter's handwriting. As Thomas is closing the door, he gets closer to read it. It says: "So you'll weep too, but rejoice!" Thomas wonders if one day he'll have another opportunity to ask Peter questions about it again at "their table" at* The Shire.

[147] John 11:35.

Chapter 12

Peace in Uncertainty

Thursday, November 30

Thomas arrives at the hospital to see Peter.

Thomas: What a fancy room they gave you—top floor!

Peter: You don't know what the best part of it is yet.

Thomas: What is it?

Peter: Look out the window to your right.

Thomas looks out the window to his right and gasps.

Thomas: You can see *The Shire* from here! And the trail!

Peter: Which means we can keep having our conversations here!

Thomas keeps looking out the window, but his body language shows he is unsure.

Peter: Which means we shouldn't have our conversations here!

Thomas laughs.

Thomas: You know what? I guess I wouldn't mind it.

Thomas is willing to talk to Peter about the big questions only because it would help Peter forget about the surgery.

Peter: I'd love to hear your thoughts now that you are an . . . atheist?

Thomas: Not really. I would say more agnostic . . . a cautious atheist even.

Peter: Oh really?

Thomas: Yeah. But before we get into the weeds. How are you? Have you told anybody you are at the hospital?

Peter: Yes, actually. I told everyone today because I wanted to spend a couple of days alone at the hospital.

Thomas: Why?

Peter: To pray.

Thomas: To pray for what?

Peter: Not "for," Thomas. I pray to have conversations with God because I love Him. Asking for things is not my priority anymore. Eternal life awaits no matter what happens, although I believe everything will go well.

Thomas: That's a change! Good for you!

Peter: Yes, it's not bad to keep a positive outlook in life!

Thomas: However, wouldn't it be better to, instead of praying to a deity, talk to the surgeon who is going to do the surgery and potentially save you from this?

Peter: I thank God for creating a world where His creation can be studied and for making us aware of all patterns of nature so that we can become surgeons and help others in His name. Helping people is a factually good thing about the world.

Thomas: Haha! Breathe! What a long sentence!

Peter: Totally! If I wrote it, it wouldn't have had any commas.

Thomas: Did you do anything interesting during the few days we didn't see each other?

Peter: Let me see . . . I had a conversation with Jim!

Thomas: Jim, the ex-pastor?

Peter: Yes, he was taking care of his mom that week and came to *The Shire* to relax.

Thomas: How many chocolate muffins did he *not* want to eat?

Peter: Haha! Two.

Thomas: Good for him.

Peter: It was a great conversation. Oh! Truman is limping!

Thomas: Oh, no! What's going on with him?

Peter: The same day I saw Jim at *The Shire*, a Thursday, I think, I realized Truman was limping and asked Lourdes about it. She told me he jumped to catch a frisbee and hurt himself when he landed.

Thomas: I need to talk to her.

Peter: Lourdes?

Thomas: Yeah. I don't think I was nice to her the day I stormed out of the coffee shop.

That's our Thomas, *Peter says to himself.*

Peter: She gets it, though, Thomas. She gets you are having a rough time. I am sure she loves you the same.

Thomas remains quiet.

Peter: What about you, Thomas?

Thomas: I just stayed home for a few days, and then I went to have dinner with my parents, soooo . . .

Peter: Soooo . . . ?

Thomas: It was tough. They are sad about me and Sofía, but I didn't tell them anything about my faith. Being yourself is almost impossible when surrounded by people who don't think like you.

Peter: Oh, yeah, that's the same feeling I had back in England, where there weren't any Christians around. But you know what? It shouldn't be like that. If we are not honest about the big questions in life and how we feel about them, how will we be honest about the most trivial things?

Thomas: I agree. But I don't want my parents to struggle beyond what's necessary. I am still on a "journey" . . .

Peter: A journey to where?

Thomas: That's the point. I don't know where this journey will take me, so I prefer not to talk about the destination until I get there.

Peter: Did you tell them that you are thinking about moving?

Thomas: No, no. I didn't.

Peter: OK. Here I go. Are you ready?

Thomas: With you, I never know.

Peter smiles.

Peter: How does it feel not to be a Christian?

Thomas sighs and thinks about it for a while.

Thomas: I don't know. It's bizarre. I think I still need time to mourn it, as I said. Changing one's worldview is not like changing how you feel about one specific thing but more like changing the filter through which you understand everything around you.

Peter: That's an excellent way to put it.

Thomas: How was it for you when you became a Christian?

Peter: I'll be honest. At first, it was a struggle because you begin to question anything and everyone you spend time with, their motives, morals, values, etc. You even risk thinking you are better than anyone because you see "the truth" and others "don't." I have met many Christians who stopped believing, and they began to see

Christians just as "people who are wrong," that's it. So, whatever worldview you come from or what worldview you go to, we all run the risk of becoming prideful. However, Jesus and the cross don't give us any room for pride, and instead of looking at people as "people who are wrong," what Jesus wants us to do is to see others as people who need Him, whether they know it or not, whether they recognize it or not, and to show them that that is true by loving them the way He first loved us. That's why I see every person as a potential follower of Jesus, a beautiful creation of God. No one will ever be perfect, but Jesus is the one who can show us there is beauty in our imperfections because of what He did for us on the cross.

Thomas: You know what? I think it's time to have a conversation about Jesus. I am not interested in historical evidence or anything of that sort, even though it's an exciting conversation. I believe Jesus existed, but I don't think Jesus "the Christ" did. However, let's assume Jesus Christ exists and you have a personal relationship with Him. Can you talk to me about that? Can I ask you questions about that?

Peter: Sure, you can. Thomas, this is the conversation and the questions that matter most.

Thomas: OK . . . so what does it mean to have a relationship with Jesus? How can you have a relationship with someone who is not physically here?

Peter: Well, to have a relationship with a person, first, that person needs to be alive, and I believe Jesus is.[148] Now, I can have a relationship with Jesus in three ways. One is through prayer.

[148] Revelation 1:18: I am the living one. I died, but look—I am alive forever and ever! And I hold the keys of death and the grave.

Two, by the Holy Spirit.[149] And three, through Scripture. Jesus sent the Spirit of God to inhabit my heart, who intercedes for me when I communicate to the Father thanks to Jesus' sacrifice on the cross. That's all theology, and it's vital. But I think you mean the relationship aspect of it; what does it look like daily?

Thomas: Exactly.

Peter: OK. Well, in that unfortunate conversation we had with Karl . . .

Peter and Thomas sigh.

Peter: I said there is evidence to demonstrate a person has a relationship with Jesus by the fruit of the Spirit, the quality of their actions, "But the Holy Spirit produces this kind of fruit in our lives: love, joy, peace, patience, kindness, goodness, faithfulness, gentleness, and self-control."[150]

Thomas: Wait, wait . . . wait a second.

Peter: What?

Thomas: It sounds like you don't have an actual "relationship." Rather, you are just following a series of behavioral patterns, like an ideal, and that ideal is changing you, not a person.

Peter: In practical terms, even if Jesus "the Christ" were not real, but only the "historical Jesus," I would still hold on to that ideal, even if it weren't "true," because I believe His way of life is better for me than anything the world has offered so far. However, I believe Jesus is "the Christ." He is God, Creator and sustainer of the

---

[149] John 14:16: And I will ask the Father, and he will give you another Advocate, who will never leave you.

[150] Galatians 5:22.

universe, with whom I can have a relationship through prayer and decision-making—not because I want to be saved—but because He has saved me already. Remember, Thomas, the premise here is that Jesus created us and died for us because of our sins so that we don't have to die forever.

Thomas: See? But you are not answering my questions. How is that a relationship and not a person following an ideal?

Peter: Because you don't pray to an ideal. An ideal doesn't have a will. An ideal never created you or me. An ideal didn't leave the throne room of Heaven to become a part of the physical world, where He, because of His great love, would offer His own life so that we could live. God did that; God is alive. An ideal would stop existing if people stopped thinking about it.

Thomas: Isn't that just the exact same case with God? If people would stop thinking and talking about it, God "wouldn't exist in a sense."

Peter: It's not the same, Thomas. The claim here is that God intervened in a radical, dramatic way in the person of Jesus. The ideal became a human being. Let me read this passage to you . . . "Though Christ was divine by nature, He did not think that being equal with deity was something to hold onto. Instead, he emptied himself, taking on the very nature of a slave. He became like human beings, appearing in human form. He humbled himself. He obeyed, though it meant dying, even dying on a cross! So, God made him the most important. God gave him the name that is above every name."[151] If we are assuming that Jesus did this, that He is alive, and that the Spirit is within me, I can have a relationship with Him and

---

[151] Philippians 2:6-9.

experience transformation through obedience. I don't only want to know things about Him, but I want to obey Him. The word *obey* has a negative connotation to some people, but Jesus created me and gave His life for me, so I have absolutely no problem obeying Him. I obey Him because I love Him.

Thomas: I'll ask you the question in a different way. What's the difference between our relationship and your relationship with Jesus?

Peter: The ability of the Spirit to dwell within me; and never being separated. Another major difference is that I don't physically see Jesus as I see you. But still, I see Jesus everywhere else.

Thomas: Uh?

Peter: I see Jesus in the beauty of creation. I see Jesus in every gesture of love and sacrifice. I see Jesus when someone's need is met. I see Jesus where there is hope in suffering. Jesus is everything a human being is supposed to be. I see Jesus everywhere. Jesus was a real human being and God, who lived a life that set a precedent for me to know what things represent Him and those that don't. So, in a sense, He is more real than you are to me, even though I cannot see Him the way I see you.

Thomas: I think you are redefining the word "see" to accommodate your bias. Why, then, don't I see Jesus, let's say, in the beauty of creation? Shouldn't it be clear for all?

Peter: Beauty is not a brute fact of reality; there is a purpose behind it. One can choose to recognize beauty simply for what it is, but the point is to recognize *why* it is there, which is to glorify who created it in the first place. When we don't see Jesus, it is because we haven't come to terms with the reality of sin.

Thomas: More things we cannot see?

Peter: Oh, you do see sin everywhere. You might have decided to change the name of it, or just call it "a bad thing; an unfortunate event," but the consequences are there for everyone to see. The world is not the way it is supposed to be.

Thomas: Sin is just another name to refer to something we all experience; bad things happen to all of us, and sometimes we ourselves cause them. Why do you need something like "sin" to explain it at all?

Peter: Because sin is what has broken our relationship with God and *introduced* brokenness into our world. Thomas, if you try to mathematically dissect every aspect of Christianity as if it were a syllogism or an equation, you won't be able to understand it.

Thomas: Oh! So, you are saying that Christianity is not rational?

Peter: Who said that?

Thomas: You did.

Peter: When?

Thomas: When you implied that you could not rationalize every single aspect of Christianity,

Peter: Your love for Sofía is not a logically sound syllogism that tracks mathematically. I think you are assuming here that something rational can only be explained empirically. But, Thomas, is it rational to say "we know something" only because we can describe it? Is it fair to say we know something when we don't have an explanation for both the person who wants to know and why there are things that can be known? Besides, rationalism is a process of understanding the world that rationalism itself cannot explain. Please don't be surprised that I cannot answer your questions as if I am supposed to know everything. Nobody knows everything.

Thomas: That's fair. So, why can't I see Jesus, and you can?

Peter: The main reason is this: Humanity has fallen short of God's glorious standard, a standard He desires for us simply because He loves us and knows it's the only way for our flourishing. I recognize this is true, and perhaps you don't. That's why. Repentance is the filter through which people can see God. It is utterly revolutionary.

Thomas: What a horrible way to look at the world, isn't it? Everyone is evil. That's a very encouraging thing to say to a child while growing up.

Peter: I know the way it sounds. But, in my case, I didn't hear "everyone is a sinner," and then I believed it blindly. Instead, I looked inside me to see if it was true. I put it to the test. And what Scripture hypothesized about me without knowing me personally, Scripture got right. There was something wrong with me. "Everyone is a sinner" is not an insult but an actual and honest description of the world. What do you see when you look inside and around you?

Thomas: No one is perfect. But the statement "everyone is a sinner" doesn't account for all the good things people can do.

Peter: Thomas, I'd rather not be that selective in understanding a statement like "everyone is a sinner" because it doesn't come out of a vacuum. Instead, it's in the Bible. We are sinners, but that's not everything we are in God's eyes. We were created to be with God, but then we sinned and keep sinning. However, in Jesus, we can find restoration from it. People think Christianity sees people as inherently evil, but that's not true. We are image bearers of God; we were created good, but we chose our own ways and ushered sin into the world. If you don't believe me, look around and pay attention to what you think about when you are alone and no one is looking. Now, sin is in us, which makes us inclined to do evil; but despite this, Jesus never abandoned us. Instead, He loved us to the point that He gave His life for us so that we could be with God again. That's the whole story. We were not created to be inherently evil, but with the potential and the freedom to choose. You could say people are evil because of the presence of sin in our lives, but not because God created us that way. Thomas, what story should we tell children instead?

Thomas: That you are not evil no matter what. That your actions define you. That you have the freedom to become everything you want to be.

Peter: I think that's a great definition for subjective relativism. Not only are we relativistic, but each person has a view of how relativism should play out. That would lead to absolute chaos. Once sin entered the world, we can see and experience that we are not good because of what we end up doing. God says in the Bible that no one is good[152] according to what we first did, not because of what we inherently were in the beginning. The whole story of redemption begins with everything being created good, including us. Everyone sins, and the evidence is everywhere you look.

---

[152] Romans 3:23: For everyone has sinned; we all fall short of God's glorious standard.

Thomas: A few minutes before, you told me you saw Jesus everywhere. So, which of the two do you see everywhere, Jesus or sin?

Peter: God planted a seed of potential in every one of us, Thomas—a future He imagined for us, just waiting to be brought to life by His love. To follow Jesus is to see that truth for yourself: to be honest about our sins while living with this incredible hope. And here's the idea that changes everything: we don't climb our way to the person God wants us to be. Instead, we just open our hands and receive it as a gift. It's a grace we could never earn, but He offers it freely. Think about it—His grace is so immense He even allows us to live as if He isn't real. He never intended for humanity to become what we are now.

Thomas: And what have we become?

Peter: Look around and then look within yourself. What do you see?

Thomas: People striving to be the best version of who they can become.

Peter: Do you really see that? What are we doing to do so?

Thomas: We fail, we learn, we try again.

Peter: If God doesn't exist, then everything we call evil has no hope of redemption. So, everything in the world that we call "evil" is something we ourselves have created and continue to perpetuate incessantly without any hope of redemption. We ourselves have invented things like abuse, adultery, unjustified anger, backbiting, bitterness, boasting, deceit, fraud, dishonesty, addictions, envy, sexual immorality, extortion, fornication, hatred, hypocrisy, self-righteousness, mockery, murder, stealing, swearing . . . and a long etcetera after that. How could I find the best version of myself if I am part of the problem and the reason these things keep materializing both in me and the world? What version of myself comes out of a world like this, Thomas? If I strive, I strive toward where . . . toward living a good life? What do we mean by "good" in the first place? And then, after all the striving to become the best version of ourselves, we die, and that's it. Gone. Now, why should I accept this as a rational position or a default position? Trust me, I see beauty in people trying to be better. I tried it myself. But when you try to improve, you think about your own version of "better," not everyone else's. My better and your better could end up being in conflict, and then we would keep perpetuating the same problem we are trying to overcome—ourselves. If we look at Jesus, though, and we follow Him and obey Him, we can find an actual definition of better, and it is all based on sacrificial love because that's how He lived and died for us.

Thomas: Are you insinuating that, without Jesus, people's lives are meaningless?

Peter: Not at all. People's lives are intrinsically valuable because God created us so. We can find meaning in some things we do, but this meaning cannot be ultimate because we get old and die. In Jesus, we can find a type of meaning in and beyond ourselves, which is eternal. Forget about me, Christianity, this or that pastor, this or that opinion . . . I am talking about the core reason for it all. Jesus said about Himself: "I am the way, the truth, and the life! No one can come to the Father except through me."[153] But *saying*

---

[153] John 14:6.

things is so easy! Our tongues can boast of such great things![154] If you are the truth, Jesus, what did You do to demonstrate it? Jesus is God, He created us, loves us, sacrificed Himself for us, gives us a chance to become a part of His family again by obeying Him and loving others, and put an end to death on the cross so that suffering can be experienced in hope for eternity. Goodness is not about boasting or deeds but about humility and sacrificial love, and God treats everyone alike. It is so counterintuitive and radical. He changed the world forever. This is gift after gift from our Creator. Why should the creator of the universe be left behind because of my shortcomings as one of His followers? Christianity is not about me, Christianity is not about Christianity, Christianity exists because of Jesus, reality exists because of Jesus. If true, could there be a love as profound as this?

Thomas: You talk a lot about sacrificial love, but what about having the option to create a world where no suffering happens in the first place? Wouldn't it be more loving?

Peter: But Thomas, is it possible to love by default? Is it possible to love without having the freedom *not* to do it? God didn't create evil, we chose it, we keep perpetuating. And then He bore all our evil on himself to save us from the condemnation we brought on ourselves. I could ask a similar question: If God could have created any world He wanted, why would He make one where He must intervene and be a part of all the suffering and struggle to save it? Wouldn't it be easier to save it from a distance? Yes! It would have been easier, but the point is to show and demonstrate the quintessential truth of the universe: Jesus, and sacrificial love. We are made to love the way He sacrificially loves us.

---

[154] James 3:5: In the same way, the tongue is a small thing that makes grand speeches . . .

Thomas: So, let me ask you a question. If everything is about sacrificial love, why don't we see it from those who claim to follow Him?

Peter: Thomas, we cannot overgeneralize like that. Some people love sacrificially like Jesus daily, but we won't see them in the news. Also, following Jesus is a growth process. Christians are not automatically mature. They grow to be more like Christ and love like Him. I grant it that this world would be different if everyone who claims to follow Jesus loved others the way He loves us. But see? You seem to be worrying about why others don't love as Jesus loves us, but I think the question is: why don't you? I am not saying that you do or you don't. I am pointing out that we can stop hoping for something to happen and make it happen ourselves. It's all about Jesus, Thomas. There are many reasons why people stop believing Christianity is true, but none of those reasons are as powerful as denying Jesus Himself, who He is, what He did, what He wants, etc. Are you mourning your experience with Christianity, or are you mourning Jesus?

Thomas remains silent for a second. He seems to be struggling with Peter's question.

Thomas: Peter, I need to take some fresh air. I'll be back in a second.

Peter: *(sigh)* Thomas, I am sorry if I said something that bothered you. I didn't mean to.

Thomas: Not at all. I challenge you all the time, and you take it so well. It's just . . . it's a lot to process.

Peter: I understand.

Thomas: I'll be back in a minute.

Before Thomas leaves the room, Peter calls him one more time.

Peter: Hey, Thomas.

Thomas: Yeah?

Peter: I am your number one fan, mate.

Thomas smiles while trying to contain his tears and leaves the room. A while later, Thomas gets back to Peter's room. As he approaches the entrance, he can hear Peter talking to a few people. Who came to see him? Should I leave? *However, he doesn't need to open the door to know who came to see Peter. Her voice makes him tremble, not out of fear but out of love. Thomas doubts about whether to open the door, but this is about Peter, not about himself.* I told Peter I would be right back. I cannot leave like this. *Thomas closes his eyes, sighs, holds the doorknob, and pushes forward to find a room full of some of the most important people in his life. Sofía, Lourdes, and Pastor John are there. Peter looks at him, trying to figure out a way to tell him with his eyes that he didn't expect them to visit. Peter quietly shrugs and smiles at Thomas, which makes Thomas do the same.*

Pastor John: Hey, Thomas! It's so good to see you!

Thomas: Hi, Pastor John. Hi, everyone.

Thomas and Sofía look at each other, not knowing what to say. There are so many things to say to each other, so many emotions to share, so many fears to face together . . .

Thomas: Lourdes . . . I am sorry.

Lourdes: *(trying to be funny)* Oh, no! What did you do to me?!

Lourdes has it. She has it. She knows how to make everyone comfortable around her. That's why The Shire *feels like home. Thomas smiles.*

Thomas: Our last conversation . . . I didn't handle myself well, I am sorry.

Lourdes: Aww, you are so sweet, honey. I know you care for me. Thomas, how often have you dealt with my nonsense too?

Thomas: A lot!

Everyone in the room laughs. It's so good to see Sofía laugh at Thomas' jokes again.

Lourdes: Come here, you!

Lourdes doesn't think about it twice. She hugs Thomas so firmly, so tightly—one hug. One hug is everything he needs to let go of his inner turmoil and allow himself to be loved. Thomas begins crying as if he had never cried before. There is nothing to hide anymore. Peter cannot take it. He gets out of the bed slowly and joins them in the hug. Pastor John does too. Lastly, Sofía hugs them all and places her hand on Thomas' head. Thomas is out of words. Everyone is tearing up and letting go of their barriers. Sofía and Thomas' relationship, Peter's tumor, all fears and uncertainties . . . There are many tears to shed and few people to do it with. But sometimes, just sometimes, in the most unexpected way, in the simplest way, everyone gets to experience the world as it was supposed to be. No arguments, intellect, knowledge, or pretensions . . . but just one hug. It is a small picture of the beauty of Heaven. After they finish hugging, Peter returns to his bed, and everyone seems more relaxed.

Thomas: Hey, Lourdes, is Truman still limping?

Lourdes: Oh, you know! This dog is more popular than me and the coffee shop together. I have had this lingering cough for a while, and no one has asked me about it.

Everyone laughs.

Thomas: Where is he right now? At *The Shire*? By the way, who is running the coffee shop right now?

Lourdes: A group from church offered to be there for a couple of hours so that I could come to see Peter. I better get back soon. I hope they didn't allow Karl to make the coffee.

Everyone laughs again.

Lourdes: Why are you asking?

Thomas: I'd like to take Truman to the vet.

Peter smiles.

Lourdes: Thomas, Thomas, Thomas. You know how to win a lady's heart! It doesn't surprise me that Sofía fell for you!

Gosh . . . Lourdes . . .

Peter: OK! OK! Lourdes! Lourdes! Let's not make it . . . weird. Filter, Filter!

Sofía blushes but cannot contain the laugh, nor can the rest.

Sofía: Thomas, can I go with you?

Silence is silent. But, sometimes, silence can be more deafening than other times. This is one of those times. After a few seconds . . .

Thomas: *(doubtful, surprised, hopeful, scared, excited)* Sure.

Lourdes claps one time. It's the loudest clap ever.

Lourdes: It's a date!

Peter and Pastor John cover their faces, blushing. Thomas and Sofía look at each other, giggling, wondering if it's possible not to love Lourdes despite her natural talent to just . . . be Lourdes.

Thomas: Peter, do you mind?

Peter: Go ahead.

Lourdes: Thank you, Thomas.

Thomas: I'll drop Truman off at the coffee shop when we finish. OK, let's go, Sofía.

It's a sight to be seen. Thomas and Sofía are together again, even for a short while. As they leave the room, Peter whispers a small prayer: Lord, help them not hurt each other. Take care of their hearts, as they are vulnerable to each other.

Thursday, November 30

Sofía and Thomas leave Peter's room together. At first, as they walk together toward the elevator, they don't know what to say and try to distract each other with everything going around them: nurses, different families in each room, people hurting, and people not hurting anymore. A hospital is a good place to start if one wants to learn about the rich spectrum of human emotions. As soon as they get into the elevator, Sofía breaks the silence.

Sofía: Do you think he is going to make it?

Thomas: Who? Truman?

Sofía smiles.

Sofía: No, Peter.

Thomas: Oh . . . he has to.

Sofía: You care for him so well. Someone should write a book about your friendship.

Thomas: I hope the author is not Lourdes, though.

They both laugh.

Thomas: Did you come in your car?

Sofía: No, Pastor John picked us all up.

Thomas: OK, then let's go in mine.

Thomas unlocks his car, and they both get inside. Spending time with Sofía again feels weird, as if nothing had happened.

Sofía: Thomas, I am so sorry.

Thomas: For what?

Sofía: My fear.

Thomas: Your fear?

Sofía: Yes. My fear. I shouldn't have left you at that restaurant the way I did.

Thomas: Then, why did you do it?

Sofía: When you told me you didn't know if you believed Christianity was true anymore, I wasn't able to think. All the fears and the awful pain my mom and I went through with Landon flooded me. My mom and I spent countless nights mourning my brother Landon, not only for his faith but for the fact he didn't want to have a relationship with us because of ours. My mom lost both her husband and her son and couldn't do anything about it. But I wasn't with you when you needed me the most. It's not that I didn't want to; it's just that I physically couldn't. The fear of having to go through the experience of losing you the way I lost my brother overwhelmed me. But internally, I knew it wasn't OK. There is one added worry to all of this. If I didn't allow you to consider your beliefs freely, would you have felt pressured to believe only because you love me? I don't think that's a good reason to follow Jesus. I am not a good reason for you to follow Jesus. Just know, Thomas, that I am working on my fear, and if you are willing, I would love to sit with you and listen to your questions. I don't know if I'll have answers or even know how to discuss any of the deep questions you ask, but I am willing to try.

Thomas wishes this had been Sofía's answer that night at the restaurant when he first told her about his faith.

Thomas: I don't know if I want or even need that anymore, Sofía.

Sofía: What do you mean?

Thomas: After all this time talking with Peter, a part of me desperately wants Christianity to be true. His whole face changes when he speaks of Jesus, his smile widens, his eyes seem to catch the light, and he describes his faith as nothing short of a miracle. I listen, but I feel no such fire. For me, there's a disconnect, an apathy that mutes the very reasons I find to believe. Yet, when I consider a life without God, that apathy morphs into a profound emptiness. It's an overwhelming void that suggests a life lived only for the next fleeting feeling, the next temporary fulfillment, before it all vanishes. I feel trapped between two extremes: a quiet apathy and a crushing emptiness. I don't know which way to turn.

Sofía looks down and tears up. Thomas remains silent.

Sofía: *(while her voice is breaking)* Was it because of me?

Thomas: *(with urgency)* No, no, no! Sofía, this has nothing to do with you! I just don't believe it's true anymore.

Sofía: *(her voice breaks even more)* Would your opinion have changed if I hadn't moved away from you?

Thomas slows down and pulls over to the side to say something important to her.

Thomas: Sofía, I love you the same. You cannot blame yourself because you couldn't physically or emotionally be with me through this. Please don't do it.

Thomas tears up too.

Thomas: Whatever happens with us, if we part ways and end up having different lives away from each other, you cannot carry my burden because my faith journey belongs to me. You didn't do anything to cause this. In fact, you showed me the love of Jesus since the first time I met you.

Sofía: So . . . *(still crying)* wasn't the love of Jesus enough to stay?

Thomas: *(eyes tearing and voice breaking)* I wish it were, Sofía. The love of Jesus is an ideal I wouldn't mind pursuing. But honestly... I don't know if I believe Jesus is God anymore. I'm not even sure I believe in God at all.

Sofía: But . . . but . . . why? What caused you to think like that?

Thomas: I don't know . . . I grew apathetic about the liturgy, the worship, the programs, the lack of deep conversations, the saying one thing and the doing another, the assuming of knowing things people don't know . . . Question after question, I felt I moved away from it.

Sofía: But why didn't you tell me before?

Thomas: I knew this would hurt you because of what you went through with Landon. I was waiting to see if this was just a transitional period that would bring me back to the faith, but it moved me away from it entirely.

Sofía: Thomas, do you have any ill feelings toward me or any of us? Would you leave us and never come back?

Thomas: Sofía, I love you. I would still marry you.

Sofía: *(crying)* There is a side of me that tells me I should marry you right now. But if I married you, I wouldn't know who I would be marrying because you still need time to find yourself in a world where God is not present anymore. Besides . . . *(she cannot contain her tears)* I cannot marry someone who doesn't love Jesus. I want the person I marry to love Jesus more than he loves me.

Thomas feels frustrated.

Thomas: But why? Why does this belief have to separate us? Doesn't my love mean anything to you?

Sofía: It doesn't have to separate us . . . we can still be friends. But I cannot join you and become one flesh with you anymore. We cannot have a marriage where one side is pursuing Jesus, and the other doesn't. I don't want our kids to grow up in a house where we only agree on the most trivial things in life. I like this or don't like that, but then disagree on the . . . how do you usually say it? . . . the "big questions in life."

Thomas: I . . . don't understand this. I am here, I am real, and I am telling you I will take care of you, but you still hold onto faith, ideas, and beliefs you cannot see.

Sofía: Jesus is not a belief to me, Thomas. He is my life. Some people don't like a specific type of personality or particular body type, and some people think about this or that in a certain way, and they break their relationships or even don't have relationships at all with those people because of those things. Jesus is my everything. If I cannot follow Jesus with my husband, then I'd always choose Jesus and walk life alone.

Thomas is frustrated.

Thomas: I wish I were so confident about something that's clearly false.

Sofía cries harder when she hears Thomas saying that.

Sofía: Thomas, I don't want to hurt you anymore. I am sorry that you feel this way.

Thomas realizes he is being unfair in the way he is treating Sofía.

Thomas: Sofía, I am sorry. I didn't want to be mean. I respect your beliefs and faith. I am just frustrated that we might lose something real because of it.

Sofía: Thomas, I cannot talk about theology, philosophy, or science. They all go well over my head . . . but my love for Jesus is the most real thing about me.

Thomas gets frustrated again.

Thomas: But how? How?! How can something be real when Jesus is not even here?

Sofía: I cannot explain it, Thomas; I am sorry. I wish I were like you or Peter.

Thomas sighs in frustration, starts the car, and keeps driving toward The Shire.

Thomas: I just . . . Everything that is going on is so strange, and I am mourning so many things, including what we had together. But . . . Sofía, you don't have to wish to be like me or Peter. We can talk about so many other things, and I still believe something Jesus said is true: "Yes, just as you can identify a tree by its fruit, so you can identify people by their actions."[155] Your actions speak volumes of who you are. Don't you ever think that knowing things and being somewhat of an "intellectual" makes a person more valuable than others. I wish I were like you in so many ways too.

Sofía tries to bring some lightness into the conversation after hearing Thomas' empathy toward her.

Sofía: I guess we still have things in common. You don't believe Jesus is real, and I don't believe the way you cook can be "for real" either . . .

They both laugh in between tears.

Thomas: Seriously, do you think my cooking skills are that bad?

---

[155] Matthew 7:20.

Sofía: In a moment like this, I think Peter would say something like *(imitating a British accent)* "Your food makes me question reality itself" or something of that sort . . .

Thomas laughs.

Sofía: I don't want to lose you, Thomas.

Thomas: Me neither. But I get why we cannot be together.

Sofía: I think you need tons of space and room to breathe away from all of us.

Thomas: About that . . .

Sofía: What?

Thomas: I don't know if I should tell you.

Sofía: What? You are scaring me.

Thomas: I am thinking about moving away.

Sofía looks out the window, seeing people, stores, and buildings pass by. She might not walk this town holding Thomas' hand anymore, nor share in life together in it.

Sofía: It hurts to hear it. But I get it. But, please, don't let your new way of seeing the world build resentment toward me, Peter, Lourdes, or anyone else. We still love you so much.

Thomas: I know. I know. Peter has helped me a lot to think through that.

Sofía: Really?

Thomas: Yes. We have been meeting every Thursday for weeks to talk about this. One of the things he said that I liked was that when your worldview changes . . .

Sofía: Wait. I learned about this when I was trying to help my brother, but I guess I have stored it somewhere along with all the pain I went through. Would you remind me again, just in case? What's a worldview?

Thomas: Oh! The filter you use to understand the world. For example, you have a Christian worldview, and I have a . . . well, it doesn't matter.

Sofía: Are you an atheist?

Thomas: Not entirely. I still see things about the world that might point to something beyond it, and I think Jesus' living ideals are good. But I don't think Christianity answers those big questions entirely. I think I am more of an agnostic.

Sofía: Oh . . . an agnostic . . .

Thomas: Yes, someone who doesn't have enough information to make a definite conclusion on either side.

Sofía: I see. Well, you were going to say something about Peter?

Thomas: Oh, yeah. Peter said when he became a follower of Jesus after being an atheist all his life, he tended to become very critical of everyone around him because he felt that he began seeing the world the way "it is supposed to be seen." But he says this happens to anyone who goes from any worldview to another worldview. And it also happens to people who stop believing. They can become highly critical or even build resentment toward people who still believe.

Sofía: What did Peter do to stop being like that?

Thomas: He said . . . everything changed once he realized Jesus didn't look at him the way Peter was looking at the world. Then he realized Jesus and Christianity are all about sacrificial love.

Sofía smiles.

Sofía: I would rather you live forever than marry me.

Thomas is speechless.

Thomas: What?

Sofía: I would rather you follow Jesus and not marry me than you marry me and not follow Jesus.

Thomas: Why?

Sofía: Because I want you to live forever. Marriage is just a stage of life. People are not meant to be married forever.

Thomas doesn't know what to think about anything anymore. Sofía says beautiful things, but he wishes he believed them to be true. Thomas pulls up at The Shire. *Many people from church are running the coffee shop in Lourdes' absence.*

Thomas: Sofía, would you mind getting Truman while I clean out the trunk of my car?

Sofía: Sure.

Thomas keeps wondering about the last thing Sofía said to him. She would rather him follow Jesus even if that meant they wouldn't marry each other. Whether that's crazy or not, what is clear is that when it comes to her love for Jesus, "When she says it, she means it," just like Peter says. I don't think I ever believed the way she does, *Thomas thinks. Sofía gets inside the coffee shop, gently puts a leash on Truman, and walks him out while Thomas makes space for Truman to be comfortable in the trunk. Everyone except for Karl is happy to see Thomas from the distance and waves at him. Truman jumps in the trunk and begins to move around and whine nervously.*

Thomas: Hey, hey, hey, Truman . . . what's up? Why are you so nervous?

Sofía: Oh, you don't know this about him?

Thomas: What?

Sofía: The only thing her former owner and trainer couldn't help Truman with was how anxious he gets in cars. He is going to be barking the whole way.

Thomas: Aww, poor thing. Is there anything we could do for him?

Sofía: If a professional dog trainer couldn't do anything . . . I think it's because it's instinct to herd things. When he sees cars passing by in both directions, he feels he needs to herd them, and it makes him feel very nervous and anxious when he realizes he can't.

Thomas pets Truman and hugs him.

Thomas: *(while petting Truman)* No worries, Truman. We are all afraid of something.

Sofía listens to what Thomas just said but decides not to say anything about it.

Thomas: OK, let's take Truman to the vet.

Sofía was right. Truman barks and whines; the poor thing cannot take it.

Thomas: *(raising his voice)* I guess we won't be able to talk!

In Truman's eyes, each car is a sheep to be herded, and it is followed by enough barking to make a person lose their hearing for a few minutes.

Sofía: Truman! Calm down, sweet boy. We are almost there.

A few minutes later, they get to the veterinarian. Thankfully, Truman is OK. According to the vet, he is getting older and needs to take it easy with the frisbee and the jumping. The vet prescribes him some vitamins for his joints and a lot of rest. The trip back to The Shire *is more of the same. Truman's Aquiles' heel is the car. But isn't it true that we all have something we need to stop fighting and just let go of? They wish they could say this to Truman. They wish they themselves could apply this valuable truth to their lives. As soon as they get to* The Shire, *they can see Lourdes behind the counter making coffee. The church volunteers are gone. Thomas and Sofía bring Truman inside, and Truman runs to Lourdes' arms as if he hadn't seen her for years. If only people would love each other the way Truman loves everyone.*

Lourdes: Truman! Truman! Truman!

Cuddles, cuddles, cuddles. Cuddles everywhere.

Lourdes: Thank you for doing this, Thomas. How much do I owe you?

Thomas: Two chocolate muffins. One for Sofía, and one for me.

Sofía smiles. Sofía and Thomas look at each other, and it seems as if nothing has changed between them for a moment.

Lourdes: Date!

Lourdes . . .

Lourdes: Sorry, sorry, sorry. I'll keep quiet. Here, here. Here are your chocolate muffins. Thomas, thank you again for doing this.

Thomas: Hey, Lourdes, how was Peter when you left?

Lourdes: He was in good spirits. As soon as he and Pastor John began talking about theology, life, death, and the "deep questions in life," I invited myself to leave as quickly as possible.

Sofía and Thomas laugh.

Sofía: You don't like those conversations?

Lourdes: Not without coffee.

Sofía and Lourdes laugh again.

Lourdes: I just wanted them to have some time together. Pastor John has become a good mentor and friend to Peter.

Thomas: Let me text Peter for a moment.

Thomas excuses himself for a second.

Text conversation.

Thomas: Peter, I will drop off Sofía at her house. Can I spend time with you tomorrow?

Peter: Yes. Are you OK?

Thomas: Yes, everything is OK.

Peter: Take care, my friend.

Thomas: You too. P.S. Lourdes has no filter.

Peter: Thank you for the reminder :D

End of text conversation.

Thomas: Sofía, would you like me to drop you off at home?

Sofía: Oh, thank you. Lourdes, thank you for the chocolate muffin. Bye, Truman!

Thomas and Sofía get back in their car and begin their way back to Sofía's house. Their conversation is light and fun, but their emotions are intense inside. A few minutes later, Thomas pulls up at Sofía's house.

Thomas: Sofía, I am sorry about what happened with Landon.

Sofía: You mean the conversation you guys had with him at *The Shire*?

Thomas: Yes. I thought he wanted to have a conversation, not a fight.

Sofía: My brother hates God, and he doesn't believe He even exists. According to him, a god who doesn't exist allowed my father to die. I tried to tell him that we don't have a relationship with God, expecting we'll have a good life, but because we love Him for everything He has done for us.

Thomas: Can I ask you a question?

Sofía: Yes?

Thomas: What has God done for you, Sofía?

Sofía: Jesus, Thomas. After all the suffering, pain, uncertainty . . . I will live forever because our Creator loves me. I don't ask God for anything; He has given me everything in Jesus. I don't love Him less or more depending on the comings and goings of my life because I have life all because of Jesus.

Thomas doesn't say anything.

Sofía: How many questions will you ask me to prove I am crazy?

Thomas: No, no! It's not that. I am just . . . I am confused.

Sofía: How?

Thomas: I . . . you, Peter, and many others talk about Jesus with such passion and love; as if you had an actual relationship with Him. I don't know if I ever "loved" Jesus or only the idea of Jesus. Hearing you and Peter talking about Him makes me feel I never fell in love with Him. I wonder why . . .

Sofía: Thomas, can I ask you a question?

Thomas: Yes.

Sofía: Are you afraid of anything?

Thomas: Huh . . . why are you asking me that?

Sofía: I heard you saying to Truman that "everyone is afraid of something."

Thomas: Oh.

Thomas keeps quiet for a while.

Sofía: Thomas, no worries, you don't have to answer the question.

Thomas: Oh, no, no. I always ask people questions, so it's only fair that you ask me questions too.

Thomas sighs and tears up. Sofía gently places her hand on his shoulder.

Thomas: I might believe Christianity is not true, but I am still afraid of what my life would look like without it.

Sofía: Yeah?

Thomas: Over the last few weeks, I have spent time with two people who don't believe: your brother Landon and another person named Jim. He is a former pastor. Actually, he drew you and Linda and showed it to us. He hangs out at *The Shire* all the time.

Sofía: Wait a second. Are you talking about this old man who sits alone at *The Shire* with a notepad in his hand?

Thomas: Haha! Yes, that's Jim. He is great.

Sofía: How did guys become friends?

Thomas: Peter and I met every Thursday to discuss "the big questions in life" and my doubts about Christianity. And one day, he introduced himself and told us he loves talking about these things too. He shared his life story and how he left his faith behind with us. He is great, respectful, and knowledgeable but . . .

Sofía: But what?

Thomas: As he was telling his story and telling us how he thinks about the world, morality, values, etc., I felt his position was intellectually consistent but emotionally inconsistent. He talked about life as if the most important things were to be right and logical about the big questions, and I respect that. But then I also got the sense that, behind his intellectual consistency, there is a person who has no real answers to why love, forgiveness, and hope drive people so much and make them so happy, whether logically consistent or not. He cares for his mom, so he knows how to love. But I don't know . . . I don't feel like life is about doing the most "pleasurable things while causing the least damage to others."

Sofía: Is that what he said?

Thomas: In a nutshell.

Sofía: Why doesn't it sit well with you?

Thomas: You are born, and you don't know why. You do "the most pleasurable things while causing the least damage to others." Then, you find others who might disagree on what things are pleasurable, and ultimately, you don't have a framework to know who is right or who isn't. In the end, you die and are forgotten forever. But, hey, at least you believe you are intellectually consistent . . . I don't know . . .

Sofía: What?

Thomas: Christianity is too much, but the world offers too little. One is outrageous, and the other one is too empty. One talks about profound spiritual truths I don't think anyone can prove; the other believes there is meaning in the day-by-day activities of life, but yet, they are all so fleeting. I just . . . some things don't make sense to me.

Sofía: Like what?

Thomas: Like . . . I have seen Peter having joy in his eyes while telling me he was afraid to die. That doesn't make sense to me. But then I think about Jim and . . . I don't know . . . He finds meaning in the little he finds pleasurable; but then I wonder, would his life have no meaning if he couldn't enjoy those things anymore? Doesn't life have meaning beyond the things we like or don't like to do? It's too empty . . . I don't know if that's the right word.

Sofía: Are you afraid of choosing a lifestyle without having all your questions answered?

Thomas: I guess so. You could say that.

Sofía: But Thomas . . . who does?

Thomas sighs and covers his face with his hands, showing he is tired, confused, and frustrated.

Sofía: I remember what my grandmother told me about Jesus; I will never forget it. I'll ask you the same question.

Thomas: What is it?

Sofía: If Jesus was in front of you, and you realized everything about Him was true: He is God, He created you, He gave his life for you, and He loves you dearly, and He wants you to live forever . . . and you could say one thing to Him, what would you say?

Thomas: . . . Thank you?

Sofía: Thank you.

They both remain silent for a few seconds.

Sofía: Thomas, I don't have all the answers; you are very smart and ask the best questions. But sacrificial love, forgiveness, compassion, life, hope are big questions for which we have found the answer.

Thomas: Where?

Sofía: In the life of Jesus. It's good to keep asking questions about things we don't know. But what about finding rest in the things we actually do?

Thomas remains silent.

Sofía: Thomas, I hope you find what you are looking for. I hope one day you can answer all your questions. I love you, Thomas.

Thomas tears up, and both hug for a few seconds in the car.

Sofía: Thank you, Thomas, for everything.

Thomas: Thank you? For what?

Sofía: For having treated me like no one ever did.

Sofía closes the door and heads toward her house, trying to find her keys to the door. Thomas stays in the car looking at her, expecting that she will turn to wave at him one last time, but she doesn't. Perhaps that's the only way to move forward: never looking back.

Thomas: *(whispering)* I love you too . . .

Chapter 14

The Day Before

Wednesday, December 13

Thomas knocks on Peter's hospital room door.

Thomas: May we come in?

Peter: We?

Thomas: Peter, some people here'd love to say hi to you.

Thomas comes in and invites two other people to do so. Peter cannot believe what he is seeing.

Peter: No way! Mom, Dad!

Peter's parents came to be with him the day before his surgery and to take care of him for a few days afterward. Peter and his parents blend into a long hug that feels too short for all of them.

Peter: Thomas! Did you plan this?

Thomas: Well, let's say I helped them a little.

Peter tears up. Thank you, Thomas.

Thomas: I'll let you catch up and visit you later.

As Thomas leaves the room, he can hear the excitement behind him, the laughs, the tears . . . However, this is not the last surprise he has prepared for Peter. Tomorrow, Peter is undergoing a complicated procedure. It seems his tumor is in a hazardous location; it's bigger than it was the first time, and the intervention is highly risky. In order to reach the tumor, they have to make a very precise incision and avoid one of the carotid arteries, which help the heart pump blood to the brain. However, there is no other way to move forward because Peter wouldn't be able to live a normal life with the tumor inside him. All of it has come to this. For some, it all depends on God's will; for others, it all depends on the surgeon's ability, but Peter is thankful for both because "God causes everything to work together for the good of those who love God."[156] *A few hours later, a huge party of people show up at Peter's room: Thomas, Lourdes, Sofía, Pastor John . . . even Jim! This is a testament to Peter's legacy: someone who can be friends with anyone and be loved by people who disagree with him vehemently about the things that matter the most. They all bring flowers, food, and of course, Lourdes is bringing some coffee and chocolate muffins. Peter's parents are in the room too.*

---

[156] Romans 8:28.

Peter: Wow! Hey, everyone!

Everyone: Hey, Peter!

Lourdes notices Peter is getting emotional; she doesn't think about it twice and leans over to the bed to hug him.

Peter: Too strong, too strong, too strong, Lourdes!

Everyone laughs.

Peter: Thank you, everyone, for being here. Jim! What are you doing here?

Jim: Thomas told me about this, and I came to support you. I want to keep having conversations with you, Peter!

Peter: Oh, man. Me too.

Sofía: How are you feeling, Peter?

Peter: I have no energy to fight any of this anymore. I let go of all my fear. I am at peace.

Lourdes: Who wants some coffee and chocolate muffins?

Peter: No! Seriously! Did you bring some chocolate muffins?

Jim: Oh, no . . .

Lourdes: What?

Jim: Now I feel under pressure to have to eat one.

Everyone laughs.

Peter: No worries, everyone. The coffee will be drinkable by the time they finish with my surgery.

Everyone laughs again.

Lourdes: "Coffee needs to be served hot to warm up the blizzard we all are journeying within us."

Thomas: There it is!

Pastor John: Thank you, Lourdes.

Peter's parents hug him again and promise to return tomorrow after the surgery to see him. They seem exhausted, but for a very good reason. Everyone is excited to see Peter enjoying being with his parents. As soon as they leave, Thomas looks worried.

Thomas: Hey, Peter, they are not staying overnight?

Peter: Well, my surgery is very early in the morning, and I just heard that only one person can stay with me overnight. I'd like for them to take care of each other. My mom needs to be with my father to take care of him and give him his medicines.

Thomas: So, who is going to stay with you?

Peter looks at Thomas making a funny face.

Peter: What do you think about one last conversation about "the big questions in life" before the surgery?

Thomas: Do you want me to stay with you tonight? Because I will!

Peter: Yes. Thank you.

Lourdes: Hey, Peter, there was someone who wanted to be with you but wasn't allowed at the hospital?

Peter: Who?

Lourdes pulls up her phone and shows him a video of Truman. In the video, Lourdes asks Truman: "Do you love Peter? Do you love Peter?" Truman is barking, spinning, and feeling super excited.

Peter: Aww . . . Truman . . . How's his limp?

Lourdes: Oh! Much better!

They all keep talking with each other. It's encouraging to see Pastor John and Jim, a former pastor, having a conversation together, Thomas and Sofía in the same room enjoying each other's company, Lourdes . . . An hour later, the nurse comes in.

Nurse: Hi, everyone, Peter needs to rest for tomorrow. You need to leave in 15 minutes. Peter, is anyone going to stay here with you overnight?

Peter: Yes, Thomas is.

Nurse: OK, thank you, everyone.

Lourdes: Peter, I'll be up praying the whole night. I wish I could stay with you. (*Lourdes begins imitating a British accent, poorly*) What a lovely chap you are!

Everyone laughs.

Jim: Hey, Peter.

Peter: Yes?

Jim: Our conversation a few weeks ago was one of the most thought-provoking conversations I have ever had with a Christian. I am glad our paths crossed, and I cannot wait to have more conversations with you over Lourdes' coffee.

Peter: Me too, Jim. Thank you.

Pastor John: Peter, may I read some Scripture to you?

Peter: Please do.

Pastor John opens his small Bible, which he always carries with him, to a passage he seems to have prepared for this moment.

Pastor John: "I am leaving you with a gift—peace of mind and heart. And the peace I give is a gift the world cannot give. So don't be troubled or afraid."[157]

Peter: Thank you, Pastor John.

Sofía: Peter, look around in this room. You have brought us all together today. God is always using difficult moments to show how much He loves us. I hope you keep resting in Him, no matter the circumstances. Thank you for being such a good friend to Thomas. I'll be praying for you all night as well. We'll see you tomorrow after the surgery!

Peter: Thank you, everyone. Every moment I spend with you is a treasure I hold dearly. Jesus' love became more and more real to me because of how you love me. Please, never stop sacrificially loving others the way you loved me, the way Jesus loved the world.

Lourdes: Let me pray over you, Peter.

Everyone holds hands. Jim and Thomas step back, feeling uncomfortable yet respectful of the situation.

---

[157] John 14:27

Lourdes: Father in Heaven, You never promised happiness in this life, but joy through suffering. We pray without expectations but out of love because of everything You have already done for us. You allow us to call you Father, and as Your children, we desire You to help Peter through this challenging moment so that we can enjoy his presence for years to come. Sometimes, it's hard to have eyes to see the infinite ways You bless us every day, but it is clear that You blessed us all through Peter. Please be with him and allow him to rest through this time of uncertainty. Thank you. Thank you. Thank you. Thank you.

All the "thank yous" remind Thomas of Sofía's grandmother's question about Jesus.

Lourdes: Thank you . . . Thank you . . . in Jesus' name. Amen.

They all blend in a hug and leave the room in good spirits. Jim approaches Peter, and they both shake hands, wishing him the best in his surgery. Thomas and Peter stay in the room alone.

Peter: Thomas.

Thomas: Yes?

Peter: I have something for you.

Thomas: What is it?

Peter: This is a small note, but don't open it now.

Thomas: What would you like me to do with it?

Peter: Look, I think everything is going to be OK. But, if I don't make it tomorrow, would you open it and read it?

Thomas: Come on, Peter, everything will be all right. Don't be a weirdo! A note? You are so cheesy sometimes!

Peter: OK, OK. I am a weirdo, cheesy, whatever you want. But would you open the note and read it if I don't make it?

Thomas sighs.

Thomas: OK, I will.

Thomas puts the note in his pocket. Peter is relieved after hearing that Thomas will do it.

Peter: How are you feeling?

Thomas: You are at the hospital, about to undergo a massive surgery, and you worry about the way I am feeling?

Peter: Yes.

Thomas: It's a lot to process. As I told you a few days ago, my conversation with Sofía went well, but I still feel weird seeing her as a friend when I'd love to marry her. However, I understand her. She never meant anything bad. She is just another person trying to find her way through a life that is sometimes difficult to understand.

Peter: I am glad you guys can move forward and keep loving each other. Who knows? Maybe one day you'll get back together?

Thomas: Well, there is only one way that could happen. She did say something to me, I . . .

Peter: What?

Thomas: I just couldn't even make sense of it.

Peter: What was it?

Thomas: She told me she would rather have me follow Jesus than marry me.

Peter: Did she give you any reason?

Thomas: She told me she just wants me to live forever.

Peter remains quiet . . . There is nothing he could add to it.

Peter: Hey, mate, thank you for helping my parents with their trip and putting together the surprise.

Thomas: It was fun to do it.

Peter: When did you start planning it?

Thomas: As soon as you told me the day the surgery was scheduled.

Peter: So, you kept working on this even after you stormed out of Lourdes' coffee shop and didn't talk for a while?

Thomas: Yes.

Peter: Thanks, Thomas.

Thomas: How are your parents?

Peter: They are struggling, but they are in good spirits. I just didn't want them to see me like this anymore. But you know? Maybe I was being selfish. I am their son, after all, and they care for me.

Peter keeps quiet for a second. But Thomas knows a question is coming.

Peter: Hey, Thomas, have you learned something valuable over the last few months? I don't mean data, but something you didn't expect to learn that might change the way you live your life from now on.

Thomas: And you say that I am the one who asks good questions.

Peter and Thomas smile.

Thomas: Yes. There is one thing I find unsettling yet fascinating at the same time.

Peter: What is it?

Thomas: No one knows truly what's going on.

Peter laughs.

Peter: What do you mean?

Thomas: If you ask any person why they believe what they believe, no matter who they are or their beliefs, they will ultimately answer, "I don't know."

Peter: Wow . . . that's true in a sense. "God has also given us a desire to know the future. God certainly does everything at the proper time. But we can never completely understand what He is doing."[158]

Thomas: No wonder that passage is so important to you.

---

[158] Ecclesiastes 3:11: Yet God has made everything beautiful for its own time. He has planted eternity in the human heart, but even so, people cannot see the whole scope of God's work from beginning to end.

Peter: The real question is: What do we end up doing with the things we claim to know? The things we know are true?

Thomas: And what is truth?[159]

[159] John 18:38

Thursday, December 14

It's 6 a.m., and Thomas has spent the night in Peter's room, keeping him company and having great conversations with him. Throughout the night, Peter sometimes opened his eyes and wrestled to fall asleep, pretending this was just a night like any other. Thomas was beside him, trying his best to sleep in the most uncomfortable chair the world has ever seen. Thomas made sure Peter knew about it, and they joked about it until one of them fell asleep. He did fall asleep after all. *Peter says to himself.* I guess the day has come once again. I'll be honest, Lord, I don't understand why You brought me to this point and how any of this would help others see You and love You more. But that's my only desire. Should I go back to England after the surgery and serve you there? Father, what if, instead of planting a church, I begin a ministry where I bring people who know You and don't know You to talk about the big questions in life? I enjoyed spending time with Jim and even Landon, to an extent. I love hearing people's stories. People are, like Americans would say, "awesome." You created us all in such unique ways. Would You help me decide what to do after my surgery? *Suddenly, Peter gasps, excited.* Wait a second! What if I went to . . . ?

Suddenly, a team of nurses enters the room to take Peter to the surgical room. Thomas wakes up wondering if any muscles in his back don't hurt at this point.

Peter: Hey, Thomas, how did you sleep? Comfy, *innit*?

Thomas: Hehe. It's OK. How do you feel?

Peter: It doesn't matter at this point. Just thank you, Thomas.

Thomas: Do your best. Please don't tell any of your jokes to the surgeon; he might doubt that helping you is a good idea.

Peter: I'll keep my mouth shut.

They both smile. Thomas keeps looking at Peter as they take him out of the room. They wave at each other. Peter gives Thomas a thumbs-up.

Peter: Thomas!

Thomas: What?

Peter: Never stop asking questions!

OK . . . Well, that's it. Now what . . . ? *Thomas thinks. Thomas doesn't know what to do with himself.* Never stop asking questions . . . I mean, that's Peter in one sentence. *Before leaving the room, he looks back at Peter's room again.* I think it's going to be OK. *According to the surgeon, it will probably take eight to nine hours to do the procedure. It is crucial to make sure they don't leave any residual of the tumor behind. A few hours later, in the waiting room, Lourdes, Pastor John, Sofía, Linda, Jim, and many people from church arrive to wait for the results. His parents are there as well. Thoughts rush through Thomas' mind: fear, uncertainty, hope, Sofía, Peter, Jesus, Jim, questions . . . and fear again.* It doesn't make sense to lose Peter. Everything is going to be OK. But what if it isn't? What would I do? Please, help him . . . Wait, who am I saying please to? *Some people are smiling, others are worried, but no one knows what to say. After nine hours of waiting, everyone is exhausted but full of hope. The door to the surgical area opens, and a surgeon approaches the whole group. As soon as she takes off her mask, Thomas recognizes her.*

Thomas: *(to everyone)* Yes, that's her. Let's go ask her!

Everyone rushes toward her trying to read the surgeon's body language to anticipate what she is going to say.

Thomas: How is he?

It takes her a few seconds to answer. Oh no . . .

Surgeon: I am sorry.

Thomas: I am sorry, *what*?!

Surgeon: Sorry, Peter didn't make it. We tried everything we could.

Thomas' world falls apart within. Lourdes gasps, and Peter's mom begins crying uncontrollably. Everyone is crying and hugging each other. Peter's father keeps asking the surgeon for explanations as if his questions could somehow bring him back to life. Sofía gently places her hand on Thomas' back, and Thomas cannot even move.

Sofía: I am so sorry, Thomas.

Lourdes: Peter . . . how? Why?

Jim: Thomas, I don't know what to say . . . I am sorry.

Thomas's mind is going thousands of miles per hour, but the world around him is moving in slow motion. Lourdes holds Thomas and hugs him.

Lourdes: *(crying)* My poor Thomas, please be strong.

Thomas is not reacting at all; at one point, he wonders if he is the one who died and if none of this is real.

Sofía: Thomas? Thomas? Are you OK, Thomas?

Thomas, almost unwillingly, begins moving toward the exit without saying anything to anyone.

Sofía: Thomas?! Please say something!

Lourdes gently holds Sofía and whispers something to her.

Lourdes: Let him go, Sofía.

Before leaving the room, Thomas looks back to see everyone again, not knowing if this moment will be his last with them. Sofía looks at him, having the same feeling. Meanwhile, Lourdes is holding and looking at Sofía, saying something to her he cannot hear. Pastor John is comforting Peter's mom, Mary. Peter's father is still trying to avoid the inevitable as the surgeon is explaining what happened to him, even though he doesn't seem to hear anything she is saying. Jim is sitting next to Peter's mom, being the pastor he once was. Thomas turns around the corner, leaving everything and everyone behind. That's it? *Thomas begins having memories of Peter: the first time they met at church, the day of his baptism, his conversations at* The Shire, *and how he would always support him through anything. Thomas gets in his car and, in between tears, begins driving, not knowing where he is going. After a few turns, utterly oblivious of what he wants to do, he realizes he is closer to* The Shire. *If there is a place to mourn and remember Peter, this is it. Sometimes, he needs to slow down to wipe off his tears. His face is red, and—at times—he cannot help but to sob. It's hard to drive around the same town where his friendship with Peter was born, where they shared so many memories.*

Thomas arrives at The Shire. *It is closed. As soon as he pulls up, he lets go of all the frustration and tension he has been feeling for months and begins yelling uncontrollably, holding on to the wheel as if it were the only thing that can keep him from dying, too. He begins looking at pictures of Peter on his phone—horrible jokes, deeply empathetic, loved like no one else . . .*

Wait a second . . .

Thomas remembers the best picture of Peter is not on his phone but in his wallet. And it's not even a picture, but Jim's drawing of Peter and Thomas conversing in The Shire. "*Bad things happen when we stop talking. May the conversation never stop!" It's cold and gray and starting to rain, but Thomas has to go to the lake. A sudden rush of fear overcomes him as he remembers . . .*Peter's note . . . *He begins walking toward the lake. The rain becomes more and more* *intense the closer he gets to the lake, as if nature were also crying for Peter's death. Thomas doesn't even know how to distinguish a tear from a raindrop on his face anymore. Soaking wet, he gets to the lake and sits down on the same bench near where Peter's tumor began hurting. He cannot stop crying. Suddenly, a gentle light falls onto the lake as the sun timidly shows up between the clouds.*

Thomas: No! No! No! No! No! No! *(hitting the bench)* "No, No, No, No, No!" *(hitting the bench even harder)* Why? He didn't deserve this! IS THIS THE WAY YOU LOVE THOSE WHO LOVE YOU?! YOU ARE A HYPOCRITE, INSENSITIVE . . . YOU ARE TRASH!

Thomas is out of control, screaming out of his lungs.

Thomas: WHY AM I EVEN TALKING TO YOU IF I DON`T EVEN KNOW IF YOU ARE REAL?

Thomas begins sobbing again; however, he doesn't have any energy left to continue yelling. He keeps talking with a softer tone but full of frustration.

Thomas: You don't care about anyone. Everything about You is "mysterious," of course it is, there is no other way to hide the fact You are not real. You move in mysterious ways, uh? Lies, lies, lies! *(hitting the bench again)* You take away Sofía from me, and now my best friend? All the arguments, all the prayers, all the "Bible" time, all to just puff up Your need to be praised, You self-centered . . . Why did You do this to Peter?! I just don't . . . I am sick of You, sick of this town, sick of pretending—sick!

After a while, it stops raining. Thomas, soaking wet, keeps sitting on the bench, trying to calm himself down. Then, Thomas remembers again. Oh, Peter's note. I can't, I can't right now. *He looks up and fixates on the island in the middle of the lake.* Why did You even bring him here, taking him away from his own family, making him lose some friends because of You?! *Thomas doesn't know why, but not feeling the rain falling on him makes him not want to keep crying anymore, perhaps because now he would feel his tears running down his face.* Sacrificial love? What does that even mean? *Thomas keeps thinking, wrestling almost in despair, trying to find the ultimate reason to forget about Christianity once and for all.* Why do the people I love the most love You? What do they see in You that I don't?! *Suddenly, images of the cross come to Thomas. Unwilling to entertain them, he does everything he can to forget about them. But he can't. The body of Jesus hanging on the cross, the nails, the crown of thorns, "forgive them, for they don't know what they are doing."*[160] *Thomas begins yelling again.*

Thomas: WHY DID YOU HAVE TO DO IT THAT WAY?!

Suddenly, a passage of Scripture comes at him, like the raging waves of an ocean, tempestuous, wild, out of control: "But many were amazed when they saw him. His face was so disfigured he seemed hardly human, and from his appearance, one would scarcely know he was a man."[161]

Thomas: WHY DID YOU HAVE TO DO IT THAT WAY?!

Thomas can hear Peter's voice answering his own question: "Because sacrificial love cannot be explained with words, but demonstrated through actions."

Thomas: THAT'S INSANE! *(he begins sobbing uncontrollably again).*

---

[160] Luke 23:34.

[161] Isaiah 52:14.

A moment later, Thomas's train of thought comes to a halt. What am I doing? *His emotions are taking the best out of him.* Peter warned me about this . . . *After breathing in and out deeply a few times, Thomas says to himself:*

Thomas: *(voice cracking)* Peter, you were right . . . I shouldn't allow myself to walk on this path of resentment because if I do, it'll destroy me. It's already destroying me . . .

Peter's note . . .

Thomas has never felt as terrified, and it's all because of a simple note. Context is so important. Thomas's hands shake slightly as he thinks about Peter writing the note while lying on the hospital bed just a few hours earlier, alive. In between tears, Thomas opens the note to find a simple question written in it:

Is it because of Jesus?

Tune In: Go beyond the book with the *Is it Because of Jesus?* podcast, your audio companion for deeper exploration. Available on all platforms.

Speak Up: Have a question, a story, or your own answer to share? Send your take to Pedro at isitbecauseofjesus@gmail.com.

Discover More: Learn more about the author at www.isitbecauseofjesus.com.